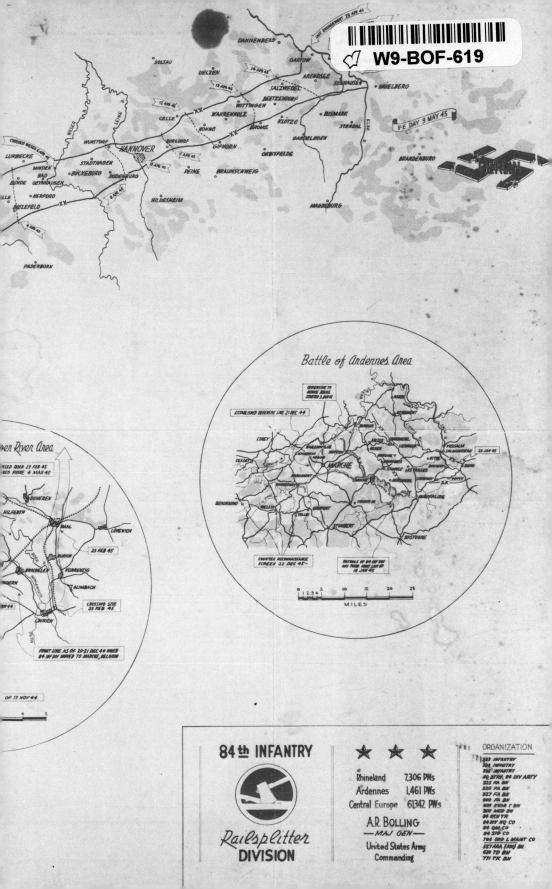

Battle of Ardennes Area

MILES

Roer River Area

84th INFANTRY

Railsplitter
DIVISION

Rhineland   7,306 PWs
Ardennes   1,461 PWs
Central Europe   61,342 PWs

A.R. BOLLING
— MAJ GEN —
United States Army
Commanding

ORGANIZATION

333 INFANTRY
334 INFANTRY
335 INFANTRY
HQ BTRY, 84 DIV ARTY
325 FA BN
326 FA BN
327 FA BN
909 FA BN
909 ENGR C BN
309 MED BN
84 RCN TR
84 DIV HQ CO
84 QM CO
84 SIG CO
784 ORD L MAINT CO
SET ABA (AUG) BN
638 TD BN
771 TK BN

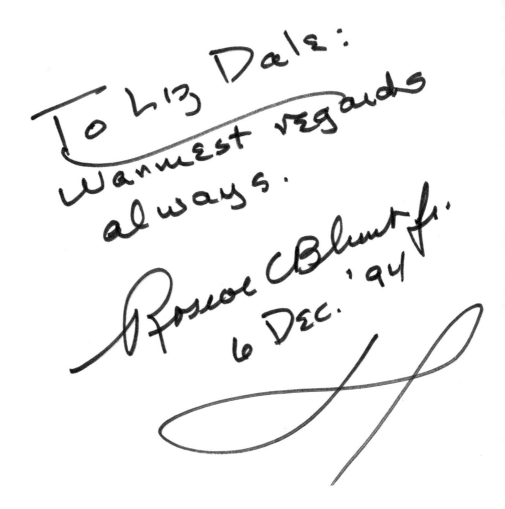

To Liz Dale:
Warmest regards
always.

Roscoe C Blunt Jr.
6 Dec. '94

INSIDE THE BATTLE
OF THE BULGE

Author Roscoe C. Blunt Jr. in Germany in 1945, soon after the war ended.

Inside the Battle of the Bulge

A Private Comes of Age

Roscoe C. Blunt Jr.

Westport, Connecticut
London

Library of Congress Cataloging-in-Publication Data

Blunt, Roscoe C. (Roscoe Crosby).
    Inside the Battle of the Bulge : a private comes of age / Roscoe
C. Blunt Jr.
       p. cm.
    Rev. ed. of: A war remembered.
    Includes index.
    ISBN 0-275-94545-6
    1. Blunt, Roscoe C. (Roscoe Crosby). 2. Ardennes,
Battle of the, 1944-1945—Personal narratives, American.
3. Soldiers—United States—Biography. 4. United States. Army—
Biography. I. Blunt, Roscoe C. (Roscoe Crosby), War
remembered. II. Title.
D756.5.A7B57   1994
940.54′21—dc20   93-2223

British Library Cataloguing in Publication Data is available.

Library of Congress Catalog Card Number: 93-2223
ISBN: 0-275-94545-6

First published in 1994

Praeger Publishers, 88 Post Road West, Westport, CT 06881
An imprint of Greenwood Publishing Group, Inc.

Printed in the United States of America

∞™

The paper used in this book complies with the
Permanent Paper Standard issued by the National
Information Standards Organization (Z39.48-1984).

10 9 8 7 6 5 4 3 2 1

I want to offer special thanks to my devoted wife Beatrice, who, soon after we were married nearly a half century ago, deciphered and typed hundreds of pages of my wartime chronicle and took my dictation while my memory was still fresh. Without her help the writing of this book never could have been possible.

and to
Joe Winston Everett
1919–1965

Contents

Preface

The first version of this book, called "A War Remembered," was written for my sons: Roscoe C. III, Randie A., and Richard D. Blunt. My purpose was to offer them an insight into a time in my life that was remote from the man they know.

I'd like to acknowledge the assistance of Roscoe, a professional writing consultant, who edited the manuscript and gave me guidance during the various stages of revision.

INSIDE THE BATTLE
OF THE BULGE

The Beginning of an Odyssey

The whistle blew. Pandemonium exploded as hundreds of men grabbed cumbersome barracks bags, backpacks, rifles, gas masks, travel orders and personal possessions, and stumbled from the tar paper–covered barracks and onto the company street.

It was 0400, September 19, 1944, a depressing, drizzly morning. All the training and preparation were behind us now and the "real thing," we all inwardly knew, was about to unfold. As I peered into the black, unyielding mist, I wondered what lay ahead. For too many, death awaited. For the survivors, a lifetime of tortured memories would be the only reward for patriotic service. Each of us stood mute with our private thoughts waiting for the next command.

After a two-mile march, we eventually boarded a transport train, 75 men crammed into each car. Those first on board grabbed the seats. Those who followed staked out aisles or platforms, sitting, sprawling, dozing or grumbling on disarrayed mountains of military gear.

We finally settled into the rough, swaying rhythm of motion typical of passenger trains in the '40s. Cinder particles from the coal-powered engine filtered through loose-fitting train windows, and covered our sweat-soaked uniforms, adding to our gritty discomfort. When the train finally ground to a halt, we saw through the drizzle that we were on the New Jersey side of New York harbor.

On the dock we stood miniaturized by the 786-foot *Edmund B. Alexander*, pressed into emergency wartime transport service; now it looked like a rusted-out old tramp steamer straight out of a Humphrey Bogart movie. Inching forward, dragging our gear behind us, 6500 irritable GIs were embarked after several hours of milling about. Everywhere was mass confusion as men fought for comfortable accommodations. Too exhausted to care, I took what was left: the floor. With my steel helmet as a pillow, I was mercifully lulled to sleep almost instantly by the heartbeat of the ship. Throbbing turbines, the creaks and groans of stretching metal provided our orchestral accompaniment for the next 13 days. The nauseating stench of diesel fuel permeated our sleeping quarters, a smell we had to live with, but never got used to, for the remainder of the trip.

My susceptibility to seasickness became apparent almost immediately. I still vividly recall the two weeks of constant, torturous seasickness experienced between the States and Europe. To compound the misery, there were daily inspections. They never ceased, even when those being inspected were totally incapacitated. It always puzzled me how the inspection-team noncoms and brass never seemed to be afflicted like the rest of us. Cherbourg, France, was our intended destination, but we learned through the rumor factory that the ship would disembark in Scotland instead because of heavy German Luftwaffe bombing at Cherbourg and Le Havre, France's major seaports on the English Channel. For once, the rumor mill proved accurate. Other units of the 84th Division were heading for Liverpool and Southampton in England. Eventually, the division would reassemble throughout the countryside surrounding the English city of Winchester, inland from Britain's channel coast.

On October 1, after a 13-day, 3300-mile voyage, we arrived in Greenock and the pastoral Scottish landscape was a quilted patchwork of stonewalled pastures, bordered by thin stands of thickly foliaged trees and hedges corralling herds of grazing cattle and sheep. It was nature's afghan of multi-hued, gently sloping farmlands giving way gracefully to cloud-enshrouded mountain ranges above them.

With a harbor pilot, I exchanged American coins for a Glasgow Sunday newspaper and a "thruppennybit" souvenir. The paper was filled with casualty lists and news from the front. As I scanned the names and addresses, I realized, in a figurative sense, my war had arrived. The long lists of British casualties had a sobering effect on me; such newspaper listings were something I had never seen in America, where the war had been far away and impersonal.

War fatalities, which had become a daily way of life for the people of the British Isles, were something I'd never had to contend with before. My mind was slow to grasp the reality that in only a matter of a few short weeks, death would become my terrifying constant companion also.

The undefined mob of hunched-over OD (olive drab) uniforms milling around the deck eventually defined itself into a single file that disappeared down the gangplank to a flotilla of military landing craft and Scottish tugboat ferries. On shore, we were shunted along the town's narrow, cobblestoned streets to a railroad station where we began a 16-hour train ride to south Central England.

K-rations were issued to everyone on the train and we got our first taste of combat field rations: a packet of lemon powder, a small can of dry cheese containing ham flecks, four dog biscuits, eight small caramel candies, four Wings cigarettes, a stick of gum, and a book of matches.

At Newcastle Upon Tyne, a few kilometers from the North Sea, the train stopped to refuel and all American troops were given chickenless chicken pie by the British Red Cross. The meal seemed sparse but in food-starved England, this was a most generous gesture. After we devoured the meal, the train continued its monotonous journey southward into London.

It was in that majestic, historical city that we saw for the first time the ravages of Hitler's saturation "blitz" (lightning) bombing designed to cower the English people. As the train moved through the city, fires under mountains of rubble burned around us while skeletal buildings defiantly remained standing, like the people, refusing to crumble. The acrid smell of destruction permeated the rail cars.

We watched armies of women and older men struggle to clear streets of debris by hand, one stone, one brick at a time. Others poked through the ruins trying to retrieve lost treasures or something from their past to hang onto for emotional strength.

It was 0400 when we pulled into Newbury, Berkshire, a town of about 5000, where we were dumped into an apple orchard at an Air Corps glider base dotted with drab, camouflaged pyramidal tents sprawled through an ocean of ankle-deep mud. Eager for sleep, we settled in, eight men to a tent. To venture outside to the mess tent or latrine was to literally "walk the plank" and pray that no one was coming in the opposite direction at the same time. If so, it meant stepping off the plank and into the muck if the person approaching outranked you or was bigger than you.

Nearby pastures were cluttered with olive drab troop-carrying CG-4A gliders and stubby-nosed British Horsa gliders. Planeloads of brass flew in almost continuously in C-47s; it was obvious that something big was in the works. The air of secrecy was intensified when questions to higher-ups produced only vague answers.

After a week, we moved to Barton Stacy camp, a former British army facility near Andover, Hampshire, 15 miles southwest by truck. With wooden barracks, asphalt parade ground, a PX (post exchange) and the town nearby, this was more like home. With the 507th, 513th and 517th airborne units we remained there for two weeks in relative comfort.

Refresher training consumed the 14-hour days. Nights were spent on a series of intensified field exercises and cross-country forced marches. The Army was getting us in top physical shape and combat ready as quickly as possible. When a call went out for volunteers for a no-questions-asked, undefined dangerous assignment, the first person to jump to his feet was Blunt. Eleven others were chosen and the cloak-and-dagger manner in which the whole episode had taken place eventually made me wonder what I had gotten myself into. The newly formed squad was whisked away by truck to Bentworth Hall, a stately English mansion in Alton, Hampshire. Without fanfare we were ushered inside, still not knowing what was in store for us in this secret "high-risk assignment." The suspense mounted.

That evening, we were informed we would be taught mine and booby-trap detection and removal and would be molded into demolitions specialists, one of the toughest assignments in the combat Army. But the extreme danger of this delicate work necessitated that it be an all-volunteer unit. We were offered the opportunity to back out. No one did.

"Here you make just one mistake. That's all," a major intoned. "Germany's most brilliant scientific minds have developed the most sophisticated, advanced mine and booby-trap systems of any nation of the world. These explosive devices defy detection and disarmament. If you're smarter than these scientific minds, you may live to go home."

One man stood up and walked out. As I found out later when our special anti-mine unit carried out its first actual combat mission into German-held territory far in front of our forward-most infantry lines, this man probably wouldn't have been able to withstand the stealth, the gut-wrenching fear and the hair-trigger pressures we felt while trying not to blow ourselves up.

The training was intensive. Live booby traps were placed everywhere imaginable, including our beds. Constant awareness was pounded into us. Our shield of vigilance had to be impenetrable. The instructors repeatedly reminded us the mines we worked on were live, not dummies, for, as they reasoned, live mines brought home the message more succinctly. When the three weeks were up, we were all relieved to graduate.

If I had been seeking the war all those months, I finally found it in London and I didn't like it, for now I was actually part of the German blitz I had read about back home. Only this time, it was not Junker and Stuka bombers raining death and destruction from overhead, but rather, the almost constant unpredictability of the German V-1 rockets and V-2 buzz bombs falling randomly on the city. The war was no longer far away. It was there and it was then.

Back in camp, preparations for our cross-channel hop reached the final stages and we were restricted to the company area with no contact with the outside world. When the move to Southampton finally came, we loaded in drizzling rain onto a Landing Ship Tank (LST) for the 26-mile channel crossing to France.

As Omaha Beach with its massive, ugly German pillboxes, hove into sight, the boat fell silent. It was November 2, 1944, D plus 146. An overturned, burned-out half-track, an apparent pillbox victim, lay partially underwater on the beach. Partially submerged German concrete anti-tank barriers snaked their way along the beach at water's edge. Twisted .37-mm anti-tank cannons and rusted-out jeeps littered the beach. Gaping shell craters on the beach still had not been filled in by the tides.

Landing Craft Infantry (LCIs) were everywhere, most of them with ragged artillery shell holes torn in their sides that sank them and their troops before they even reached the beach. Now, as we watched, they were still being rolled from side to side by the surf. Ammunition crates, sandbagged machine gun emplacements, rolls of barbed wire—all the signs of what once had been.

"Hit the landing net," a loud voice barked out, and over the side we went, clawing, slipping and falling. An LCI took us within 50 feet of the sandy high-water mark where we jumped into chest-deep water, half paddling, half wading, half drowning, spitting and gagging out mouthfuls of cold sea water, stumbling, bobbing up for air but eventually getting a foothold on the beach. At long last, we were on the Continent.

Looking much like a rag-tag mob, we climbed over the debris-strewn landscape, and started the most spirit-shattering, grueling march I had ever undertaken, a 50-mile hike inland during which I collapsed repeatedly beside the road and was left behind by my company. Before it was over, despair overwhelmed me. My boots were soaked with blood from blisters.

Devastation was everywhere. The road, pastures, and orchards were pocked with artillery craters. Scarcely a tree remained. Horse carcasses rotted under the sun. Burned-out German Tiger and Panther tanks and American Shermans were everywhere, grotesque testimony to the earlier Normandy warfare.

The column filed through a small, totally destroyed town with no sign of life anywhere. A street sign in the mud read "Caen." What the Allied bombing had started, the artillery barrages, the tanks and infantry had completed. As we shuffled along, French farmers toiling in their barren orchards pelted us with stones and rotted apples, blaming us for the Allied bomb damage to their land.

When I collapsed from exhaustion, I came to again in a "meat wagon" (ambulance) with a medic cutting my uniform shirt off me and dressing my shoulder and foot blisters. "You're done walking," he reassured me. I refused his offer and returned to the column as soon as the open sores had been treated. The forced march eventually stopped about midnight, 15 hours after it had started. I learned later that nearly a quarter of the GIs in the march inland had dropped out and had been trucked to our eventual destination.

LOVE Company's first sergeant called me to the tent that served as a CP (command post). "You're being transferred, Blunt, to Anti-Tank Company. Report right away. Here are your orders," he growled, barely looking up at me. Ironically, I was now assigned to a company that traveled in trucks, not on foot. It was maddening to realize that all this excruciating pain could have been avoided if only some rear echelon clerk had done his job more efficiently.

But I soon stopped feeling sorry for myself when I realized how many hundreds of miles remained before us. Actually, the transfer from LOVE Company to Anti-Tank Company simply meant moving from one apple orchard to another, from one pup tent colony to another, from one mess tent to a different one and having to contend with a new batch of officers.

On the move again, lurching along crater-pocked roads, from the rear of the truck, I recognized the men of LOVE Company miserably slogging their way forward through deep mud, with heads bowed in resignation. I hesitated to look back at those who once had been my buddies. Repeatedly we had to tumble off the truck, which almost constantly became mired in the mud, and push it out. The rear wheels, whining and spinning wildly in search of the grip of solid ground and traction, flung half of the mud of France in our faces every time we grunted and shoved.

When the truck finally stopped for the night, I jumped out into the deep ooze and slithered underneath to escape rain pouring down. I managed several hours of sleep before the bone-jarring ride continued. As we neared the war zone, convoy movements were made at night and under blackout conditions. Even so, many roads along the route were lined with civilians throwing flowers and bottles of wine at us. In repayment, we threw gum, candy, food and whatever else we had back at them.

Since the people of this region had not been free of German occupation long, their joy at seeing the reinforcing American liberators was still overwhelming, a far cry from what we had experienced days earlier in

Normandy. It was not until we heard the roadside reception committees shouting "Viva le America. Viva le Belgique" that I realized we had crossed from France into Belgium. I had heard that the people of Flanders were demonstratively emotional and now I was convinced. However, I felt guilty accepting this adoration for I hadn't really done anything to deserve it.

As we drove eastward, I noticed a new twist to the landscape: dozens upon dozens of small, crude wooden crosses made of sticks or small tree branches and crowned with helmets appeared in the ditches. Many were adorned with small bouquets of flowers. These, I learned, were American GIs, buried hastily where they fell and the Belgian people were honoring their memories. These were the first actual American graves I had seen. The war was now very near, I knew, and as we crawled past these roadside graves, the whole truck fell somber and silent, staring at the ditches.

The war had been through the region only days earlier and many of the smashed vehicles from both armies were still smouldering and giving off the stench of death. The graves with no crosses or flowers, we soon figured out, were those of Germans. When the convoy stopped, I inspected some of the graves more closely. They were simply made by grateful Belgians mostly from scrap wood and bound together with twine or wire. None were identified, not even with dog tags.

The convoy had barely started up when it slammed to a halt again.

"Hit the dirt," men screamed. Instinctively, we dove overboard and into nearby ditches. Already, the instinct of preservation was taking over. A constant roar, similar to that of a large diesel truck, could be heard. The rumbling roar grew louder, then stopped.

Looking up, I spotted an ugly, cigar-shaped German buzz bomb with a piggyback rocket compartment and short, stubby wings. It was about 400 feet directly over our heads and had already started its awkward tailspin spiral toward earth. It hit the ground and exploded with a concussive force a half mile away that shook the earth beneath us. I had heard these unguided bombs in London but I had never seen one. The realization hit me that I had finally arrived at the war. It was no longer something "out there somewhere." It was the first frightening sound of war I'd heard. The buzz bomb, I reasoned, with its one-ton explosive load, 100-mile range and fuel for a 20-minute flight, had been aimed at London but had malfunctioned along the way and fallen short near our convoy. Once we were back on the trucks, the convoy pushed relentlessly toward Liege at the junction of the Belgian-Dutch-German borders. The city was devastated, plastered repeatedly by German Stuka dive bombers years before during the German invasion of the lowlands. It was a case of a quiet, innocent city caught in the struggle between major nations at war. The destruction was even worse than London. Hardly a building was left standing.

There were no cheering crowds greeting the American liberators. The people there had suffered too much. There were only the silent staring eyes of people in utter despair who were now merely existing and waiting for the war to end. It was the hopelessness of people whose nerves had been shocked almost beyond human endurance. For most practical purposes, the war was over for them, but it had left a mark that would take generations of forgiveness to erase.

By midnight, the truck column pulled into a war-ravaged village and we unloaded. As we tumbled out of the trucks onto another of Europe's inevitable mud-carpeted streets, a bitter wind blistered our faces. While slogging around looking for a place to hunker down for the night, I called out to Captain John C. Bowen, AT Company commander, "Hey, Cap'n. Where the hell are we?"

"At the end of the line. Holland," he barked out.

The impending war was just around the corner. I could hear it in the distance now and I could smell it. It wouldn't be long.

Our platoon bivouacked in an apple orchard and I tried to pitch a pup tent in an ice-encrusting sleet storm but was thwarted by the mud, the wind and the cold. When I awakened in the morning, I found the tent blown down on top of me. But it mattered little—I was by then too exhausted to care much about anything, much less a tattered GI pup tent whose pegs wouldn't hold firm in the soft Dutch earth.

The date was November 11, 1944—Armistice Day back home—and the first snow of winter was falling heavily.

After a few days, the rest of the Army caught up to us and we received mess-kit hot chow again. In the field, when finished eating, soldiers dumped unfinished portions of food into a swill barrel and then sloshed mess kits in a barrel of soapy hot water.

While dumping my uneaten food into the barrel the first day, I was overrun by several severely undernourished Dutch children from nearby Heerlen who darted up to the garbage bucket and frantically scraped handfuls of garbage up and gorged them down. Then they scraped the sides of the pail with small spoons trying to get every last remaining scrap of food. As fast as they had appeared, they were gone again, bolting away through the apple trees. The sight was pathetic.

During the ensuing days, the platoon began beckoning to these urchins whenever they reappeared and offering them mess kits full of hot food. As long as we were in the orchard, we were determined not to let these babies scrape garbage barrels again to stay alive, at least not in front of us.

From the company field kitchen, I "liberated" sugar, flour, butter and coffee and, with my weekly ration of cigarettes swapped for candy bars, was able to supply my newly adopted children with items they had not seen during the five-year German occupation.

From a Heerlen family, I learned of German occupation atrocities, the scorched earth policy, hastily executed when the occupying forces withdrew before the Allied onslaught. The Germans burned practically every building and barn and then fired phosphorus shells into the orchards to burn the soil, making it useless for planting for years to come. They slaughtered livestock, poultry and even pets, anything that could be eaten. They crushed apple trees with tanks and ground apple crops to pulp with vehicles. Farmers were forced at gunpoint to shake apples from their trees so that the fruit could be sprayed with acids. Mattresses and blankets were slashed with bayonets.

In a premeditated, systematic plan to reduce a whole nation to starvation, the Germans had even contaminated wells and poisoned vegetable and fruit crops. They plundered everything.

Orders came to break camp. This was it: our entry into combat. We loaded onto trucks under cover of darkness and moved slowly eastward on a road even more shell-pocked and rougher than those in the rear area. Our blacked-out truck tipped and groaned furiously as the driver tried, without headlights, to navigate twisting roads. In the distance, we heard almost continuous muffled explosions and could see flashes of light silhouetting nearby low-lying hills. Other than the buzz bombs, these were the first actual sounds of war we had heard. No one spoke; the time for horsing around was past.

The convoy slowed to 10 miles an hour as the road worsened. The battle had passed through the area only hours before and the stench of smoke and fire was overpowering. The artillery blasts grew louder until they were almost deafening. Finally, the convoy halted in Marienberg, a battle-ravaged village with more muddy streets and buildings leveled by violence.

Again, I asked Captain Bowen where we were—Holland or Germany?

"Right on the border," was the only answer I got. Later, a map indicated that we had crossed a mile into Germany.

It was slightly before midnight November 18 when we were advised to find whatever shelter we could for the night. I entered a bombed-out house and staked out a kitchen couch. A still-warm wood stove showed the previous German occupants had fled a short time before. Explosions and gunfire echoing back through the blackened town indicated that fighting was still raging just over a nearby hill.

We were told not to get too comfortable for we would be pulling out in a couple of hours. Sleep refused to come: there were just too many jumbled thoughts racing through my mind.

The Jump-off

"Off your cocks and grab your socks. This is it, the big one you've all been waiting for," yelled a faceless silhouette behind a bright flashlight.

Operation Clipper was underway. It was Sunday and cold, rainy, dismal and gray. A perfect beginning.

Being awakened so abruptly, I felt a sudden wave of nausea wash over me. It wasn't fear as much as the culmination of total physical exhaustion and a lack of proper food since coming ashore on the French coast 17 days earlier. The accumulated loss of sleep and the cold, greasy C-rations were ganging up on my stomach, and the stomach was now starting to fight back.

As I collected my gear by candlelight and staggered out the doorway, the platoon sergeant said, "Blunt, you're on temporary assignment to BAKER Company for this operation. Move out."

BAKER Company, some units of which were still milling around on a nearby street, was already probing its way forward when I arrived. I joined 200 strangers without the slightest idea what I was supposed to do or even who to report to. In cases like this, the wisest thing to do in the Army is to shut up, tag along and wait for an order. The Army isn't noted for telling its soldiers much, and when it does, it's often gibberish or nonsensical.

I fell in at the tail end of the nearest column and started following in the tracks of the dark forms shuffling along in front of me. The silence was eerie, broken only by the occasional clanking of rifles slung against steel helmets and the uneven squishing patter of thousands of footsteps on the muddy street.

The nausea got worse as the ruins of the town slowly fell behind us and the column became enveloped in a black void. With the rain, there were no stars in the sky to offer some bearing or perspective of where we were. Just a blackness that was so total it was difficult to distinguish the GI walking only a few feet in front of me. I struggled as best I could to keep up with the pace set by someone up front. To lag behind, even a few feet, would be to lose sight of the column completely.

After all these months of preparation, the fear of the unknown was finally hitting me and I recognized it for what it was. I didn't feel the least bit ashamed of myself for this emotion. The apprehension was building up too suddenly and was too great. My heart was pounding as I plodded into the unknown. I tried to subjugate my fear by forcing myself to think about home, but it didn't help much. The instinctive feeling of impending death and the ink-like blackness took over my emotional being. I had never been afraid of the dark before, but I was this night.

The column in follow-the-leader fashion silently veered off the road, possibly to avoid mines, and started climbing a gently sloping hill to our right. Just as we reached the crest of the hill, we were suddenly, without any warning, bathed in daylight with grotesque, moving black shadows being cast every which way around us by gigantic floodlights.

"Jesus Christ," someone in front of me muttered. "What the hell's going on? Every gawdamn Kraut in Germany can see us."

But it was not the GI's privilege to question the wisdom of Army brass, just to obey it. In military terms, it's known as "do-and-die blind obedience."

The rumor filtered down through the ranks that Brigadier General Alexander R. Bolling, commanding general of the 84th Division, had been given permission from Corps to use this highly unorthodox "artificial moonlight" to enter combat. To this day, I still can't fathom the rationale behind the maneuver.

Slipping and sliding through the mud tired me quickly, for it was 0230 and I had been up since the previous night with less than an hour of sleep.

We crossed a long, flat open stretch of land, still basking in the glare of the floodlights, and eventually entered the town of Palenberg about 1000 yards from Geilenkirchen. The column was half way through it before I realized the ruins had once been a town. All that remained were a few jagged piles of masonry. The town had been literally flattened.

As we climbed another sloping hill away from the brilliance of the floodlights, the darkness was reassuring; at least now we had some protection and wouldn't make such easy targets. I came across a GI asleep on the hillside and as I walked past him, I nudged him with my foot. "C'mon, man. You can't sleep now," I said under my breath. Then I saw it, an inverted rifle with GI helmet perched on top jammed into the ground beside the face-down sleeping form.

It took a few moments before it sunk in—I was looking at my first dead American. The patch on his jacket indicated he was a Railsplitter. The war was now very close. The corpse was not that of a stranger; this was one of our own. Without looking back, I continued on, but having now actually touched death, I was even less confident of my own abilities. Nearly a half century of time has failed to erase the memory of that first dead GI.

Through the night and the glare of the floodlights behind us, I sensed that I was passing the skeleton of what had once been someone's home. In my mind I damned the floodlights again, for now even though they were far behind us, they still cast us as perfect silhouettes against the terrain for the Germans we knew were waiting up ahead. As we continued across a sugar beet field on the far side of Palenberg, I was startled by a huge, black form that emerged out of the darkness before me. It was a smouldering American Sherman tank at the junction of two stone walls and I had almost bumped into it before seeing it. I would have to learn to rely in the future on smells as well as visual observation.

As we marched, the cadence of our footsteps played a duet with artillery shells swish-swooshing lazily over our heads. Much to our relief, it was all "outgoing mail" and after the first few passed overhead, we ignored them.

Climbing over a wall beside the burning tank, I tripped and fell flat on my face. When I landed, the ground felt different somehow. There was not the normal splattering sound usually heard when one plops down into European mud. I felt the earth with my hand and discovered I was lying on a well-manicured lawn. Moving more cautiously forward, I eventually made out the form of a large mansion, similar in appearance to those of the Civil War era seen in the American South.

The column halted and we were told to dig in. Soon, this once-magnificent estate had dozens of GI foxholes punctuating its lawn like a colony of gophers, another small price of war being paid by some anonymous German family.

Eighty-one millimeter mortar emplacements dug in around us started thwopping away at the German forward positions. As we crouched in our holes, enduring the concussion of each explosion battering our bodies, watching and listening to the sounds of war, it was brought home to us that the enemy was only a few yards in front of us and waiting. As each explosion blinked a millisecond of light, I peered intently into the night trying to see him, but I could detect no one.

It was 0430, and we had been on the move about two hours. Strangely, the nervous fear had disappeared, replaced by a strange elation, almost a euphoria. I started to settle down, knowing that I had successfully gone into combat and nothing had happened to me. I dozed off, but a moment later a blast from a German shell landing nearby blew my helmet off and sent it flying. The parapets of dirt I had thrown around the rim of the hole while digging in had been blown in on top of me, leaving me even more exposed to the German artillery.

The first shots and the first cannonades of my war had been fired. I learned afterwards from grizzly old regular Army non-coms that an infantryman is considered a veteran if he survives his first day of combat.

German artillery was zeroed in on our position. The element of surprise, if there ever had been one, was gone. A steady rainfall had nearly filled my improvised foxhole. With each artillery explosion, the only protective alternative was to cringe forward, bury my face and hold my breath as long as I could before the next shell landed.

I proved, then and there, to myself and the world that a five-foot, nine-inch soldier could compress himself into a three-foot-deep foxhole. I did it, but I also soon learned to dig holes deeper, no matter how much work was involved, for the German shell exploding near me had shown that deep holes could make the difference between life and death.

When the shelling stopped a few minutes later, the ensuing silence was louder than any I had ever heard. All I could hear was the ringing in my ears and my thumping heart. It took only a few minutes to realize that German .88 artillery barrages are nothing at all like the basic training .105-mm shellings we had experienced back in Alabama.

After 20 minutes of figuratively holding my breath, the shelling started up again, only far worse this time. But, again to our relief, it was ours and we were battering the Germans three rounds to their one. The shells exploding only a few yards in front of us pounded our position almost as badly as the German barrage had earlier.

I mistakenly thought the American shelling was retaliatory, but it turned out to be the softening-up process preceding our attack. A combat infantryman's comprehension of the war extends only as far as the foxholes on either side of his position, not into the map rooms at Battalion, Division or Army. What a combat GI sees, he can attest to, and nothing more, for he is never privy to the overall picture. After a while, he doesn't even try to figure anything out; he just exists by rote and waits for the next command.

The barrage continued for more than a half hour. Curled up in the fetal position with eyes tightly clamped shut in our holes, we were being knocked almost senseless by the concussion from each explosion. As each detonated, I was pitched violently from one side of my hole to the other, back and forth until mercifully, the shelling finally stopped. When I was satisfied the barrage was over, I peeked out of my hole and saw that dawn had broken.

BAKER Company commander jumped out of his hole, yelling, "Let's go! Let's go! This is it. We have a city to take!" I looked at my watch. It was 0600 on the dot, and we were "going over the top," just like in the movies. Men all around me were scrambling out of their foxholes and surging forward en masse. On November 19, 1944, the day I had waited for so long, I met and fought the German on his own ground, even though I had yet to see him or fire a shot.

The ground attack started slowly, picking up momentum as we moved forward. When the city finally came into view, smoke filling the sky from one end of the city to the other, we broke from a fast walk into a frantic sprint, darting jaggedly back and forth across a 200-yard-long sugar beet field.

I galloped across a dirt road and catapulted myself blindly into a ditch, trying to escape from that exposed beet field as quickly as I could. But I should have looked before I dove; the ditch was half-filled with water. I came up drenched, chilled and miserably uncomfortable.

I jumped up again and sprang across another field where I saw a BAKER Company rifleman lying face down on the ground. As I ran toward him, I yelled, "C'mon. Let's keep moving." Then I saw one of his legs had been blown off below the knee and the bloody foot stump was on the ground several feet away. He was still alive. Shuddering at the sight, I yelled, "I'll get you a medic," and kept running.

My heart jumped into my throat when it finally occurred to me I was running full tilt in a field infested with hundreds of wooden Schu mines. "Mines! Mines!" I screamed at the other GIs around me, but for the legless GI I had just passed, it was too late. I skidded to a stop and stared at the ground. Some were buried shallow, the rest just planted on the surface in no particular pattern.

The apprehension I had felt back in Palenberg almost paralyzed me now. I stood frozen, afraid even to put my foot down. Slowly, I inched my way forward, putting as little weight as possible on each step. At that moment, I realized for the first time the insidious psychological effect mines have on a soldier. It struck home. I would take my chances with small arms fire or even artillery rather than these silent, deadly devices.

I was pushing my feet along the ground, not wanting to lift them, when an explosion about 100 feet to my left signalled another victim of the German mine field. This man didn't have to worry about being an amputee—both his legs and groin area had been blown away and he was dead before he hit the ground. I was instantly sickened when I shot a glance in his direction and saw his body still twitching on the ground, even in death.

The sight of this second shattered body unnerved me. This was a rotten war, and mines were a stinking way to die.

The loud snap of a whip close to my head brought me back to reality fast. It took a few seconds for me to react; this was a new sound to me, a sound not described in Army training manuals. It was a sniper bullet, probably from somewhere in the city a few hundred yards before me.

I threw myself on the ground, the mines be damned. The hidden German sniper fired again and dirt kicked up in my face, only inches away. I was his sole target and at that moment the war had become one-on-one and I knew he would never let up. I was out in the open, totally exposed with no place to hide, and still had no idea where the shots were coming from.

Frantically, I started to crawl forward, rifle cradled in my arms. Every snake-like motion of my body meant I might be crawling over a mine, but I had to make it to the comparative safety of a small ditch-like canal about 100 feet in front of me. The sniper fired again and again, each time the bullet peppering me with chunks of earth.

Finally, unable to take it any longer as each slug chewed up the ground around me, I jumped up and ran in a headlong dash for my life. No zigzag this time, just a mad burst of flailing legs, a desperate will to escape. I made it to the Wurm River and jumped in, wading furiously through three-foot-deep water and flopping against the far bank, out of sight of the sniper.

For several minutes I lay there panting and trying to quiet my galloping heartbeat, all the while furtively snatching glimpses of a quaint, water-powered mill beside a spillway about 100 feet from me. This had to be where the sniper was concealed. The lack of sleep and food and the tension of the past few hours were apparently too much for me. As I crouched half-submerged in the canal water trying to regain my composure, nausea swept over me again and I started to gag.

From the intermittent firing on both sides of me, I knew the attack was still underway. Peering over the edge of the canal embankment, I saw men on both sides of me running toward the city. For a fleeting moment, I thought of remaining safely in the canal until the attack was over. No one would ever know—the confusion surrounding me would shield my location and identity. I watched dozens of GIs advancing on both sides of me past the canal and toward the city, relieved that I was not alone. My eyes scanned the windows of every building facing me for several long minutes and I saw no signs of life or movement from any of them. I watched for puffs of smoke signifying a machine gun or a sniper from a number of wooden sheds scattered randomly in some of the closest yards, but they all appeared to be empty.

Off to my left, American troops, their M-1s held across their chests, were running crouched low among the buildings without firing. When all the shooting finally tapered off and there still were no signs of German troops anywhere, I opted to try for a railroad trestle bridge, a clump of shattered trees and another canal directly in front of me. It seemed like a safe route and if I made it, I too would be inside the city.

We had advanced more than 4000 yards from Palenberg.

I glanced to my right and saw ABLE Company working its way toward a row of pillboxes set slightly apart from the city. I made it to the bridge and swampy canal and started wading my way closer to the outlying buildings. I crawled up an embankment and out into the open again, pausing only a moment to look around before running again, this time firing my M-1 from the hip at an invisible enemy. When there was no return fire, I threw myself to the ground behind a low stone wall enclosing a backyard vegetable garden and emptied a clip at windows and doors about 50 feet away. Still receiving no response, I fired another clip as I sprinted to the closest building, where I crashed through the back door and crouched in a hallway, again struggling for breath.

I had reached the city alive, but what was I supposed to do once I got there? There was no one in sight anywhere. I got the sinking feeling I had been left behind somehow, totally isolated from the others. I cautiously inched myself deeper into the building and found myself in a demolished grocery and remnants store with shelves and merchandise scattered every-where. Through a shattered window, I saw a slight movement in a doorway across the street. I drew a bead on it and paused. Lucky I did—it was another GI.

I yelled across to him, asking whether he could see anyone. I got my answer when a bullet ricocheted off a door casing near my head. "He's in your building on the second floor!" I screamed, cringing against a wall for protection. I heard three fast shots and moments later I spotted the GI waving an OK sign at me from a gaping hole on the second floor from which the sniper had been firing. He had eliminated the sniper and I felt safe in pouncing back out onto the street.

I had broken one of the first rules of combat by giving away my position and, this one time, I had lived to tell about it. It had been lesson number one in combat and a mistake that I wouldn't repeat again. With each passing hour I was learning the rules of survival.

I doubled back across the street and joined the other GI who had taken down the sniper. He was from BAKER Company and informed me it had taken his company two hours to fight its way to the center of the city. He also said that most of the city had been cleared except for a few diehard snipers here and there. To play it safe, we decided to check out some buildings on his side of the street. He went first while I lay in a doorway ready to give him covering fire.

As we leapfrogged our way down the debris-cluttered street, I spotted movement out of the corner of my eye. I whirled around and saw Sergeant Norman Betz, our squad leader and a retread from ITEM Company, sauntering down the street without a care in the world and accompanied by several other members of the mine-removal squad from which I had been detached back in Marienberg.

He greeted me like a long-lost cousin and handed me a "vacuum cleaner" mine detector with the casual wisecrack, "Here, Blunt, I'm tired of carrying this gawdamn thing for you." With that, he disappeared with the others down the main street past a grassy, triangular patch of trees at an intersection across from the *Geilenkirchen Beobachter* (Geilenkirchen Observer).

After several buildings were searched and cleared of German stragglers, I signalled to the BAKER Company GI that I would check out a cellar near the square. As silently as combat boots allowed, I tiptoed down the cellar stairs and listened at a door where I could hear movement and muffled voices inside.

"Kommen Sie heraus mit hande hoch" (Come out with hands high), I yelled at the top of my voice. Only then did I remember that Betz had swapped my rifle for the mine detector. The door opened a crack, a white handkerchief tied to a stick poked out, and behind it emerged a shabbily uniformed Wehrmacht soldier. Trapped in a situation I couldn't back away from, I pointed the mine detector at him and asked him if he was alone. Looking terrified at the new "secret weapon" I held in my hand, he said there were others. When I reassured him they would not all be shot, 21 more bedraggled, unshaven soldiers filed out. They had never seen an American mine detector and thought it was a weapon of some sort.

They were the bedraggled remnants of First Company, 343rd Infantry Regiment of the 183rd Volksgrenadiers Division, their identification books indicated.

I stripped them of their knives, pistols, "potato masher" grenades and rifles and marched them down the main street with their hands folded over their heads. Seeing Betz returning from a sight-seeing tour of the city, I turned them over to him and reclaimed my rifle. At this, the prisoners finally realized they had been duped. Betz walked away, laughing. "Only you, Blunt, only you could pull this off."

"Stadt name?" (What city is this?) I asked the prisoners.

"Geilenkirchen," one mumbled back.

They told us they had been left behind to defend the city at all costs while the main body of troops had pulled back. They had lost their will to fight, mostly because of hunger and the artillery barrage that preceded our attack. They were just glad to be alive and know that their war was finally over.

These frightened, half-starved Kriegs Gefangener (war prisoners) didn't look at all like the images of vicious German soldiers with cruel, distorted, snarling faces displayed on posters back in basic training lectures. Facing them close up brought the war into sharper focus for me. I was dealing with men just like ourselves, only in different uniforms, speaking a different language and fighting for a different cause.

When everything finally quieted down and I collected my thoughts, I realized my baptism of fire was behind me. I felt proud. I was finally able to sling my rifle over my shoulder instead of constantly keeping it pointed at the ready.

Geilenkirchen was a major rail and mining center with a population of about 20,000. It was also one of Hitler's bastions in his Siegfried Line defenses. In an attempt to bolster divisional pride, word came down from 84th headquarters that Geilenkirchen was one of the first and largest German cities—second only to Aachen—to be taken by American forces during the furious fighting to breach the Siegfried Line and push on to the Roer River.

The streets were filling up fast with men from ABLE and BAKER companies. With the city now secure, I went back into the cellar to sort over the arsenal of weapons I had stripped from my 22 prisoners before other GIs found them. There were enough rifles, grenades and machine guns in the cellar to hold off a battalion, had the prisoners wanted to. I claimed all the pistols, a German paratrooper trench knife, and a Schmeisser burp gun before smashing all the other weapons against the walls. Then I checked out the rest of the cellar, to see just how German snipers operated.

The concrete cellar foundation was an unbelievable six feet thick with four-foot-square openings on the inside that tapered to about a foot square at the outer wall. The sniper merely positioned himself in these openings and had an excellent field of fire in practically all directions while being offered full protection from artillery.

One by one, I started searching other buildings for loot that would be useful to me. As I started down one of the streets, I heard a prolonged burst of machine gun and M-1 rifle fire. I pressed against a wall and listened. When it stopped, I cautiously moved forward, my rifle up to my shoulder, not knowing what to expect for I had been told the city was cleared of Germans.

I snapped a quick glance around a corner and saw about 30 GIs guarding a group of German prisoners taken from the cellar of a bookstore. On the ground a dead American lieutenant and a German soldier were lying in a large pool of blood. The group told me the Germans had surrendered under a white flag, and while they were being searched, one had stepped from the back of the group and shot the lieutenant in the head with a concealed pistol.

The GIs had riddled him with more than 100 bullet holes and were staring at the German prisoners, hoping someone else would make a move and give them an excuse to slaughter the whole lot.

I searched another building for souvenirs and hit the jackpot. It had been a Gestapo headquarters and was filled with Nazi flags, pictures, whips and other torture devices. In a safe, I found bundles of money, which I threw out a window to the winds, for there was nothing to buy in the city and the money was worthless to us. Perhaps if the civilian population ever returned, they could reclaim it. I just knew it was fun to throw money away, even if it was German Reichsmarks.

I took several flags and destroyed everything else before I left. If I ever met any of our rear echelon troops, I figured to be in good bargaining position with the flags.

I entered another building and stumbled over another German whose war was over. The building contained one of the plushiest apartments I had ever seen but the war had passed through and not much of the elegance remained. Not being a particularly religious man, nonetheless I found something I still treasure. It was a small crucifix from Lourdes in France. I shoved it in my uniform watch pocket and carried it through every battle. Often, I pulled it out and looked at it for strength.

With the city now secure and with my anti-mine squad nowhere to be found, I decided to try out my newest trophy, the German Schmeisser "burp" machine gun—so called because its rapid fire, coming in short bursts, sounded like bbbuuurrrppp.

I made my way to the Wurm River I had forded earlier coming into the city and fired a few bursts into the water. I was enjoying myself when someone grabbed me by the shoulder and yanked me around. It was BAKER Company commander, who chewed me out for firing a German weapon near American troops. I didn't understand why he was so upset until he pointed out the possibility of some trigger-happy GI, hearing the sound of a German machine gun and thinking it was a German, pumping me full of lead. Shocked at my own stupidity, I quickly threw the gun into the canal. After all, I was going to get all the target practice I needed in the coming months.

About this time, I heard "Hey, Blunt!" It was Sergeant Betz and the mine squad again. "C'mon. We've got a mission." I ducked into a nearby building, stashed my flags and weapons where no one could find them and rejoined the squad. We picked up our gear and started out on what we later called the "Betz Salient."

Our objective was to scout along a railroad track between Geilenkirchen and Suggerath, about two kilometers away, to assess the enemy strength in that area. We moved out slowly in squad formation—two men walking point, two others on the flanks for security, and the rest bringing up the rear.

Betz and I took the point, running crouched low on either side of the tracks. About a half mile from Geilenkirchen, we came to a gate tender's shack. While I covered him, Betz crashed his way inside. It was vacant.

Finding no German opposition, we stopped to rest and eat a K-ration. With my helmet as a pillow, I promptly dozed off on the rail tracks, warmed by the November sun. Fifteen minutes later, Betz moved us forward again. In single-file formation, we moved toward Suggerath. A whip cracked again beside my head. The GI about six feet in front of me suddenly cried out, "Oh my God. I'm dead." By the time he pitched forward and slumped to the ground he had already been cast into the black abyss of eternity from which there is no return. As we threw ourselves prone on the ground, I saw only a small, bloody bullet hole in his back. He never made another sound after his initial exclamation. Before the shock of losing one of our squad had time to hit me, I wondered if he had cried out before he died or afterward.

When a medic finally ran up to examine him, Betz moved the patrol forward again, each man solemnly glancing back at the corpse on the ground. The shot could only have come from a sniper in the gate tender shack that earlier had been checked out, now about 100 yards behind us. We doubled back and laid down withering rifle fire at the building. A white flag started waving from a window and the sniper surrendered. We surrounded him and then, in a spontaneous outburst of hatred, every man in the squad fired at once. It was an eye for an eye. Many times later I learned that snipers were seldom taken alive unless they were needed for information.

When we returned to the field where our squad had suffered its first casualty, one of the other men was cradling the corpse in his arms as if to comfort it. He had been the dead man's friend back home, had been inducted with him, trained with him, shipped out with him and fought with him. And now his friend was dead after only two days of combat. The man sobbed like a baby. We pushed on silently, leaving him to his private grief. We knew that Graves Registration would be along soon and the two friends would be separated.

The Anti-Mine Squad was now down to 11. Who would be next? I remembered that shortly before, I had carelessly slept on the tracks a mere 75 feet from the sniper's position, a perfect target. The fates of war had decided that death, though walking close beside me, instead had chosen someone else.

As we came around a nearby barn, I found we were in another Schu mine field, only this time the mines had all been hastily thrown on the ground. Picking my way cautiously around them, in my concentration I was oblivious of small arms fire all around me. But I was startled back to reality by bullets splintering a barn wall above my head. The fire was coming from a huge pillbox before me. Men everywhere were hugging the earth and crawling to the rear. I sprinted about 30 feet and dove into a ditch where I could see the German machine gun barrels poking out of the pillbox. I was still exposed and knew I had to move.

I zigzagged across a nearby road and threw myself into another ditch, where I embraced the ground as bullets kicked up dirt over my head. We were pinned down. Also in the ditch with me was an ABLE Company officer who was trying frantically by walkie-talkie to get a flame-throwing Crocodile tank to burn the box. A British-accented voice answered the urgent request with, "Send in more infantry. They can be replaced." The infantry was American, the tanks were British—another bitter incident of war that remained with me for a long time. At the time, we were unaware that the 84th Division had been under temporary British command for more than a week.

The officer then called for artillery support and within seconds it was whistling overhead. After 10 minutes, the barrage ceased. Men around me charged directly into more murderous German machine gun fire. Those who were not cut down during these aborted charges repeatedly withdrew to whatever cover they could find. Eventually, they stopped trying and we all squirmed in the roadside ditch waiting to see what would happen next. The pillbox had effectively stalled our advance.

That day we learned that artillery is largely ineffective against underground pillboxes, and the alternatives were to lie there and take it or retreat and work our way around and bypass the fortification if possible. Pillboxes could usually be taken, we found, with satchel charges by approaching from the rear and throwing them through the gun apertures or ventilating systems.

I started to dig in with my bare hands and then with my helmet. In a half hour, I had a hole deep enough to feel a little safer. Soon, I dozed off again but was awakened by a hideous roar. Two British tanks were flame-drenching the facing of the box for us while engineers crawled behind it with demolition charges. The charge was detonated and through the smoke, a single-file of about a dozen Germans surrendered.

The flames, they told us, had shut down their air supply and they had not been able to breathe. One of the GIs from the attacking force marched them back to Geilenkirchen.

As we advanced once again toward the sloping hills of Suggerath, we heard German anti-aircraft guns in the village. In a ball of fire, a P-51 American fighter plummeted from the sky, trailing flames and black smoke behind it and slamming into the hill about a half mile in front of us. Even though we kept looking up hopefully, there was no sign the pilot had been able to bail out.

A stream of .57-mm tracer shells cut into Suggerath as the wind picked up and it began to snow lightly. I passed another GI with his dog tags wrapped around his rifle stock and thought how peaceful he looked. Little by little I was beginning to accept death for what it was: a by-product of war—some of them, some of us.

When I reached the top of the hill, shivering from the weather change, I was greeted by one of the prettiest sights I had seen so far. The town was aflame from one end to the other and I was momentarily held entranced by the red glow illuminating the night sky as the buildings were being consumed by flames. Beyond the village, the flames painted dancing shadows on a pine forest bordering a sloping snow-covered meadow. In all its savagery, the scene was quite beautiful, almost like a violent etching.

I wanted to get to the town as fast as I could to be warmed by the flames. In frontal formation, we drew no enemy fire as we moved in. As I walked down the central street of the inferno the flames felt good. The column halted and spread out, keeping distance between us in case of a mortar barrage. A nearby GI informed me I had inadvertently filtered back into LOVE Company and he asked if I had anything to eat, saying that he had not eaten all that day. I broke out a D-ration hard chocolate candy bar I had in my field pack and gave it to him.

In a ditch beside the road, I closed my eyes again, warmed by burning buildings all around me. I had been awake, except for a few catnaps, since leaving Holland the day before.

Sometime afterwards I awoke and found the other GI still in the ditch with me asleep. I looked around but could see no one else. I got the disturbing feeling the town had been abandoned by LOVE Company. I shook the man beside me to whom I had given the ration and asked where everyone was. Then I saw the dented helmet and the bullet hole in it. My ditch companion was a corpse, meaning there was a sniper somewhere in the flaming buildings around us. I rolled him over and saw his bulging cheek. He had been eating my D-ration when his life ended. His eyes were wide open in death. I hadn't heard the shot nor had I heard him die. The sniper had apparently seen me and thought I was dead and not worth wasting a bullet on.

For a moment, I wondered whether I had made my unknown dead companion's last minutes on this earth happier with my D-ration.

Breaching the Siegfried Line

LOVE Company had pulled back during the night, leaving me alone in a Suggerath ditch with a dead man. They apparently had seen me asleep in the ditch and had assumed I was just another corpse to be picked up later. It took me a few minutes to collect my wits before deciding to go back and look for my old company. I wasn't even sure if they had pulled back or had pushed on farther. I decided to try backward. The known was always safer than the unknown. I walked back up the slope from which we had come some hours earlier.

I passed through an undefined line of foxholes and stumbled onto DOG Company. When I told them I was lost, they showed me where I could dig in, but I was too exhausted and just stretched out in the snow to sleep.

"Hey, Blunt. C'mon over here. I've got room in my hole." It was Joe Everett, of Madill, Oklahoma, another member of the Anti-Mine Squad. When I had been temporarily assigned to BAKER Company back in Marienberg, Everett had been similarly sent to DOG Company for any mine-removal duties needed there.

During the trying times ahead, Everett and I shared many foxholes and tried to maintain our sanity by arguing often whether older or younger women were more desirable. Being only 19, I voted for older women. Everett, on the other hand, was six years older than me and adamantly argued the virtues of dating young Choctaw or Chickasaw Indian girls on a Saturday night in Ardmore, Oklahoma.

The reunion was warm. Since the jump-off had started two days earlier, I had mostly been alone, surrounded by strangers trying to kill strangers.

When daylight came, I could see Suggerath still smouldering before me and the ruins of Geilenkirchen in the distance behind me. About 600 yards to our right, another string of pillboxes looked like a row of unnatural humps in nature's landscape. No matter how cleverly disguised the German fortifications were, we were already learning to spot them from a distance. The survival instinct was gradually developing within us.

I could see groups of German soldiers walking back and forth between the pillboxes, silhouetted against the cold and cloudless blue sky. I fired off an M-1 clip of harassing fire at them, perhaps out of spite or because it seemed the right thing to do at the time. They obviously couldn't even hear me as they continued going about their business, but I felt better having fired at them. After all, wasn't that what I was supposed to be doing?

I broke open a can of C-rations and tried to eat it but the hash inside stuck in my throat. As I spit it out, "incoming mail" (German .88s) started pounding our position. Everett and I crouched against each other, crammed in the bottom of his hole, trying to crawl inside our helmets. The unmerciful beating we took was the worst shelling since the jump-off had begun. The Germans knew precisely where we were.

The most terrifying aspect of an artillery bombardment is not that your mind goes blank, which it does, for all thoughts of home and family and the fear of dying are blown away when the first shell hits. Nothing remains. Nothing. The worst aspect is cringing in mortal fear, knowing that the next shell will land on top of you. Such absolute fear brought on a mental paralysis, a form of shock that blotted out all senses or emotions.

A near-miss caved part of the hole down on top of us. I shall never forget the screeching whine of incoming .88s, "screaming mimmies," that intensified until eardrums wanted to burst. After one such blast, I blacked out. When I came to, I was still in the hole and Everett had his arm protectively around me.

I couldn't focus my vision; everything looked fuzzy gray. Even though not a word was said to me, I knew I had been crying. I could hear voices around me but I couldn't distinguish them. Everett shed some light on what had transpired after the artillery shell had exploded outside our foxhole. The explosion had blown me partially out of the foxhole, and when the smoke settled, I had jumped up and started running around shaking my fists in the air and cursing the Germans. Everett said I was yelling, "Come on, you bastards. I'll kill you all!"

Everett had jumped out of the hole amidst the bursting shells and grabbed me. When I struggled, he overpowered me and dragged me back to the relative safety of our foxhole. There, he pinned my arms back and sat on me until the shelling stopped.

Peering over the rim of our foxhole, we saw a group of American GIs running away from the distant pillboxes. In Army manuals, this was called a "strategic advance to the rear," but actually it was men running for their lives. The Germans had overrun their position and scattering GIs were hightailing it for the relative safety of our hill. Within minutes, they were streaming through our positions and still heading west as fast as their legs would carry them.

When a DOG Company lieutenant panicked and yelled for us to join the retreating troops, Everett pulled me down the hill. We joined the rout until we came to a culvert beneath the Geilenkirchen-Suggerath railroad track. Crawling through it to a gravel ditch on the far side, we found a medic bending over a GI whose elbow had been shattered by artillery fire.

I ran crouching along the ditch and skidded to a halt as I came face to face with two German soldiers who probably had been American prisoners and who were now both victims of their own artillery shelling. One had an arm and leg blown off and had apparently died moments before.

The other had been disemboweled and his mouth, nose and jaw had been blown away. How, I don't know, but he was still alive and as I stared at him, his eyes followed my every movement. With each breath, foamy blood drooled from his mouth onto what had once been his chest. Only a foot-wide gaping hole of bloody meat remained of what had been his upper chest, and his intestinal tract lay stretched out on the gravel like long twisted links of sausage. I could not take my eyes off this gruesome scene.

Everett broke the trance I was in when he returned to see why I hadn't kept up with him. The retreat didn't end until we reached the outskirts of Geilenkirchen and found reinforcements.

During the confusion, my head cleared—except for an excruciating headache—and with a few minutes of free time on our hands while the situation stabilized, Everett and I went loot hunting. We reentered Geilenkirchen proper. In a priest's former home that was quite elaborate we found chinaware and tablecloths on which to eat. We located the Anti-Tank Company kitchen and treated ourselves to the first hot food in nearly a week. DOG Company, if they needed us, could wait—the opportunity for hot food came too seldom. Someone approached me and said there was a medic back at the priest's home looking for me.

The medic greeted me and informed me I was being sent to a field hospital back at Marienberg for mental evaluation because of the artillery shell incident that had blown me from my foxhole. I protested the evacuation, saying I wasn't crazy, but he shut me off. "You either come with me now or the MPs will take you back. Which will it be?" Saying good-bye to Everett with the flippant remark, "Hey, Joe, keep the war going for me," I followed the medic to a Red Cross marked jeep and climbed in. The trip took only a few minutes.

The hospital was a partially bombed-out building that had been scrubbed clean and was filled mostly with patients being treated for wounds serious enough to send them back to England or the States. I felt out of place; I hadn't been wounded, only subjected to a close one.

I was given a hot shower and a fresh change of uniform, both of which lessened the stigma of my forced trip to the rear. After a long soak, I shaved. The stillness of the field hospital was difficult to become accustomed to. I was put to bed and slept straight through from noon one day until 0700 the next.

After a breakfast of bacon, eggs and coffee on plates and eaten with utensils, a captain stopped by and told me I had an appointment at his office at 1000 so he could ask me some questions. I asked a wounded soldier in a bed beside mine who the captain was.

"A psychiatrist," he said.

I relished the breakfast I had been given and pondered whether I should string along for a while at least with what the Army considered was best for me.

The doctor, a friendly sort, offered me a cigarette, which I declined, and had me sit down. He asked me to relate in detail what I had done since going into combat and what I thought of combat and the war in general. He kept nodding his head and taking notes.

Finally, unable to stand it any longer, I demanded to know, "I don't belong here. I haven't cracked up, have I?"

"No, I don't think so but you have experienced a very severe shock to your nervous system," he replied. "Your answers haven't all been completely rational but I think with a couple of days rest you'll be just fine." When he dismissed me, I headed back to the hot food chow line again.

After three days of these question-and-answer sessions, I was deemed cured and told I could return to my squad. That was fine with me; I was starting to get a little itchy from the inactivity. A jeep returned me to Geilenkirchen and dumped me off where I had been picked up. Fortunately, the Anti-Mine Squad was still there so I rejoined them. I found Everett was back after deserting DOG Company when it moved back on the line.

Interested in what I had been doing in Marienberg, the others envied my stories about the field hospital beds and hot food. Soon after I bunked into Everett's billet, the Germans began shelling the city and I found myself cringing with every shell burst, a reaction I hadn't experienced before being subjected to the peaceful atmosphere of the hospital. I retreated into the cellar hoping this jumpiness would go away when I again acclimated myself to combat conditions.

While my squad huddled in a room at the priest's house, a loud crash sent them all sprawling onto the floor. When the dust settled, they found an artillery shell dud imbedded in the floor near the doorway. It was another unexplained mystery of war. Had it detonated, it would have destroyed half of our squad.

In the cellar, I made a bed out of straw and tried to get comfortable. With me were the two squad members who were closest to the sniper victim a few days earlier in Suggerath and who now were unable to cope with their loss. When both eventually became too terrified to venture out onto the street, some of us brought them their meals. Whenever a shell exploded in the city, they cowered in a corner trembling.

The company officers became aware of this and the two men were transferred back to Marienberg to guard Anti-Tank Company equipment and barracks bags in the rear area. I was glad they could still contribute to the war effort without being stripped of their dignity and pride.

Battle fatigue hit men of all ages and in many different ways. No one ridiculed them. We all knew it could happen to anyone at any time, and we realized that understanding was called for. The mind and body could be tortured only so much before they reached their tolerance limit and snapped. Psychological or emotional wounds healed slowly. With their leaving, the squad was down to nine and our war was only five days old.

I spent much of my free time exploring and searching for souvenirs. The people of the city were quite religious. Every street intersection had cruci-fixion statues mounted on posts, and most homes were adorned with ornate wall crucifixes.

In one building, I found several Hitler Jugend (youth) snare drums used at political rallies. I had carried a pair of drum sticks in my pack all the way from the States so I had a ball for myself making enough racket at the billet to emulate World War III. After someone took my picture with them I shoved one in my dufflebag to keep. I hoped that when my family back home saw the pictures they would think everything was a lark in Germany.

It was amazing how much a barracks bag would hold. Mine was soon filled with war booty for most Army gear had already been discarded. While liberating items from practically every building I came across, I found a toy-size spoon that would be handy for eating C-rations. I stuffed it into my uniform watch pocket with the crucifix. I still have both.

The next day, troop convoys rolled through the city headed back toward Holland, away from the battle. Rumors were rife that we were being pushed back by the Germans and that soon Geilenkirchen would be overrun by their tanks. Orders came soon afterward to be ready to move out in 10 minutes. As we loaded onto a troop carrier, I discounted the rumors, figuring the area had been cleared and our unit was now needed elsewhere.

We bounced along for some time when a non-com in the truck broke open a case of K-rations and flung them around at us. "Here. Now you guys can celebrate."

"Celebrate what?" someone asked.

"Didn't you know? It's Thanksgiving. Here's your turkey dinner," he answered, sarcastically.

Later, I read in the military newspaper, *Stars & Stripes*, that all European troops, especially those in the front lines, had been supplied with full course turkey dinners with all the fixings. At least, this is what the Army wanted the people back home to believe, so in my next letter, I described in great detail the dinner I had allegedly been given from nuts to cranberry sauce. I felt justified in telling them this small lie for the truth would have served no purpose. Many white lies were told in letters home to spare my family from anxiety.

When the convoy arrived at its destination it was getting dark. We tumbled from the trucks and tried to find shelter from the cold. Locating a house with a section of the roof still intact, I cleared debris away from a corner of the kitchen and dropped my gear. Within minutes, I proved that even a pile of rubble could make a good bed. After someone found a lantern, we were quite cozy. Blackout conditions were fine for the rear echelon troops, but comfort, something seldom achieved, was of primary importance up front.

Morning came much too soon, about six hours later. Curious as always, I went outside to explore and was met with the most gruesome sight I had yet seen. A building sign identified the town as Prummern. We were told that the fiercest battle fought so far by the 84th had been there by elements of the 334th Regiment against SS troops and Panzer Grenadiers the day before our unit moved forward.

American and German bodies lay scattered everywhere, usually side by side and some with knives still in hand attesting to the fierce hand-to-hand fighting that had taken place. Abandoned rifles all had bayonets attached. More than 100 bodies littered a two-acre plot. Every house, room, street, alleyway, foxhole and shell crater contained at least one body, it seemed.

The name Prummern would be remembered in 84th Division history; it had been written in blood. The grotesque sights there will be in my memory as long as I live.

I came upon a decapitated German corpse, slumped face forward in a foxhole with a Schmeisser machine gun pointed at four dead Americans who had obviously tried to rush his position. The German had a holstered pistol and trench knife attached to his ammo belt and I wanted them.

Fearing the body might be rigged with a booby trap, I noosed a long piece of wire gently around the German's arm and crawled a safe distance away. I tugged at the wire repeatedly until I was convinced the corpse was not rigged with explosives to maim souvenir hunters. I crawled into the hole, picked up the still-helmeted head, studied it a moment and then threw it away.

Minutes later, I had my first Luger pistol and another Kraut trench knife. I took some blood-stained writing paper off the body and eventually wrote a letter home on it. My parents never knew what the brown stains on one of my letters were.

I found some of my squad members gathered around a dung heap in a courtyard at our temporary billet. While they admired my Luger, a German .88 shell landed in the manure pile and detonated before we could react. Though covered with manure and severely stunned by the explosion, not one of us suffered a scratch.

GIs had a saying: the Germans were so accurate with their artillery, they could put a shell in your hip pocket. It was also believed that with a muzzle velocity of 3600 feet per second, you never heard the .88 that would hit you. When you heard the whistle, it was already too late, it was past you. The incident in the courtyard proved the saying. We had heard nothing before the explosion.

Word was passed around that hot chow, the first in several days, was available at the company field kitchen. As I walked back to my billet with mess kit full of field slop, picking my way over dead bodies lying on the muddy street, I saw another GI carrying a mess kit coming toward me on his way to the kitchen.

Faintly in the distance, I heard the swish of a mortar round about to land. Instinctively, I dove for a doorway. The GI, apparently unaware, kept walking. As I crouched watching, the shell landed in the street, a direct hit. The man disintegrated, leaving only patches and puddles of flesh and blood spattered in the mud. Graves Registration wouldn't find this one, not even his dog tags. Another unknown soldier. I sat and ate my food, for I hadn't known him. Combat was becoming quite impersonal.

Later, I tried to write home by heavily shaded lantern light, but concussion from an artillery barrage blew out the lantern. The building shuddered convulsively as shrapnel ricocheted off what walls remained. When more of the roof collapsed, some of us withdrew to the cellar. Twenty minutes later, the shelling stopped. When we tried to make our way out of the cellar to make sure the barrage was not a prelude to a German counter-attack, the trapdoor at the head of the stairs was buried with debris. No matter how hard we pushed, it wouldn't budge. We were trapped. Fortunately, a cellar window was just large enough to crawl through to the street. An artillery shell had completed the demolition of the house in which we had been temporarily sheltered.

I pulled two-hour guard duty one night, midnight to 0200, in an area overshadowed by a huge defense bunker. I walked alone watching spasmodic bursts of anti-aircraft fire illuminating the night sky. To escape a cold, drizzling rain, I thought about entering the bunker for shelter. But the prospect of joining four dead, grenade-killed Germans inside in the dark deterred me. I continued to walk my post, feeling quite alone.

Orders came to rejoin Anti-Tank Company for another territorial move. I was starting to accept the middle-of-the-night, nomadic life-style of the combat infantryman. It meant only more sleep lost, more mud, less food, more cold and worse living conditions. We pulled into another sea of mud in the town of Immendorf just before daybreak in the waning days of November.

To understand the billeting procedure, I should first explain how German houses were usually disassembled by war. First, the doors and windows were blown out with bazookas and grenades to eliminate possible snipers. The roofs and floors usually burned their way into the cellar, with the remaining exterior walls collapsing outward onto yards and streets. All that normally remained of the houses after a battle was rubble.

Soldiers seeking shelter either could clear debris away from a corner of the building and sleep against a wall, or they could try to get into a cellar and exist for a few hours by candlelight. Cellars were preferred by some for they offered shelter from the elements, but in the event of a lightning enemy counter-attack, those living in cellars were most vulnerable for they couldn't evacuate the building as rapidly. I used candlelight whenever possible for the effect it had on me, both physically and psychologically. Candles were wonderful for warming numbed hands and even feet, and they could partially dry out wet clothes. Candles could also warm C-rations slightly but, most importantly, they offered a flickering flame of hope where often there was nothing but darkness and despair. Candles were excellent morale-builders.

Candles had as many varied uses for the combat GI as his helmet, which was alternately used as a frying pan, shaving basin, toilet, pillow and even, sometimes, as head protection.

We were fortunate, for in Immendorf I found a mostly intact billet consisting of three walls, a roof and cellar for my squad. I say fortunate, for according to Army plans, we were to spend several days there. As Spartan as the living conditions were, it was a relief to be able to stay put in one location for more than a few minutes and to figuratively catch our breaths.

The company kitchen was dispensing hot food with a new twist: pancakes and occasionally some bacon for breakfast. I quickly learned how to beg, steal or barter empty C-ration cans of pancake batter for butts, booze or candy with the company mess sergeant. This enabled me to make myself pancakes over an improvised portable stove as a midnight snack back at the billet.

And, as luck would have it, my most recent Christmas package from home had contained some small maple sugar figures which I melted down and poured on my clandestine meals. Nothing ever tasted as good as those pancakes in the cold snows of the Roer River plains in early December 1944.

I don't remember whose idea it was, but about this time the mine-removal squad started meeting each night to read the Bible aloud. After each passage was read, squad members stopped and discussed it. We seemed to gain an inner strength, a peace of mind that pushed the war away for those special few minutes each night. The squad consisted of several Protestants, several Catholics and two Jews. None missed the nightly Scripture readings. Some even commented that perhaps our Bible studies might offer us some sort of special divine protection from above.

At a central crossroads in Immendorf I came across a burned-out German Panzerkraftwagon (tank) with the charred remains of two dead soldiers propped upright inside. Both, either killed instantly or unable to escape, had been reduced to lumps of cinder when the tank had exploded and burned. Their heads were no more than two hunks of charcoal, their arms were burned off at the elbows, their legs at the knees. I climbed inside and studied the ghoulish scene. Each day in combat, it seemed, I witnessed every face of death imaginable.

One evening, I went into the courtyard to relieve myself. The night was clear, cold and silent. Suddenly, an anti-aircraft battery nearby opened up and I bolted back to my billet. The artillery fire had unnerved me completely. Only then did I realize it was ack-ack firing at a marauding German observation plane. After everyone had a good laugh, I returned to the courtyard to watch the fireworks display quietly.

A platoon leader, a typical 90-day wonder, came by and asked for volunteers to accompany him on a reconnaissance patrol. Still not very wise to the ways of the army, I volunteered. He said we would be reconnoitering in front of CHARLIE Company. I was to wear only a field jacket, wool cap and carry no weapons. We were to scout the area on an intelligence-gathering mission and not engage the enemy; and if we were discovered, we were to try to escape rather than put up any resistance.

Not too pleased about infiltrating unarmed behind German lines, I stuck a knife in my boot, a P-38 German pistol under my shirt and a D-ration chocolate bar in a jacket pocket. The lieutenant briefed me on the terrain we would cover and the password for the day. We would be back before dawn, he said.

We walked outside into a hard, cold rain. Ideal weather for such a mission, he claimed, for the Germans would not be expecting a patrol and perhaps, if we were lucky, German outpost sentries might even be seeking shelter somewhere from the elements. Often, our unorthodox methods of fighting caught the Wehrmacht off guard and I hoped this would be one of those times.

At the edge of town we started to crawl, and soon I was covered with mud, nature's own camouflage. I made my way through a break in a stone wall and over a hump on the ground. It was a dead German. I recoiled, but after my heart stopped pounding and I settled myself down, I continued on. After a hundred yards or so, I was exhausted with mud down my back and thoroughly soaked by the rain when suddenly, I heard a whispered challenge, "Orphan." "Annie," I responded quickly. It was a CHARLIE Company forward position. I told him I would be out in front of the lines for several hours and to pass the word along in case there were any trigger-happy new replacements on the company line.

As I crawled, I instinctively felt before me for trip wires, mines or barbed wire. I tried to orient myself with landmarks I had studied on the map at the briefing, but I couldn't see anything. It dawned on me as I continued to crawl forward that I was lost, so I decided to abort the mission and crawl back to our lines. Every direction I probed seemed strange to me and I couldn't find any landmarks. Also, I hadn't seen or heard the lieutenant for quite a while. An American machine gun opened up in the distance, but the echo distorted its direction. I dug my face into the mud and waited for the firing to stop.

Sensing a form before me, I hoped it was one of the buildings in Immendorf. It turned out to be a huge tree. I didn't remember any that large left standing back in Immendorf. I had been crawling deeper into German territory and away from our lines in Immendorf. I became aware of other forms and knew that I was in a wooded area where, I hoped, I could get some shelter from the rain. I crawled to the base of another tree before realizing the tree was a Wehrmacht sentry towering above me only inches away, huddling from the weather.

Sizing up the situation quickly, I realized I couldn't go back and I couldn't move forward or around him without being discovered. There was only one alternative: to eliminate him silently. Slowly rising to my feet with P-38 in hand, I hit him as hard as I could at the base of his skull. He collapsed without a sound. I took my knife, rolled him over and drove it into his throat with a vicious twist. In the rain I heard a soft gargling sound as I plunged the knife repeatedly up to the hilt into his chest. Stabbing him took all the strength I had in my arms.

I lay on the ground panting, my heart again pounding in fear. It was my first kill with a knife. I had been baptized with the sentry's blood all over my arm. I was near sheer panic, but I had to find a way to get away from there as fast as I could.

"Wer ist da?" (Who is there?), a muted voice called out.

"Es ist nur mir" (It is only me), I answered in frightened desperation. "Ich musz pisse." (I have to piss.)

"Sei ruhig" (Be quiet), the voice admonished.

In a rush, my breath came back, for I had been holding it for what seemed like five minutes. My mind became twisted with terrified thoughts. Daylight was starting to come on and I remembered a dead GI I had seen who had been found by the Germans with a German pistol in his possession. They had rammed it down his throat and fired it, blowing the back of his neck off.

I didn't want to be captured with a P-38, but I hung onto it anyway. At least if I had to, I could give it a fight as long as the eight-round clip lasted. My chances of making it back to my lines were growing slim and I forced myself to face my dilemma.

I crawled into a dried-up brook bed and waited, trying to figure a way out of my predicament. Bushes on both banks offered excellent cover that I hoped would buy me some time. In the pre-dawn I could make out a German bivouac with men washing, shaving and cleaning their weapons about 150 feet away. From their routine manner, it appeared they had not missed the sentry yet.

I could see a tank, two .88s, stockpiles of ammunition and supplies and a large group of soldiers digging in. They had slipped in during the night and apparently were planning to defend the area. This information was needed back in Immendorf, but there was no way to get there and no one to give it to.

Later, the early morning sun warmed me slightly and started drying my soaked uniform. About noon, I tried to break off pieces of my D-ration and soften them in my mouth without being seen, but the brook bed was only about a foot deep.

As I watched the Germans, a commotion started and two of them came into the bivouac area carrying the dead sentry. I heard the word "Patrouille" (patrol). They were unaware the sentry's killer was still only a few feet away and, fortunately for me, they didn't bother to search.

At the sight of the dead sentry, a wave of nausea came over me. I quickly scratched out a hole in the gravel, placed my face in it and vomited up pieces of the D-ration I had been eating. They didn't hear me. I decided to wait until nightfall and again try to make it back to Immendorf.

At dusk, I chanced raising myself up—hopefully still hidden by the bushes—to search for Immendorf. As I did so, a Mauser rifle shot cracked near me. I slammed my face back into the gravel, angry that I had given my position away. The shot was only a German soldier shooting at a rabbit for supper.

With each call of nature, I could not move, not even roll over without being seen by the Germans, so each time I was forced to wet my pants, the price I paid to stay alive.

I lifted my head slightly, shooting quick glances around the countryside. Behind me to my left I could see rolls of defensive barbed wire, meaning the American lines had to be in that direction. I waited until it was pitch black and started crawling. My body ached all over from lying cramped in the ditch for so many hours. I crawled as far as I could on my stomach and then scrambled to a kneeling position. I wormed my way through the barbed wire and, thinking I was safe at last, stood up and started walking toward the town.

"Buck," a voice barked out.

I forgot, the password is changed every day. "Orphan Annie" was no longer the password of the day.

"Rogers," I gambled.

"Buck," the voice repeated. The outpost hadn't heard my reply.

"Rogers," I yelled back. "I'm an American. I've been lost on patrol since yesterday. I don't know today's password. For Christ sakes, let me in."

"Buck," he yelled back for the third and last time before I knew he would start firing.

I dropped to the ground and yelled, "You dumb son-of-a-bitch, I'm an American."

"Advance and be recognized," the voice instructed. I stood up and approached the outpost.

"What's your company?" he quizzed me.

"Anti-Tank."

"What's your company commander's name?"

"Captain John Bowen."

"Where ya from?"

"Worcester, Massachusetts."

"Where do the Red Sox play?"

"Fenway Park, Boston."

"OK. C'mon in," the sentry said, apparently satisfied.

"The password is 'Buckshot' not 'Buck Rogers,' " he told me.

I had guessed incorrectly, and had almost been shot because of it. I had crawled back through DOG Company's line, about a quarter mile off course from where I had started the night before.

The lieutenant had returned without me, giving me up for dead or captured. When he saw me, he was anxious to get any information I might have. I described what I had observed, even though I was confident the lieutenant would take full credit when the information was passed up to battalion.

Then I wolfed down some food and returned to my billet to change uniforms and sack out for a few hours, only to find all my gear missing. The squad, thinking I was dead, had divvied up my possessions. Begrudgingly they returned everything, even my Christmas packages from home.

I was instructed to show company officers on a map the coordinates of the German position. A few minutes later, the area was pounded by 105-mm and 155–mm howitzers. They must have hit the supply dump, for I saw black smoke curling upward from where I estimated the German position to be.

The men in my squad made me some pancakes with bread, bacon and coffee and for a time treated me as someone special. It was an overwhelming relief to be back. Company command told me I had earned time off back in Maastricht, Holland, to rest from my ordeal. When I arrived there, after a short truck trip, I was given a shower, hot food, another fresh uniform and told my time was my own.

I located a theater and treated myself to a foreign-language movie. It seemed so strange after the experiences of the last few days. When I wrote home next, I casually mentioned I had been too busy to write.

Recreational passes have a strange way of being curtailed and rescinded. Almost as soon as I arrived in the Dutch city, I was ordered back to

Immendorf. My reward for giving up half of my brief furlough was to pull guard duty at a forward position as soon as I arrived back.

As I tried to get comfortable in a foxhole that someone else had dug out of the frozen ground, my eyes pierced into the night. Hearing a slight sound behind me, I whirled around and shoved my rifle right under the nose of General Bolling, division commander, who had crawled forward to check his troops. The star on his helmet didn't intimidate me, but the fact that I had almost shot him did.

He asked me how I felt, whether the food was good, how the officers were treating me and if I was homesick.

I answered, "Good," "Not too bad," "As well as can be expected," and "No," respectively to his questions. He patted me on the shoulder, smiled and disappeared again into the darkness.

Seemingly all alone, I stared back into the night and, after about an hour, I noticed the silhouettes of sugar beets in the field before me were moving. I blinked and the movement stopped. Then as I stared at them some more, the movement started all over again. I closed my eyes for a moment and when I opened them again, the beets were gone. Hallucinating had never happened to me before, and I felt silly. This was a malady usually experienced by green troops their first time on the line.

Almost motionless, I continued staring into the blackness. Suddenly, loud German cursing erupted right in front of me. Instinctively, I fired a whole M-1 clip at the voice and other GIs along the line joined in. Gradually, the firing died out and the night quieted down again.

In the morning, I found a dead German about twenty feet in front of my hole, his body riddled with bullets. While on patrol, he had stepped on a shovel and it had come up and hit him in the face, making him instinctively cry out in pain. The others in his patrol had managed to filter back to their own lines.

I removed his Soldat Buch (soldier book) from him and kept his picture as a souvenir. Then I left him in peace. I collected many more such pictures in the following months.

During a temporary lull in the fighting, I was called to the company CP and handed an all-too-familiar Army notification slip. Wondering what the brass had in store for me this time, I read that effective December 11, 1944, I had been awarded the Combat Infantryman Badge for "exemplary conduct in action against the enemy." It was the most coveted medal by fighting troops and I felt an inner pride and satisfaction of achievement as I returned to my billet.

Walking to chow one muddy day, I heard a tremendous explosion and saw a cloud of black smoke coming from a nearby field. A tank destroyer loaded with men had taken a shortcut through a hedgerow bordering the street and had run over a stack of discarded mines that had been cleared earlier from roadways.

The sight stunned my eyes. The vehicle was burning furiously upside down and scattered around it were the remains of six dismembered GIs. The hedgerow was red with their blood but the most sickening sight was a headless, armless, legless torso that had been thrown up in the air and was swinging to and fro, balanced on a temporary overhead telephone line. I turned away; I could take only so much gore.

Life in Immendorf was never quiet, for there was always the nuisance shellings by the Germans and occasional aerial strafings by Messerschmitt fighters. During one such episode, while reading the Bible one night, we all dove for the floor when we heard the approaching planes. A .50-caliber bullet tore through the roof, shattering the shoulder of one squad member. He writhed in pain moaning on the floor until the medics evacuated him. The wound was severe enough to earn him a trip home and a discharge. The squad was now down to eight.

Rumors were rampant that German paratroopers in American uniforms were infiltrating the area, but nothing ever came of it.

On another night the stove in our billet, for some reason, blew up and ignited a wall. We grabbed our possessions and equipment and scrambled out of the building as what remained of it burned down. It didn't matter much to the squad because we had been told we were pulling out soon anyway. That proposed move, wherever it was to have been and for whatever purpose, was eliminated from General Bolling's strategy plans in an instant by a turn of events we wouldn't even be aware of for hours to come.

The next evening, as I walked through the mud to the field kitchen for supper, frantic troop movements erupted all around me. The field kitchen was being hastily struck, officer and communications jeeps careened around company area streets every which way, men were hastily clearing out their billets, drivers sprinted for their trucks, and tanks were jockeying for road positions trying to form a convoy.

"Moving out in 10 minutes," platoon sergeants started hollering. In what was undoubtedly the fastest troop movement we ever made during the whole war, we gathered up our gear and clambered onto a line of trucks and prepared for travel, again as always, to some unknown destination where we were needed. It was something big, no doubt, but we had no idea what. All we knew was we were on the move again with uncharacteristic urgency.

When the trucks started rolling, I reckoned from the winter sun disappearing through the trees on the horizon that we were headed south.

We knew other elements of the 84th had been able to overrun and occupy Lindern, Prummern, Linnich, Beeck, Wurm, Leiffarth, Mullendorf and Gereonsweiler, practically the whole area west of the Roer River. But the convoy wasn't headed in that direction.

All we were told were bits and pieces of information indicating that 20 German divisions had broken through on a 60-mile front in the Ardennes Forest of Belgium three days earlier, and if they succeeded in their offensive, the Allied forces could be thrown back to the English Channel. We were told the 106th "Golden Lion" Division had been overrun, its troop strength decimated during the German counter-offensive and had been pulled back 30 miles to rally its forces.

The pulverizing force of Field Marshal Karl von Rundstedt's spearhead, Operation Wacht am Rhein, had caused two of the division's regiments to practically no longer exist. The division had been so badly mauled, it had to be withdrawn from combat and reorganized. When the division re-grouped, only 600 men remained to fight again. The others had been killed or captured. Battalions of new 75-ton King Tiger tanks were storming over the countryside pretty much at will, we were told.

It was Adolf Hitler's final desperate gamble to win the war, an all-out attack with every available Panzer and infantry division he still had. With this massive push through the defensively vulnerable Belgian Ardennes Forest, he had promised the German people his armies would be in Paris in three weeks.

The bulk of von Rundstedt's force was centered between Monschau and the northern tip of Luxembourg between Belgium and Germany. Our convoy commander eventually passed the word along that's where we were going. None of us in the convoy truck were strategists, but we all knew apprehensively that the 84th was about to participate in one of the most crucial, major battles of the European campaign so far.

The date was December 19, 1944, and it was obvious that minutes meant lives and hours possibly the war.

The convoy moved as rapidly as mud-slicked road conditions allowed. There were no rest breaks along the way, no delays of any kind. When men had to relieve themselves, they did it off the back end of the truck while trying to hang on at the same time.

The convoy tempo never slackened as we chewed up the kilometers steadily throughout the night. We huddled together as the cold in the back of the trucks worsened. Hours dragged on into more hours as Germany moved further behind us. Mostly, men sat silently contemplating what lay ahead, for we had been told to keep noise to a minimum.

Eventually, far into the night, the convoy slowed to a crawl and continued to grind southward.

Just before daylight, after 75 miles and about 10 hours on the road, the convoy stopped. In hushed tones, we unloaded.

I wandered into the closest house I could see for shelter from the bitter cold. There I was greeted by a young, attractive dark-haired girl sitting in her kitchen by candlelight. She smiled a tired welcome and said, "Entre," a word I had learned earlier in France. I asked her if she was "Française" and she answered, "Non. Belgique." We had arrived in the town of Haversin, she said. Like so many other villages and towns I had been in, I had never heard of it.

We were soon to learn what an important cog the 84th would become in the most crucial phase of the entire European campaign. The weeks to come would also prove to be perhaps the darkest interlude in the division's history, a time of untold suffering, staggering manpower losses and a period when the 84th's mettle would be tested. It would be a time of valor. A time of pain.

Operation Wacht am Rhein: Hitler's Final Gamble

There was no fire in the house, but at least I was sheltered from the biting snow and cold wind. Using mostly sign language with the woman living there, I learned the Germans, only hours before, had fought their way back into the area and were all around us. This news snapped me back to my senses fast. I took up a guard post outside with the jumpy feeling the enemy might appear at any moment out of the fog-enshrouded night.

It wasn't long before I heard in the distance the sound of German tanks approaching the town. Moments later, a voice ran through the darkness yelling, "Load up! Everybody load up!" We were hightailing it out without even a fight.

Haversin, we were told, was not considered militarily important enough to defend and the decision had been made to let the Germans have it uncontested.

Snow was falling quite heavily as the convoy lumbered along at a walking pace for two hours through what was fast becoming a zero-visibility blizzard. From the tailgate of the truck, I could see the convoy was inching its way along beside a fast-flowing river at the base of jagged mountains framing the winding road on both sides. Wind-driven snow squalls beat sharply against our eyes, and soon visibility was restricted to only the two pinpoints of light peeking out at us from the blacked-out headlights of the convoy truck behind us.

The Germans, who were advancing almost unchallenged westward toward the port city of Antwerp, were boasting they would occupy Paris by New Year's. With the intensity Hitler's generals were pouring infantry and armored divisions into the Ardennes Forest and the reports we received of massive breakthroughs all along the front, the boast was becoming a more distinct possibility every hour.

As the truck column continued cautiously forward, my thoughts turned to the convoy truck drivers. They had been in unheated cabs for more than 14 hours, navigating with taped-over headlights on narrow, unfamiliar, German-infested, slippery roads teetering inches away from sheer ravines and all the while knowing that around the next bend in the road could be a Tiger or Panther tank waiting for them. They were surely some of the unsung heroes of the whole campaign to retake Belgium from Hitler's troops. Our lives, and the success or failure of what had already become the bitter struggle for Belgium, truly rested in their hands.

About 0400, December 20, the convoy halted again and we were told furtively in hushed tones to bed down in a nearby barn. Having been without sleep for 23 hours, I didn't argue. I found a hayloft and before my head hit the hay, I was asleep.

I don't know how long it was, but I was awakened by a strange weight pushing down on my chest. Raising myself slightly, I found a chicken had roosted during the night near my chin. My sudden move startled it and it flew away with a scolding cackle.

Hunger welled up inside me for I had not eaten since noon the day before, and my candy supply from home had been depleted by the many missed meals prior to the desperate troop movement south away from the Siegfried Line. At a farmhouse beside the barn, an elderly couple and their two grown daughters, after more sign language, offered me a breakfast of ham and eggs with fresh, cold milk, the first I had had since England. The family seemed oblivious of the impending danger and I couldn't tell whether they knew the Germans were coming back or just didn't care. I thanked the family the only way I knew, with a simple "Merci" and a pack of cigarettes.

They informed me we were in the village of Heure.

At a platoon briefing, we were told that the Germans had the village encircled and that an attack could come from any direction at any time. Our job was to slow the German advance in that sector at all costs, any way we could. To guard against the possibility of a surprise German tank assault, we placed "daisy chains," ropes with anti-tank mines tied every two feet, at all strategic roads leading into the village wide enough to accommodate Hitler's vaunted mechanized juggernauts.

As we did this, company officers also planned contingency retreat routes if we were unable to repulse a full-scale German attack. Better to fall back and fight another day than to be captured and lost for the duration was the unwritten judgement. But these avenues of escape were to be used only as a last resort; our orders were to hold, no matter what. If the Germans hit us with superior strength, our chances were slim—we were few against many, and we knew it.

Those of us in the daisy chain detail took a position in ditches beside the roads and waited as the heavy snowfall tried to bury us. If the Tigers came, the chains would be pulled into the path of the lead tank at the last possible moment. At the same time, another chain would be pulled behind the tank, boxing it in. If the mines didn't damage or destroy the tank, a bazooka team lurking nearby would try. The tactic then would be for the daisy chain teams to "shag ass" as fast as they could before the tank machine gunners could zero in on them.

Snow, nature's camouflage, blanketing the pine boughs we hastily cut to cover us as we huddled in the ditch, offered us almost undetectable conceal-ment. As we shivered in the blackness from cold, and perhaps impending fear, the sounds of small arms fire and the harrruuummmpp of artillery everywhere around us in the forest, we knew the wait wouldn't be long. The breath-holding agony stretched into hours as our eyes strained to penetrate the mist around us. The fearsome blackness gradually became the gray of dawn and the dreaded German tanks never materialized. Almost without notice, the cacophony of war had quieted down throughout our vigil and the forest was still once again.

Perhaps, as the American Army had concluded in Haversin, the Germans figured Heure wasn't strategically worth fighting for. Combat continually offered isolated instances of unexplained fateful luck to both sides.

The next night, we moved out again under cover of darkness as the snow persisted and the temperature dropped below zero, producing conditions we would have to contend with almost the entire time we were in Belgium. The column soon halted in a large city where we were dropped off in front of a school and told to get some sleep for we would probably need it later.

From a bronze plaque in the school corridor, I learned we were in Marche, Belgium. As I read the inscription, I had no way of knowing the significant role Marche would ultimately play in the outcome of the war in the European theater of operations.

No sooner had I closed my eyes, lying atop two tables pushed together in one of the classrooms, when I was told I had guard duty. After some customary Army bitching, I stumbled out onto the street and ambled over to an arbor spanning a frozen brook where I could see in every direction, at least within the limitations of the constantly falling snow. I figured that if I had to give up my sleep this way, at least I could try to make myself comfortable.

I paced my post back and forth, just fast enough to keep from becoming frozen to the ground, all the while hoping the exertion would keep my circulation pumping to warm me. Dragging my feet from exhaustion, I shuffled past a door at the rear of the school building and decided to check it out. As I swung it open, a bright light blinded me. Being so indoctrinated to blackout conditions, I slammed the door shut again instinctively. A moment later, I laughed to myself—the blinding light had only been an electric light bulb in the school boiler room. I couldn't believe I had become unaccustomed to electric light in such a short time.

The boiler room was so toasty warm, I was seduced into goofing off for a few minutes. I pulled up a wooden crate, leaned back against a wall, took a half-frozen D-ration from my coat and started thinking about home until my eyelids drooped. Almost instantly, I was lulled to sleep.

Without warning, my eyes flew open as a burst of burp-gun fire rattled throughout my snug hideaway. My heart raced. I couldn't tell where the machine-gun fire had come from and I had left a whole platoon unguarded and unprotected.

I jumped back outside and, crouching almost to the ice-slicked ground, crept around the building, M-1 at the hip, trying to adjust my eyes to the blackness while searching for the machine gunner. I found no one; everything appeared to be all quiet outside. Apparently, the firing I had heard had only been an echo. Needless to say, I didn't fall asleep again that night. I had involuntarily been reproached by a distant German machine gunner who had shown me he had more battle savvy than I did.

Day and night, the roads leading west from the town were clogged solid with refugees carrying their worldly possessions on their backs, in baby carriages or in wagons dragged through the snow usually by the strongest family member. Despite our reassurances that American troops were there to stay and that the Germans would not reoccupy the city, the people continued evacuating in droves. Living under Germany's cruel military domination for four years, the people reflected no confidence in our ability to overwhelm their former oppressors. Their opinions were recited in the defeatist tones of those who had endured too much too long.

The cold silence of night was broken by the familiar sound of German tanks again. I ran from room to room, rousing the others in the platoon. Other GIs throughout the sector, also hearing the tanks, were taking hasty defensive positions.

Batteries of .57-mm anti-tank guns—scant protection against the awesome Tiger tank—had been placed in strategic locations when we first arrived in the city. As bazooka teams raced to their pre-determined positions at intersections, rifle squads dug in to establish a firefight line to support them.

Orders, direct from General Bolling we were told, were disseminated from foxhole to machine-gun emplacement to artillery battery. Marche was to be as far as the Germans advanced toward Antwerp and Paris—the end of the line. We were ordered to blunt their forward progress and stop them there. As in war movies, there would be no retreat. It was to be a fight-to-the-last-man affair.

I grabbed some explosive primer cord, several pounds of nitro-starch, my M-1 rifle and P-38 and several grenades before scratching, slipping and clawing my way up a steep, ice-encrusted hill behind the school. The high ground was strategically the best place to be, even though there had been no orders issued or detailed battle plan given. It was, as was so often the case in Belgium, every man for himself, each an army unto himself.

I joined a bazooka team already dug in at the crest of the hill where we could see in every direction. It was a perfect position with a commanding view of the main road as it snaked its way into the city from the east.

With only a few minutes to secure our position, the bazooka team ammo carrier and I also scouted an alternate position to which we could fall back and which could be used in the event we were overrun. Then we waited, fidgeting in the snow nervously as the tank roar grew louder. In the distance, we could hear the intermittent chattering of slow-firing American machine guns answered by the belching sounds of German Schmeisser burp guns.

As the nerve-taut wait continued, our eyes gradually became accustomed to the first glimmer of daylight. We saw that our hill was cradled by rugged mountains on all sides and our position was in a deep ravine-like valley. The oncoming tanks could enter the city only by a narrow, winding road below us and that factor, we knew, would weigh heavily in our favor. The monstrous German armament would be unable to maneuver, just come at us head-on.

The German offensive had already crushed its way 40 miles westward and the Allied position, which only days before had been steamrollering its way practically unimpeded eastward with devastating strength, was now tenable, even critical. It was imperative that Hitler's forces be stopped at Marche, for if they penetrated our position further, the entire Allied campaign would be in jeopardy and in danger of collapsing.

German SS troops, fortified by several seasoned Panzer divisions, attacked in full force for 12 days. It wasn't until January 3 that American and British forces could regroup, be reinforced and mount anything resembling a counter-offensive.

As dawn broke December 21, the fog started to lift and word was passed along the line we would be facing elements of the 2nd and 116th German Panzer divisions—both with reputations as crack outfits in German Field Marshal Karl von Runstedt's arsenal. The 84th, we were told, was totally isolated and the impending battle would be, for the most part, bitter, personal and unsupported. If the uniform was gray, you shot at it; if it was brown, you didn't. That was all we had to know. We were not offered the luxury of backup units; there were none. Cooks, mess sergeants, company clerks, truck drivers, supply personnel—everyone who could walk had been issued weapons and pressed into the line.

So weak were our defensive positions that, in many reported cases, for the first 10 days of the German counter-offensive, American foxholes were spaced 150 yards apart as American divisions occupied positions with severely decimated forces. As a result, German patrols penetrated our lines pretty much at will.

North of us, an entire division reportedly had been captured by the Germans almost intact during the initial hours of Field Marshal von Rundstedt's unheralded explosion out of Germany. Top divisional officers called the impending battle at Marche the turning point of the entire war in the European theater of operations.

Most American units in the Ardennes had been severely mauled and depleted by combat losses or by those cut off and captured during the two-week-long total confusion at the outset of the breakthrough. To survive the hit-and-run battles that were being fought over much of Belgium, American forces constantly changed positions and regrouped until some semblance of collective military reorganization and direction was restored. It was during this stage of the campaign that the battle for Marche unfolded.

The approaching tanks rumbling at us through the snow-blanketed evergreen forests below were a prelude to some of the fiercest hand-to-hand combat we had experienced since jumping off from Marienberg four weeks before.

"Here they come," one of the bazooka men yelled as we counted nearly a dozen Tigers and half-track armored vehicles appearing around a curve in the road less than a half mile away. Thin threads of German infantry trudged along behind, properly spread out to minimize losses from artillery fire.

At the same time, a squad of SS troops in frontal attack formation appeared through the snowdrifts to our rear, firing as they came.

"They're behind us!" someone screamed. We had been outflanked and the German infantry was about to overrun our hill position. Caught totally by surprise, we opened up with withering fire as the Germans broke ranks at a dead run toward our position. Their sheer numbers overpowered our position as both sides tangled with bayonets, knives, pistols and bare hands. In less than a minute, the blur of violence was over and half of the Germans who had come up the hill were scrambling back down, leaving four comrades and two GIs behind sprawled grotesquely around our position. Physically and psychologically drained, we sank to the ground, buried our faces in our arms and tried to lick our wounds and resume breathing again.

Our hilltop outpost was littered with SS and American dead and wounded but we had held our position. But there had been no winners. The next action would be by Graves Registration.

Confident that the foot troops would not hit us again, at least not for a while, we turned our attention to the tank column approaching the city below us. German troops stretched as far as we could see in the first gray light of morning. Anti-tank guns and bazooka teams were firing as fast as they could reload while support riflemen were cutting the Germans to pieces. But still they came fanatically, wave after wave of them. Half of the estimated 100 attacking infantrymen were outfitted in white camouflaged ski suits. These, we learned afterward while searching the dead for unit identifications, were SS troopers, the most bestial element of the German Army.

Not realizing how heavily defended Marche was, the German Tigers were not in battle formation, but instead entered the city single file. As a result, they were sitting-duck targets.

A German half-track at the rear of the column exploded in a blinding flash and black smoke started curling up through the forest. Belching orange flames could be seen through the towering pine trees. With the last vehicle knocked out and blocking any withdrawal route, the armored column could only move forward directly into the sights of our guns. Several of the standing tanks started arcing their turret .88s defiantly back and forth, seeking out those who had destroyed the armored vehicle.

The bazooka team on the hill beside me fired at the lead tank below us and its tread unraveled from its bogie wheels. Its menacing .88 cannon pointed at us and fired. The shell slammed into the ground about 30 feet below us. Before I could react and cradle my head in my arms, my helmet was blown off and rolled down the snow embankment. An indistinguishable helmeted German head appeared in the tank turret and pointed toward our position. We had been spotted. I fired several rapid shots at him and he slumped forward, jackknifed dead over the turret hatch rim.

He disappeared in a flash of flame and smoke a moment later when the bazooka team fired off another round, this one hitting the turret dead center and tearing a hole in it. Another German tankman tried to squeeze out of the hatch to escape, but he was cut down by rifle fire from below us. I crawled down the hill to within 20 feet of the disabled tank and threw a grenade against the rear engine grillwork. At that moment, the tank exploded in a ball of fire, but probably not as a result of my lobbed grenade. There were no survivors. My rushing the already burning and about to blow up tank with a fragmentation grenade was a totally irrational action, perhaps even irresponsible. I can only rationalize that I had grossly endangered myself because of the incoherent rage of battle. It had been my first direct involvement with a German tank, the most feared adversary faced by infantrymen in combat. A GI feels completely vulnerable against 50 tons of roaring armor spewing death in all directions from an arsenal of cannon and machine guns.

Slipping and sliding, I scrambled back up the hill only to face the biggest damn screaming, black-uniformed SS trooper I would ever see running at me. Behind him were more SS troops, also yelling shrilly and almost on top of us.

I emptied my M-1 from the hip without even taking the split second needed to aim. Those who remained at the hilltop bazooka position were pouring rifle and pistol fire into the attacking German formation as fast as they could reload their weapons. The closest German trooper grabbed at his stomach and skidded face first toward me in the snow, his burp gun landing a few feet away. Since my M-1 was empty and there was no time to ram another clip home, I threw three quick fragmentation grenades blindly at the yelling Germans.

Then I ran, tumbling over and over down the hill behind the school. I landed in a heap near a line of GI foxholes. The bazooka team, unequipped to fight foot troops, had already hightailed it off the hill.

The snow was crimson with American and German blood. Most of the mechanized column had been destroyed and several dozen SS troopers had been cut down. The colors of the uniforms and the shapes of the steel helmets testified to the overwhelmingly lopsided losses: four wounded or dead Germans to each GI. Medics scrambled about tending to the American wounded. Here and there, clusters of GIs bent over their buddies offering whatever comfort or first aid they could while waiting for medics to get to them.

As they worked, I crouched in a ditch beside the road, fascinated as exploding ammunition in one tank gave off a violent pyrotechnic barrage. In one of the many paradoxes of war, I glanced behind one of the furiously burning armored vehicles and watched a GI tending to a wounded German.

Bone weary and sore all over, I climbed back up the hill to relieve the trooper who had charged at me of his Soldat Buch and pistol. I also relieved him of a small brooch with three gold-colored stones, which I later sent home to my mother who, as far as I know, never figured out how I had acquired it. Around me, other GIs were busy lifting souvenirs from German corpses.

After repeated probing attempts to enter the city, the SS troops, fighting without the advantage of armored cover, finally pulled back and decided to bypass Marche in search of a weaker point in the American defenses. The 84th had held firmly, had taken the full weight of von Rundstedt's effort and now was lashing back with whatever resources and manpower remained.

Stars & Stripes later reported that the 84th Division was credited with stopping Hitler's salient westward at Marche. Unable to advance further in that area, German commanders had split their forces, circling north and south around us in a pincer maneuver trying to outflank and entrap American forces.

This made it possible for American troops to methodically dissect these weakened pincers and isolate much of the German strength into small pockets that, when eventually eliminated, produced thousands of prisoners and seriously weakened Hitler's military strength in Belgium.

It was about this time that the 84th was awarded another badge of honor of sorts, one that inflated our exhausted egos and enhanced our divisional pride. Interrogated German prisoners revealed that German divisions facing us called us "The Hatchetmen"—possibly because of our "Railsplitter" insignia—and "The Terror Division." I liked those descriptions. They made me sound fierce.

We were given two days to rest and regroup our forces, but we all knew our break would be short-lived. It was only a matter of time until we were needed elsewhere. The Germans were still in control of the campaign and occupied practically all of southern Belgium. The Battle of the Bulge was far from over; in fact, as far as we were concerned, it was just beginning.

Remarkably, considering the fierce struggle raging between two armies around them, the Belgian people managed to adhere to their normal routine. Stores and markets remained open as shoppers walked the streets. I swapped cigarettes for a loaf of hot, fresh Belgian bread and a bottle of port wine, which I was told would warm my feet during those bitter Belgian nights.

The quality of the bread was poor but a vast improvement over C- or K-rations. As I had done back in Laon, France, I devoured the whole loaf by myself—only this time, I went back to the bakery and got another loaf for Joe Everett.

In the midst of all the last-ditch combat defending Marche, we were told by company officers of a pleasant Christmas surprise opportunity. For $10, we could wire flowers home for the holiday. I learned afterward that the telegram and flowers had frightened my mother to tears; she thought they were notification of my death.

When reinforcement troops arrived to occupy Marche, we prepared to move out again. Meticulously trained German paratroopers, dressed in American uniforms and speaking perfect English, were infiltrating our lines everywhere to sabotage our efforts and assassinate our high-ranking officers. They carried dog tags and IDs taken from prisoners or our battlefield dead.

The German werewolf plan, as troublesome as it was before we were able to get a handle on it, failed dismally because of American diligence and ingenuity once the plan was discovered. But it was, I must say, a strange feeling to be stopped and interrogated by our own MPs everywhere we went. They often threw baseball questions at me, and I sometimes had difficulty verifying I was an American. I wasn't much of a baseball fan.

The convoy hesitatingly explored its way along a planned route throughout the night. At dawn, we were informed the vehicles couldn't be risked any further in the daylight and we would have to hoof it the rest of the way to another undisclosed destination. Even though we were sorely cramped and frozen numb in the wooden bench-seat truck, it felt good to stretch our legs and try and get some circulation going again.

Under combat conditions, GIs could carry whatever gear they wanted. Accepting the fact there were only three kinds of combat infantrymen—the quick, the lucky and the dead—I always traveled light for speed when conditions allowed. Usually, I carried a helmet, rifle, cartridge belt with first aid kit, trench knife, canteen, pistol, two grenades and as many candy bars from home as I could cram into my pockets. Blankets, mess gear, shovels, extra ammo, field rations and raincoats could always be stripped off American dead if the need arose.

In severe winter weather, I added a sleeping bag, extra blankets, an overcoat, scarf, mittens, overshoes and as many pairs of dry socks as I could lay my hands on. Like most other GIs, I often obtained overshoes, ammunition or rations from American casualties. Combat was a time to be realistic; dead GIs no longer had need of clothing and gear. Conditions during the Bulge reduced most of us to insensitive, unfeeling, basic survivors.

We marched past a road sign: Hotton, 1 km. From a map, I found Hotton on the Ourthe River about six miles northeast of Marche. Small-arms fire and artillery shelling could be heard, and .105s arcing over our heads indicated possession of the town was still being contested. It was just another unfamiliar town, but with the distinction of being one I would never forget.

We crossed some railroad tracks and an arched concrete bridge spanning the Ourthe River that divided the town. Scarcely a building was left intact. As we ambled past a burning Sherman tank, I reached up and grabbed a Thompson .45-caliber submachine gun from the dangling arm of a dead tanker. I carried it for several weeks before finally discarding it because of its weight and the unavailability of .45-caliber ammunition for it.

FOX Company had faced four Mark V Tiger tanks, a half-track and 20 German infantry in the small river community. Before it was over, three of the tanks had been destroyed and the infantry routed. The carnage of the struggle covered practically every street. Smouldering tanks draped with bodies, bullet-riddled overturned jeeps and wagons, horse carcasses, grotesque brown and green uniformed corpses littered streets and clogged doorways everywhere. Dozens of furiously burning fires were devouring what remained of the town. The intensity of the fighting only hours before was total.

In an army, certain elements come under the heading of first things first: a place to bed down and food to eat. I found a partially intact house and inside I found two dead Germans. I dragged them out onto the muddy, snow-slicked street, relieving one of his helmet to be mailed home as a souvenir.

GIs from the Graves Registration unit began removing our dead from the town. Besides the three destroyed German tanks, two American Shermans were burning beside the river.

Exhausted from the march, I sat down against a building along the river's edge and let the sun warm my face. Without warning, beset by depression and frustration, tears started flowing down my cheeks. I buried my head and quietly cried for my mother. Combat was a constant roller coaster of adrenalin-pumping highs and soul-searing depressions.

My thoughts poured one over another of how I had made an accounting of myself the past few weeks. I had taken German lives, helped destroy a tank, captured prisoners and garnered vital military information. I admitted to myself that this all came about because of my penchant for getting lost at the right time and volunteering for details at the wrong time. To me, killing had become a thrilling sport—but I tried not to dwell on what this blood lust was doing to me as a human being. As an apparent mental defense mechanism, I had learned to cast such disagreeable thoughts out of my mind.

As I rested, I hoped the temporary lifting of the fog and the improvement in the almost impossible weather would allow Allied planes to fly again.

They had been grounded in England since the outset of the German breakthrough. Military advantage wouldn't be ours until our planes again ruled the skies.

Another close call in my military life came when a new replacement shavetail lieutenant, fresh from the States, wandered past me looking at the destruction around us and sniffed, "Hm. Fort Benning was worse than this." Enraged after what I had endured, and the losses we had sustained, I lunged at him. A GI nearby tackled me just as I threw a punch at the moronic, fuzzy-cheeked officer's face. The startled lieutenant glared at me but let the incident pass without retaliation.

Through the grapevine, I heard later that Captain Bowen, upon hearing about what had nearly transpired, had privately admonished the opinionated officer to keep his mouth shut until he found out what war was all about. I felt somewhat vindicated. The consequences of my actions would have been severe.

Exploring a wooded area at one end of the town, I discovered six German Tiger tanks lined up in a row, with no outward signs of damage. Crawling inside the first tank and fidgeting with the controls, I located the starter button but got no response from the motor. In one of war's many coincidences, the tanks had run out of gas simultaneously as they reached the outer edge of town.

Had this not happened before they could reinforce the other four attacking Tigers, the outcome of the struggle for Hotton probably would have been different. It was a case of simple logistics. While the German was moving forward, his supply lines were being stretched beyond their limits while ours were being shortened as we were being driven backwards.

I joined a lieutenant from the Corps of Engineers and we planted TNT in each .88-mm gun barrel, blowing them up and rendering them useless. With additional charges we then blew up the motors and turrets. If the Germans ever retook the town—and that distinct threat existed every day we remained there—the six tanks would not be part of their reclaimed booty.

Realizing I had not eaten for some time, I left the demolition project and headed back to my billet to break open a K-ration. As I walked, I heard a muted wwhhuummpp. Overhead, a crippled B-17 Flying Fortress had exploded and six parachutes trailed down behind the lazily disintegrating aircraft.

I watched in silent fascination as parts of the plane plummeted to earth over my head. Almost hypnotized, I didn't know whether to run for safety or stand fast. The bulk of the plane's fuselage landed about 200 yards away with an earth-throbbing crash and started to burn. The tail section separated and fell swishing back and forth into woods thought to be occupied by the Germans, while a wing landed about a half mile from the town.

Some of the chutes seemed to be coming down in American territory, close enough, it seemed, that we might be able to find them. I ran to the billet to enlist Everett's help. Grabbing our rifles and some grenades, we were ready for "Operation Rescue."

We legged it to a sawmill at the edge of town and then slowed down to a cautious walk, entering the woods using dead reckoning as an azimuth. Having no idea where the German lines were, we split up, walking about 150 feet apart through the dense forest to reduce the possibility of capture. I followed a narrow fire break leading up a hill while Everett, much larger and stronger than I, crashed his way through the pines and plowed physically through waist-deep snowdrifts.

We walked close to a mile up what might be considered a small mountain, crouching low, scrutinizing every tree, every bush for signs of movement. I followed a sharp turn into a gully and paused as my sixth sense that had saved me so many times before warned me again. I froze against a tree and listened. I had a premonition of danger, that someone was out there. All I could hear was Everett, now almost 200 feet above me on the hill, bulling his way noisily through the underbrush.

I swung my rifle around at a voice that said softly from some bushes, "Man, am I glad to see you." One of the aviators for whom we had been searching from the downed B-17 had spotted me first. I had sensed someone's presence but had not seen him wrapped in rolls of his parachute for warmth and camouflage. He was a master sergeant radio man on the crippled Fortress and his face had been chewed up by the trees through which he had fallen. Fortunately, he had had presence of mind enough to crawl into the bushes to hide and assess his situation.

In a loud whisper, I called and signalled to Everett. All smiles, he waded through the drifts toward us.

"Man, all the way down all I could think about was German concentration camps," grinned the Air Corps sergeant lying in the snow. I dressed his wounds, gave him a candy bar and some water from my canteen.

He told me his plane had been on a bombing raid over southern Germany when flak had made a sieve of the plane and had torn off two of its four engines. The Fortress had been forced to fall back out of formation and, in doing so, had been at the mercy of swarms of German Messerschmitt ME-109s. When a third engine caught fire, the crew was ordered to bail out while the pilot and co-pilot remained at the controls, trying to reach American lines. Minutes later, the plane had exploded. This all happened at such an extreme altitude, I had not even heard the aerial dogfight before the bomber exploded.

After a short discussion, Everett took the sergeant back to Hotton while I continued to search for other Air Corps chutists who might have landed in the same vicinity.

Following the direction the sergeant had pointed me in, I worked my way deeper into the forest. The snowdrifts deepened and the hills became steeper. Then I saw him. He was lying rolled up in his parachute in a small clearing with a .45-caliber pistol in his hand.

I softly called to him but, without first looking, he answered by snapping off a shot at me. I dove into the snow, yelling "Take it easy you dumb son-of-a-bitch. I'm an American. I've been searching for you."

After profuse apologies, he said he thought he had fallen behind German lines. I was fortunate the Air Corps never taught its officers how to handle weapons or shoot accurately.

As I walked toward him, I could see he was in considerable pain. I checked him over and found he had a compound fracture of one ankle that was bleeding profusely. I gave him a shot of morphine from my first aid kit and applied a makeshift splint made from a small tree sapling and torn strips from his chute. During his painful ordeal, he didn't utter a sound of complaint. The Germans, I knew, must have heard the shot and I was anxious to get back to the safety of the town. Half-lifting, half-carrying, I helped him hobble back down the mountainside. On the steep slopes, I laid him on his back, grabbed him by the scruff of his neck and dragged him toboggan-style through the drifts without a pain-induced sound. The morphine had taken effect and my little fly-boy louie was morphed to the gills.

The physically taxing trip, about a half mile but fortunately all downhill, took more than an hour before we finally made it back to the warmth of the company aid station. Everett, who in the meantime had started back into the forest looking for me, met us at the outskirts of the town where we had stopped to rest. Seeing the lieutenant's bloody and broken leg, he ran ahead to get help from the company's medics. Within minutes, they arrived and carried the airman into town on a litter.

When I arrived back at my billet, I began to laugh.

"What's so funny?" Everett asked.

"Nothing," I answered.

The lieutenant I had rescued had been dressed in full uniform, complete with combat ribbons, 50-mission crushed officer's cap and shined brown oxfords. He could have been an advertisement for best-dressed man of the year.

Then I looked at those around me dressed in smelly, mud-covered, baggy uniforms that hadn't been changed in weeks, bloodshot eyes from lack of sleep, scraggly bearded faces creased by fear, exhaustion and hunger. "What are we walking advertisements for, death?" I muttered out loud. The question set off a round of laughter.

The Air Corps radio man, after being treated for his injuries, remained with us about two weeks to fight on the ground where he could actually see the enemy rather than impersonally bombing him from 30,000 feet. He took part in several skirmishes with German infantry and during that time, he grew a beard and become just another mud-belly GI.

Eventually, the Air Corps caught up with him and he was returned by the MPs to his squadron in England for punishment . . . but what stories he would have to remember and tell.

Someone in the squad piped up, "Hey, guess what I found out today? Field Marshal [Bernard] Montgomery was billeted in this very room a couple of weeks ago." I supposed that even the brass had to rough it once in a while.

As we talked, the distant roar of a buzz bomb interrupted our conversation. I stood in the doorway watching it. With my longtime, youthful interest in aviation, I was fascinated by this new 25-foot-long, rocket-like plane thundering overhead. Its stubby, 16-foot wingspan made it appear almost awkward, surely not aerodynamically correct. But, at the time, I knew nothing yet about jet propulsion. As far as I knew, the United States had not been able to develop anything like it as a potential weapon.

When its engine quit overhead, the silence was unnerving.

"It's coming down here!" someone hollered. "It's falling short!"

As it tailspun to earth, we scrambled down a flight of cellar stairs. Nervously we counted the seconds ticking away until we heard the 2000 pounds of explosives detonate and felt the earth shudder. The house shook violently and plaster cascaded onto us. We dusted ourselves off and ran upstairs to see where it had landed and how much damage it had done.

From smoke in the sky we could see that it had slammed into the earth about a half mile away at an artillery battery. It left a crater large enough to accommodate a small house. It also ended the war violently and instantly for the crews of three 105-mm howitzers. More telegrams would be sent to mothers or wives back home. Buzz bombs, like land mines, were unpredictable and you grew to hate them more every time you watched them kill. Called "robot bombs," "whizbangs," or "doodlebugs" by the British, many had been shot down by the Royal Air Force over the English Channel before they reached the island.

One day, walking along the street in Hotton, I was greeted by a recruit soldier I had trained as a cadreman at Fort McClellan. He had joined the 84th that day from a "repple depple," a replacement depot, and he said another of my trainees had also been assigned to KING Company. I promised to visit them.

The next day, I located the company just outside of town. When I inquired about the new replacement by name, no one had heard of him. I questioned the company first sergeant who said only, "So that's what his name was." For a moment, I didn't get the implication.

"He was killed last night by artillery," he told me simply. He hadn't even seen combat and, in fact, his name hadn't even been entered yet on the company duty roster.

I returned solemnly to my company area and sat under a tree, my head on my folded arms in quiet reflection. I became depressed from frustration at the total waste of war, especially for those like this man whose face I hadn't even remembered.

I pondered whether he had been given his pre-combat indoctrination by a combat-wise non-com to whom he would be assigned. If so, he was probably counselled not to fear dying but not to taunt death either. Replacements were instructed what to watch and listen for in a firefight and cautioned not to forge close friendships. They were usually told the first day in combat was no worse than any other day, that eventually all become the same and after the first day you're an old-timer.

It is a truism in war: artillery fire respects no one. You age quickly into manhood after the first shots are fired.

The Battle of the Bulge

One thing about a combat infantryman is that he quickly develops an intuition soon after his initiation into war. It was evident even to the lowly GI huddled in his foxhole during the punishing December nights that the tide of battle was shifting, that the end was nearing for the soon-to-be-vanquished German military forces.

For two days, I had been uneasy about something I couldn't put my finger on and time eventually proved me right again. A lieutenant came to our quarters and informed us the Germans were planning a massive tank assault and we were to lay an extended defensive mine field in front of EASY Company's lines.

Biding our time, we waited for darkness, knowing that the area where we would be working was under German surveillance. Forming a human chain at the rear of the supply truck delivering the explosives, we started sewing a systematic pattern of alternating anti-tank and anti-personnel mines. The plan was for one line of mines to cripple approaching tanks and the next string to stop the accompanying German infantry, allowing EASY Company bazooka teams, riflemen and machine gunners to take their toll.

As we positioned each mine, we heard German voices being telegraphed by the calm, bitter cold night. Apparently, even in the well-disciplined German Army there were those who were careless about giving away their position with their chatter. This prompted us to be even more stealthy as, one by one, the mines were buried in the snow.

"Incoming," someone whispered under his breath. We hit the ground, but there was no cover anywhere, just the exposed snow-covered field. As soon as I heard it, I knew it was the one with my name on it. My heart didn't even have time to stop before the .88 hit practically on top of me.

When I came to, members of the squad were bending over me and reassuring me I was alive. The shelling had stopped but I couldn't stand up for dizziness. I had been unconscious, they told me, for quite a while and it was later determined at an aid station that I had suffered a concussion but no shrapnel wounds.

The shell, exploding only a few feet away from me, had thrown up a basketball-size chunk of frozen earth that hit me on the head. My cheek was gouged out and blood ran down my neck from a cut jaw. I was not wounded, only injured. There would be no Purple Heart this time.

I was taken to a nearby ambulance where I rested and was kept warm until my head cleared somewhat. Throughout the long night, 1,147 mines were put down by the members of our squad. EASY Company rested easier that night.

From the ambulance, I could see anti-tank guns and bazooka teams digging in to offer deeper defense for the rifle company. Even in the silence of the night, I could also see reinforcement rifle companies moving in silently under cover of darkness. I didn't really care which companies they were; my head still hurt badly and my ears still gave off strange tingling sounds.

But although still dazed and unsure of my reactions, I was reassured that when the Germans mounted their offensive and finally came at us, we had a big surprise waiting for them.

By dawn, we were fully prepared and waiting, all eyes on the woods in front of EASY Company and all ears cocked for any tell-tale sounds that signified Germans. We could not move for, again, we knew we were being watched. We kept low in our foxholes and kept the tank companies hidden in the woods to our rear. Everything had to give off the appearance of an unoccupied position. We broke open K-rations for breakfast and waited. Trapped in a foxhole, when a man had to defecate, he did it in his K-ration box and threw it over the side; when he had to urinate, he did it in a C-ration can, his helmet or in the bottom of his hole. Conditions were primitive and you improvised.

The morning wore on slowly and our necks, bent below the rims of our holes for hours, began to ache.

"Hey, Blunt," someone whispered from the next hole.

"What?" I whispered back.

"Merry Christmas."

Most of us hadn't even remembered what day it was. Under combat conditions, every day, week or month becomes the same. The days of the week or dates of the month had no particular significance to the foot soldier. Why bother keeping track of the date, for you had long since resigned yourself to the fact you were going to die that day anyway. Of this you were always certain.

I removed a small, four-inch artificial Christmas tree from home out of my pack and stuck it in the snow at the lip of my foxhole. Also from my field pack, I took some newly arrived candy bars, a can of C-ration pork and beans, a small can of fruit cocktail, some crackers and some peanut butter fudge my sister June had sent me. I passed some of my cache over to Everett in the next hole and we had a party.

I spent the next few hours staring at my little symbolic Christmas tree and thinking of home, but they were lonesome, melancholy thoughts as I wondered if the family had received my holiday flowers and telegram.

As important as our mission in Europe may have been, crouched in a frozen foxhole in Belgium was no way for anyone to spend Christmas. I had trouble reconciling the birth of Christ to all the killing around me.

The best Christmas present we were given, though, was to look up into an almost cloudless blue sky and see it filled with contrails from fighters and B-17 bombers so high we couldn't even hear them on their way to German cities. Showers of shiny tin foil, much like Christmas tree tinsel, rained down from the bombers attempting to confuse German radar.

The rain and fog back in England, which had kept all aircraft grounded except the Luftwaffe since the Bulge had erupted nine days earlier, finally lifted, and now squadron after squadron of Allied aircraft were streaking east and southward over our heads. What a beautiful, morale-boosting sight it was.

The Germans also wished us a Merry Christmas, a brief artillery barrage that stopped as fast as it started. We knew they were just sending over greetings on this special holiday.

All day the anticipated attack never materialized, but still we remained trapped in our foxholes, for we knew it could still come at any moment. As daylight faded into Christmas night, we heard a new sound in the sky, not a buzz bomb or a German fighter, but a whistling roar that made us all look up. A German plane was streaking across the sky faster than anything any of us had ever seen before. We watched the plane fly from one horizon to the other in a matter of seconds, almost like a bullet.

"What in the hell was that?" someone asked incredulously.

"It beats the hell out of me," another answered. "Must be another one of Hitler's secret weapons."

"How come we don't ever have any secret weapons?" the first voice asked sarcastically.

Someone piped up saying he had read about some jet propulsion system the Germans had been working on, something like a rocket plane. "That must have been one of them," a voice from an adjoining foxhole reasoned. It was the first jet aircraft that any of us had ever seen. Though it was still in the developmental stage, Germany's scientists had managed to get a prototype in the air and into limited service during the last five months of the war but too late to turn the tide of aerial warfare in their favor.

That night, I huddled in my snow-filled foxhole wondering how my family back home celebrated the holiday. I hoped that unlike me, they were sitting down to a turkey dinner despite all the ration point restrictions and war shortages on the home front.

Lost in my thoughts, I became aware of a high-pitched screaming noise that grew in intensity as it got closer. The screeching noise was coming straight at me. I curled into a ball, my tightly folded arms pulling my helmet almost down to my shoulders, and cringed against the bottom of my hole. Just when I thought I would be smothered by the sound, it ended with a splintering crash and was replaced by overwhelming silence.

I knew that cold night air magnified sound, but this was something different. Hardly daring to breathe, I listened for other disturbances or motions that would tell me what had caused the ear-piercing racket. Cautiously, I peered over the rim of my foxhole but nothing in the dark offered a clue. For several minutes, I remained motionless, M-1 gripped firmly in hand, ready for anything, still waiting for something to happen next—but all I could hear was the sound of my own heavy breathing and the rustle of the night winds in the pines around me.

When I couldn't stand the suspense any longer, I crawled out of my hole and bellied my way slowly through the snowdrifts toward the last splintering sound I had heard before everything had grown silent. Having no idea what I might encounter, I hooked a grenade onto my cartridge belt.

The soft crunching of the snow under my belly was amplified by the cold, and I was sure anyone nearby could hear me. I crawled through low-lying, ground-cover evergreens for a few hundred feet and then, deciding there was nothing out there that posed a threat to me, started to slither back to our lines. I was sure I must have at least reached the German outpost lines and I didn't want to celebrate my holiday there. But again, my usually good sense of direction failed me.

I crawled in a circle and tried to find the path that I had plowed through the snow with my body, which would lead me back to my hole. As my eyes tried to pierce the night, I faintly made out an image that was strangely out of place in the forest's natural setting. I paused, held my breath and stared at it. In the darkness, I could make out the shape of a strange, eight-foot, shiny silver-colored metal object shaped like a cigar—or maybe like a torpedo—protruding out of a snow drift at a 45-degree angle. I lay there listening to the object for several seconds and when I heard no sounds emanating from it, I figured it was a dud bomb of some sort.

Not knowing any better, I inched my way closer and closer until I could almost touch it. Only then could I make out the letters stencilled clearly on its side: "U.S. Air Corps."

How foolish I felt when it dawned on me the sound that had practically caused my heart to jump into my throat in my foxhole was nothing more than an empty aviation gas auxiliary belly tank jettisoned from a P-51 fighter returning to England after an extended flight protecting B-17s over Germany. Sheepishly, I knew this was not one of my finds I could brag about to the squad.

On December 27, our problems in the field were compounded when it started to snow heavily again. If there was anything the American GIs in Belgium didn't need, it was more snow. But we couldn't do anything about it, just slouch shivering in our holes, throw anything we could find over our heads for protection from the elements and continue to exist and endure.

During this time, we received some good news to offset the ferocities of the Belgian winter. Captured Germans were beginning to tell our interrogators that the 116th Panzer Division no longer existed as a viable fighting force. Months in combat, most recently against the 84th, we were told, had decimated it to where it was only a numerical designation or a thumbtack on a strategy map in German high command headquarters.

This news, coupled with Hitler's 2nd and 9th Panzer divisions being systematically destroyed by our forces every day, fueled our speculation, and deepest hopes, that the tide of battle truly was turning in our favor at last.

But I'm not sure whether any of us fully realized just how long the road before us still remained. The euphoria of achieving victory after victory against the German Army in a steady succession of Belgian cities, towns and villages was misleading and offered only a sense of false hope. But our confidence was high, and that had to count for something.

From our positions inside our holes in the earth, even we could sense that the momentum had shifted and was now gradually becoming ours and, as a result, Hitler's dream of walking again before the Eiffel Tower in Paris was only that: the fantasies and ravings of a demented madman.

The German assault we had been waiting for never materialized and gradually we resigned ourselves to spending another night in our earthen homes. With each hour, the temperature plummeted.

There was no way one could keep warm, even with a candle, for the light it would give off in a foxhole could reveal our position to the ever-present German eyes. For the same reason, it was not advisable to stand and stretch or to exercise. One thing you learned early on in the Bulge was to not unnecessarily stand up, making yourself a better target for some Mauser rifle.

I tried to stamp my feet on the bottom of the hole, but the pain had become too severe.

It continued to snow heavily. All we could do was just crouch low and endure it, waiting for it to blanket us. Perhaps the mantle of snow would bring some deceptive warmth with it. When my feet went numb, I was relieved to feel the pain subsiding, but I was also weakened enough by exhaustion not to realize what was happening to me.

Snow and sleet filtered down my back and froze on my cheeks. Soon, my feet were encased in snow and ice and I could no longer move them and, more disturbingly, I just didn't care anymore.

As the temperature dropped well below zero, I wasn't aware of any feeling in my body and I gave in to the sheer fatigue that had been building up in me for days. I lapsed into sleep. Some time later, I was awakened by Joe Everett punching me and telling me to move or I would freeze to death. I tried to but couldn't, and I fell back into an unconscious sleep. The mind-numbing cold had finally conquered my instinct to survive and I just lay in the hole letting the cold render me helpless.

Several hours later, Everett was hitting me about the body again. It was almost daylight and the snow hadn't slackened off at all. My face was frozen stiff and my eyebrows, cheeks, and jaw were encrusted with ice. I could not turn my head, for my snow-drenched overcoat collar was frozen stiff as a board. My glazed-over eyes could see only 20 to 30 feet in front of my foxhole.

My feet were encased in a block of ice up to my ankles in the bottom of the hole. Everett pounded on my legs but there was absolutely no feeling or movement. He and another nearby GI chipped away at the ice with their bayonets, lifted me out of my hole and dragged me across the frozen ground. I tried to stand up but my legs repeatedly buckled under the weight of my body.

The two men worked on me until eventually, supported under the armpits, I was able to stand up and hobble around slightly. By now, the snow around our foxholes was more than two feet deep and extreme pain in my feet and legs was shooting throughout my body. I couldn't fully comprehend what was wrong with me, just that my mind was confused and I couldn't stand up unassisted.

I was carried to an ambulance hidden in a clump of trees not far away, where I was fed a mess kit of hot oatmeal and coffee and told to rest awhile to thaw out. When circulation began to return to my legs, excruciating pain that had been dulled by the numbness gradually became almost unbearable.

The medics, seeing my discomfort, covered me with several more blankets to hasten the warming process and turned up heaters in the patient compartment of the ambulance.

After a medical conference, most of it held out of earshot, I was moved to a field hospital tent about a mile behind the lines to continue thawing out. A team of doctors examined and probed at my legs. Later, by chance, I overheard them discussing the probability of evacuating me to a rear area hospital where the badly frozen legs could be amputated.

I was able to sit up enough to look down at my feet. The sight that greeted me was unnerving: both feet had been reduced to ugly, purplish-blue mutations with large blistered pieces of torn skin peeling off them.

I stumbled off the cot I was lying on and started almost hysterically pleading with the doctors not to do this to me.

"I'm a musician, a drummer. I have to have my feet," I implored, now crying unashamedly. "Please, don't do this to me. Please."

"We'll give your feet one more day but then the decision, whatever it is, will be final," one doctor said impersonally, as he walked away to tend to other patients. I was given a pain killer and soon dropped off to sleep.

The next day, I was examined again, and terrified at what the doctor might say, I heard one doctor mutter to the other, "There appears to be some improvement. Let's hold off awhile." The surge of overwhelming relief, the sudden realization that I would be spared from being footless the rest of my life, brought on an upheaval of emotions. Tears filled my eyes as I stared at the ceiling, reciting a prayer of thanks. Then I shut my eyes and allowed the tears to flow down my cheeks onto the pillow.

Three days later, I was released, heavily bandaged, back to my unit. Frostbite and trench foot during the Battle of the Bulge disabled more GIs than the enemy did, I was told afterward, and men who sustained minor non-life-threatening wounds often froze to death quickly if left unattended for more than a few minutes. Others froze when they became too fatigued to keep moving.

Most of those living and fighting in foxholes during December 1944 and January 1945 in Belgium learned quickly the only thing worse than not being able to sleep during the sub-zero nights was being able to; quite often those men never woke up.

These were without doubt the darkest days for us and for the division, the days when GIs urinated on their M-1 rifles each morning to free up ice-encrusted chambers; the trying times when it took several hours to dig a two-foot-deep foxhole into the deeply frozen earth . . . but by that time you were usually on the move again. Laboriously scratching foxholes into the frozen earth was a constant and futile process.

Hot food, during the rare times when it was available, solidified in our mess kits before we could eat it and water froze in our canteens. It was later published in Allied military newspapers that the winter of 1944 was the worst on record in 40 years for snow and bitter cold. *Stars & Stripes* wrote of 40-below-zero temperatures recorded during the Bulge.

We experienced constant food and ammunition shortages, since supply lines could not be kept open in blizzards. Getting supplies through usually meant long, arduous trudging through waist-deep snowdrifts with ammunition crates on our shoulders. GIs were turned into human pack mules. Nothing mechanized, not even tanks, could move during most of these savage storms. In one sector, American dead were evacuated to the rear on captured sleds pulled by horses. For nearly a month, we went with little hot food.

To this day, whenever my feet are subjected to extreme cold, the pain returns, a constant reminder of what once was.

When I returned to my squad, Everett, as always, was waiting for me and soon was regaling me with more stories. No one, but no one, can inject humor into a story better than an Oklahoman.

On January 3, the 84th mounted an attack in sleet and snow supported by the 2nd Armored Division. By nightfall, the Germans were driven from the village of Odeigne; the Allied counter-attack to crush the Nazis was on. In my foxhole, I knew I couldn't survive another ordeal like that during Christmas, but my gloomy meandering thoughts were abruptly interrupted by the sound of approaching German tanks.

The long-awaited German assault was finally underway, but the snow whipping our faces blinded us, making it nearly impossible to see from which direction. Our anti-tank guns opened up at targets their crews couldn't see, and spasmodic German infantry return fire along the line indicated they too were blinded by the snow but were shooting merely to intimidate us as they felt their way forward. Even though we couldn't see them or determine precisely where they were, several loud explosions in the snow squalls before us signified that German forward unit tanks had entered the mine field we had put down days earlier. The swirling snow was working to our advantage—the tank crews were unable to spot the mines in their path.

Interspersed with the sounds of battle were eruptions of a different sound, German tanks being destroyed by their own exploding ammunition. The mines were doing their job far beyond our wildest hopes. Panzer-mounted .88s fired blindly through the squalling snow in our direction, in most cases without clearly defined targets in sight, just where they estimated we might be. Most of their bombardment fell ineffectively off to our side.

The hills echoed and re-echoed with the thunder of battle as I strained my eyes trying to see even a single German to shoot at, but I too was held sightless by the white avalanche of blowing snow.

A roar behind me spun me around in my hole only to see a Sherman tank from the 2nd Armored Division bearing down almost on top of me and overrunning my position. I curled up against the bottom of my foxhole as the tank rumbled directly over me, searching for a Tiger to engage. Being overrun by a tank was no big deal; we had practiced this tactic many times back at Fort McClellan during basic training. The only problem then, and it surely wasn't one with the Bulge's rock-solid earth, was being buried by the dirt the tank treads squashed down on top of you during the pass over.

After about 20 minutes, the German tanks and infantry withdrew and I still hadn't fired a shot. But the standoff didn't last long—the Germans regrouped and hit us again behind an artillery barrage. When the snowstorm eventually eased somewhat, I surveyed the carnage on the battlefield. Smashed and burning tanks were everywhere. The main thrust had been about 200 yards off to my right where the 2nd Armored, we were told, had taken a beating by a superior German force.

There were at least a dozen destroyed tanks from both sides, with American losses outnumbering the German two to one. For the first time, I had witnessed a major tank battle, or at least the sounds and results of one.

There had apparently been only a few Wehrmacht troops trailing behind in support of the Tiger and Panther tanks, and it appeared the heavy snowfall and the American resistance had reduced the ferocity of the infantry engagement between the two adversaries. A terrible price, however, was paid by both tank companies and the outcome of the engagement still wasn't determined.

A company of Sherman tanks, reduced in number by the initial battle, repositioned itself in woods to our rear to await the arrival of reinforcements. Medics wandered about the battlefield checking the dead and attending to the wounded.

We waited nervously for the next onslaught.

"Hey, Joe, say something funny. Make me laugh," I called over to Everett's hole during the lull in the fighting.

"Did I ever tell you about the . . . ," but he never finished his sentence. The lumbering German tanks were moving at us again with a decimated line of infantry straggling along behind them.

This time we could see them, but they were still beyond effective rifle range so we held our fire. The tanks laid down a withering field of machine-gun fire cover for the infantry and they were getting close enough for us to actually see the tank guns belching flame at us.

Almost holding our breaths, we waited for the lead tanks to enter what remained of our mine field so we could open up with everything we had. When the German tankers saw our Shermans now out in the open and maneuvering for position, they swung into a frontal line from one extremity of the battlefield to the other, a length of about 200 yards.

This, I knew, would surely be a battle to the finish, and for all practical purposes, it was. The more maneuverable Shermans weaved and dodged around the Tigers, choosing their targets at will and sniping away as fast as their .76-mm cannons could be reloaded.

As each enemy tank erupted in flames or was disabled, we picked off crew members attempting to escape, and as each American Sherman was knocked out, we laid down intense covering rifle and machine-gun fire for the crew members frantically trying to scramble back to our lines. The smaller .76-mm cannons and light armor of our Sherman tanks were no match for the reinforced armor and larger .88-mm cannon-equipped German Tigers.

When the German Mark Vs stopped to avoid our mine field, the German infantry picked up the momentum and broke into a running, frontal assault. Our rifle barrels became hot as we fired as fast as we could expend one eight-round clip and reload another. Our machine gun emplacements cut the Germans down like a scythe through wheat while riflemen lobbed fragmentation grenades at any Wehrmacht attackers who managed to penetrate the machine-gun fire.

The Germans withdrew, firing as they went and turning only occasionally to hurl potato masher concussion grenades at us. Most of them fell short of our positions and exploded harmlessly, throwing up fountains of snow. Not anticipating such defensive strength and determination, the German commanders pulled back to probe for a weaker sector. We knew we had broken the back of their attack. The German fanaticism we had observed during the initial stages of the Ardennes campaign had waned considerably during the more recent fighting. By now, more often, if they were beaten back once, they probed for less heavily defended avenues of approach. The Wehrmacht was no longer throwing itself ferociously and blindly into hails of American bullets as we had seen weeks earlier on the Siegfried Line.

When we were confident the Germans had withdrawn and weren't coming back, Everett and I assisted medics searching the Shermans for possible survivors. None were found. These armored vehicles were aptly called "steel coffins" by the infantry.

In the distance, German medics also carried away their wounded unmolested. Correctly, as has been the custom of armies throughout the ages, no one fired a shot from either side. Beyond the mine field lay at least 30 SS and Wehrmacht troops in the snow. It had been a senseless slaughter. The contrasting colors of black uniforms, white snow and red blood painted a ghoulish beauty on the landscape.

When the American lines were finally pulled back, I was taken by jeep to Hotton; my feet were still too swollen and painful to walk. While someone in the squad lighted a coal fire in a potbellied stove in our billet, I tried to pry off my overshoes, but my feet and ankles had become so enlarged that I couldn't get the shoes off. Everett cut them off with his trench knife and then wrapped my feet in strips of drapery material soaked with canteen water.

Miraculously, my feet started to feel better.

I snuck a candy bar out from under my sleeping bag where I had hidden it and the sweetness settled my upset stomach. I stretched out on the floor, planked my head down on my overturned helmet and fell asleep.

No sooner had I closed my eyes when someone was yelling, "Fire! Fire!" From instinct, I jumped up. The room was illuminated by a red-orange glow that can only be produced by flames. Pungent, lung-constricting black smoke curled along the ceiling and cascaded back down walls all around us. The coal stove had become overheated and had ignited a wall. Almost instantly, the heat was searing our throats with each breath. I grabbed my gear and fled barefoot across the street to another squad's billet where I watched our building burn to the ground. When there was nothing else to watch, I fell back asleep.

Precisely at 0600 every morning, the Germans sounded reveille for us, a single artillery shell exploding in the middle of the street nearby.

As I walked to chow one morning, I heard group laughter coming from the distance. Wandering in that general direction, I found a platoon sergeant dancing a burlesque routine in old-fashioned women's clothing. Anything to keep our flagging morale high, he strutted around bumping and grinding like a burlesque stripper. The men were convulsed with laughter. It was good medicine for our sagging spirits.

Later that day in a freak accident, a jeep ran over the sergeant's foot, crushing it, and his dancing days on the Belgian stage were over. I never saw him again. Now the squad was down to seven and the war was still a long way from being over.

Orders came that we were to move again, this time to fill in as riflemen in a decimated company on the line until replacements could be brought in from France. I tried to beg off because of my feet, but I was assured we were traveling by truck and besides, I could still fire an M-1. I carried only a sleeping bag, rifle, and ammo, hoping the assignment would be temporary and that soon I would be back with my own outfit.

Dressing properly for the winter of '44 in Belgium was a study in improvisation. I wore several variations of layered clothing trying to stay warm: long-john underwear, woolen uniform pants and shirt, a sweater, field jacket, full-length wool overcoat, two pairs of gloves (American wool and German leather), wool knit cap, helmet, two pairs of wool socks, combat boots wrapped in torn-up woolen strips, and oversized galoshes. Then, if I was to be positioned in a foxhole, I wrapped as many blankets as I could find around me cocoon-style.

For the temporary transfer to the rifle company, I bound my feet in more drapery material and pulled two pairs of oversize socks over the wrapping. I left my boots behind in favor of overshoes packed full of newspaper. Only then was I ready to go.

We arrived at the other company—I never learned which one for it no longer mattered to me—and were told to dig in. After 20 minutes of only being able to scratch the frozen surface, I hit upon an idea. I still was carrying a small quantity of nitro-starch with me since Marche. I wired it up, placed it in the hole I had started, warned those around me, and fired it. A second charge blew a hole below the frost line and the rest of my digging was comparatively easy.

Almost as soon as I finished digging, my eyes started to droop and I was fast falling asleep. I felt a hand on my shoulder and looked up to find the company commander bending over me. "I understand you're out on your feet, but stay awake if you can. The Germans are all around us and very close," he said. That's all it took. I was wide awake again and staring into the woods surrounding our position.

Eventually, dawn came and with it came the fog that had plagued us daily since arriving in Belgium. Out of the gray mist, the outline of a man emerged unexpectedly who threw a K-ration in my hole and disappeared again as the mist closed in around him. It was a mess sergeant offering room service to the troops.

Somewhere in the fog shrouding the trees before me, a short burst of machine-gun fire shattered the morning stillness. Later, we heard that six Germans dressed as Americans had tried to pass through our lines, but when an alert sergeant had challenged them and their subsequent actions were not American, he had cut them down as they went for their weapons.

That night, some of us were moved again to reinforce another company about a mile away; we had become, it seemed, a bastard squad without a home. At the new relocation, I found a barn with a hayloft, and having been awake for nearly two days, I was finally able to catch a nap away from the company brass.

When Everett, that master Oklahoma scrounger, found a field kitchen with hot food, we hobbled there and filled up on bread, oatmeal and black coffee. With stomachs now full, the world looked a little brighter. The mess sergeant said he had been told we were in the town of Briscol.

On the way back to the barn, Everett and I heard the laughter of men whooping it up. A Belgian farmer was chasing a GI around in circles threatening him with a pitchfork. Then the farmer broke off the chase and came running into the barn where we were quartered. When he screamed and shook his fist at me, I let out a threatening bellow and fired a pistol shot into the wall over his head. With me chasing him, he stumbled back outside where other GIs took up the cue and started firing their weapons in the air. The farmer kept running first one way, then the other in fear and anger, then fell clumsily on his face in the snow.

From the French-speaking GIs in the platoon, we learned that he blamed Americans using his barn for the damage the Germans had done to it with artillery fire. I had more important things to worry about than one irate farmer and his dilapidated barn.

I ventured into a nearby bombed-out home, where I found a Victrola and a cracked French record. I placed it on the turntable, and pushing it around manually with my finger, I could make out a scratchy French version of the "Woodpecker Song," a faint reminder of home.

Investigating several rifle shots in the village, I found that a cow and some chickens had been shot and were being prepared for cooking. It appeared that at long last we were going to get some decent meat to eat.

Smelling smoke, I turned and saw the farmer's barn on fire. Some GIs had decided that if the farmer hated us that much, they might as well give him a good reason. Everett and I barely managed to salvage our gear from the barn before it burned to the ground, much to the delight of the entire platoon. We never did get any steak from the cow, because right after breakfast we were told we were moving on foot to the nearby village of Manhay.

The steady slapping and crunching of feet in open-file formation on hard-packed snow brought us closer every minute to where we hoped opposition from the Germans would not be heavy.

As we approached the village, I glanced into a ditch beside the road. The body of a naked woman in her early 20s lay face up, with terror permanently contorting her face. She had been slashed wide open from throat to crotch and her breasts had been cut off. The woman's body was the centerpiece of drifted snow, dyed crimson with her blood.

Beside her lay the crushed body of an infant boy about 18 months old, its head bashed in unrecognizably. A nearby tree against which the baby apparently had been swung by his feet was covered with blood and patches of flesh.

The Germans had evacuated the town only moments before and had left this gruesome remembrance for us. They should have known that each one of these grisly scenes only intensified our hatred for them and strengthened our resolve to fight. I had not truly known why I was fighting in Europe until I began witnessing these atrocities. I couldn't comprehend what kind of sadistic beasts could do this. For what possible crime had the woman been subjected to this unspeakable punishment?

Shaking my head in disbelief, I walked on without even a backward glance.

Farther down the road, my wonderment was answered by the scenes of sheer, total atrocity that I would see repeated in several towns ahead of us, and then again, months later, when the 84th liberated concentration camps on the northern plains of Germany across the Rhine River.

But in Manhay I had not seen it all yet. In the village just ahead was a heavily damaged church and in a snow-drifted graveyard beside it reposed the frozen, snow-covered bodies of nearly two dozen elderly people, their hands tied over their heads. They had been lined up systematically and machine gunned, apparently in retaliation for some crime against the Germans. We were told it was German practice to retaliate against a village by executing inhabitants whenever German military equipment was sabotaged.

In the center of town, an elderly man sat in the remains of what had once been his home. He cradled a lifeless, blood-covered infant in his arms. Despair in his eyes portrayed a grandfather in shock. I silently walked around him to not disturb his grief.

The most comfortable billet I could locate for us in Manhay was a gristmill containing a pile of grain that made a most comfortable bed.

That night, I lighted a candle and caught up on my journal and correspondence home. In my letters, I soft-pedaled the truth considerably as I related the events of the past week. Again, nothing, I felt, was gained by detailing the unspeakable horrors I had experienced and endured. I wrote of peaceful walks in the woods and good food. Stretching the truth a little didn't bother my conscience. I figured the end justified the means.

In youthful patriotic fervor, I also did quite a bit of opinionated flag-waving in my letters home. It would take many years after the war to eradicate my memories and to mellow my intense, stubborn beliefs.

My father wrote to me daily, no matter how late he had to stay up at night to do it, to ensure I had a letter each day. With such devotion, there was nothing I couldn't endure. I knew why we were fighting and the cause, I felt, was just. As I wrote, the night was still and I was hungry. At the company kitchen I got a K-ration and hot coffee to wash it down. I was hungrier than I realized. The cold cheese ration actually tasted good.

Because of my feet, I was excused from guard duty and was able to sack in back at the gristmill until about 0430 when I was awakened and told we were moving out again, this time to a town that was "hot." We were warned to be ready for anything. Slowly, the truck convoy probed its way along another shell-cratered road lined by towering pines, their snow-covered boughs displaying a gentle serenity that was beautiful, but deadly, for they sheltered the Germans. A road sign told us we were in the village of Grandmenil. All I knew was the name sounded French, the country was still Belgium and the Germans lay in wait for us around the next bend in the road or in the next town.

The Ardennes Salient
Crumbles

The convoy stopped short of the town and we were told a line company recon patrol would be sent in to probe for Germans. We were already sharply aware the enemy could be driven from a town and then stealthily reoccupy it a few hours later. We had been waltzing around in circles with the Wehrmacht and SS like this every day since the massive German breakthrough in the Ardennes three weeks before. Grandmenil would be no different.

Accurate military intelligence was at best sketchy, for the whereabouts of German troops—or our own, for that matter—was always in doubt. Defined front lines were nonexistent. Rear echelons were vague and seldom were there distinct company or battalion boundaries, or safe or unsafe sectors. The Germans were everywhere, and so were we.

It was not unusual for platoons to function independently from their companies, and it was almost customary for squads to be separated from their platoons during these most complicated and confusing early weeks of the Bulge. Furthermore, because of the fluid situation, inter-platoon communications were often fragmented at best or practically impossible at worst. It was hoped that German commanders and their troops were as confused as we were.

The recon party consisted of a jeep for the company commander and his radio man, an infantry squad and a jeep for a demolition specialist bringing up the rear. I loaded a mine detector onto our vehicle and, accompanied by a lieutenant observer, cautiously approached the town. At the brow of a long sloping hill offering a commanding view of the village, we paused momentarily to make a final observation, but as we did so, the command jeep impatiently motioned us forward to check for mines.

Before we could react, the captain's jeep at the front of the patrol exploded in a ball of smoke and fire. It had been blown onto its side and was burning furiously with its passengers scattered about on the ground. While the infantry squad rushed to their assistance, the officer in our mine detection jeep and I dove for a nearby ditch as several riflemen pounded away at an unseen target in the village. With binoculars, we located a huge Tiger tank cozily tucked between two bombed-out buildings about 300 feet away. We found out later it was one of the new, gigantic super tanks developed by Hitler toward the end of the war, another of his so-called Geheimnise Waffen (secret weapons).

In front of the tank position were two burned-out American half-tracks. The tank commander had obviously been picking off American vehicles pretty much at will as they entered the village. They too had probably been part of an advance unit reconnoitering the town.

The German tank turned its attention to the infantry squad with us that was laying down heavy but ineffective return rifle fire: .30-caliber bullets against a steel-enforced Tiger tank were about as troublesome as fleas to an elephant. We found ourselves in a highly exposed position and unable to move forward or backward. The lieutenant motioned for me to follow him in a flanking attempt around one of the buildings shielding the tank, while our driver crawled to the rifle squad and told them to keep up the cover fire.

I hastily described my swollen feet to the lieutenant and told him I couldn't make a dash for the nearest building. The only other alternative was to crawl a circuitous 400-foot route over open fields using any defile we could find along the way for concealment.

As we crawled forward, I wished for one of the white ski suits I had seen used by the German Sturm Schutzel (storm troopers) back in Marche. All I had was the highly visible full-length brown wool army overcoat, which I was sure would make me a prime target against the snow-covered field.

Fortunately, the tank crew, its visibility restricted by partially buttoned-up gun apertures, concentrated its machine-gun fire on the riflemen; streams of bullets could be seen raking the roadside where they were positioned.

Our only chance was to get unseen behind one of the buildings concealing the tank before the tank crew diverted its fire in our direction. When we finally reached a point about 15 feet behind the tank, the deafening roar of the .88 pounding the hillside almost lifted us off the ground each time it fired. Seeing us, the rifle squad stopped firing.

Communicating by hand signal and eye language, we quietly swung ourselves on top of the tank. When the lieutenant pulled the tank's heavy, round hatch cover partly open, we heard yelling inside and saw a pair of hands grab at the cover in a tug of war with the lieutenant. I pulled the pin on a fragmentation grenade and shoved it under the hatch cover just as the lieutenant released his grip. The grenade was wedged between the hatch cover and the hatch rim, keeping the cover from being slammed shut.

With only four seconds before detonation, I gave the grenade a hard sideways kick and it fell inside as the lieutenant and I dove head-first off the tank and rolled behind one of the buildings. With the muffled explosion and the screams from inside, the hatch cover flew open and white smoke billowed out. We clambered back onto the tank and emptied our pistols down the turret hatch to finish the job.

Then we waved forward the riflemen who were crouched in ditches watching us. The command jeep casualties had already been evacuated in our jeep to a rear area aid station.

Infantry manuals said tanks can't be knocked out with a fragmentation grenade but now the book would have to be rewritten. For this exploit, I heard later the lieutenant awarded himself a Bronze Star for his bravery. His citation hadn't mentioned me; the only award I received was the thanks of the infantrymen in the recon patrol after the firefight was over, none of whom had been killed or even wounded.

With the lieutenant skulking around, it was impossible, and probably improper, to lift the Soldat Buchs from the dead tankers as my Tod Preisen (death trophies). It is apparently a strange quirk in some men's personality that prompts them to collect trophies when an adversary has been vanquished. Hunters collect animal heads, fishermen mount prize catches, gunfighters of the Old West notched pistol grips after each shootout. I wasn't notching my M-1 stock but, instead, lifting Soldat Buchs from dead Germans I had faced down.

After checking out all the destroyed buildings for possible snipers or German stragglers, I found one house mostly intact. It became my first choice as a billet. To inspect it closer, I lighted a stubby candle I always carried with me. I recoiled slightly, startled when I discerned a pair of wide-open eyes staring at me. After slashing my M-1 toward the eyes, I found a terrified Belgian woman huddling in a corner and wrapped in a blanket, obviously very sick. I assured her we were Americans and told her I would get her medical help when I could.

With no dry wood around with which to kindle a fire in the kitchen stove, I broke off chair legs and stripped off window ledges. Within minutes, I had the woman warm and smiling weakly. I opened a C-ration and placed it on the floor beside her.

"C'est le Guerre" (That's war), I said, admittedly a rather stupid remark, but it was all I could think of to say at the moment in my extremely limited

French. She just kept staring at me, probably afraid and, having just watched me burn pieces of her home, uncertain about what was to happen next.

When a French-speaking squad member arrived, the woman said she was an elementary-grade schoolteacher who had been too ill to evacuate the town with the others when the Germans and Americans had faced each other in a seesaw battle there earlier. The Germans had not discovered her and, satisfied there were no Americans remaining in the village, had withdrawn quickly, leaving one harassing tank behind to impede our advance. Once relaxed, the woman said she had not eaten for two days; the C-ration was a banquet for her.

By nightfall an infantry company was occupying Grandmenil and the threat of a German counter-attack was past, but intense German artillery fire kept us pinned to floors and in cellars most of the time. When it subsided and shifted to LOVE Company position in another sector, we ventured outside and saw our artillery already in place and returning the fire. The blasts of fire from the 105-mm howitzers illuminated the snowy forests, giving them a deadly, but beautifully serene, appearance.

Everett and I pulled outpost guard duty together at one approach to the town. Trying to keep our spirits up, we were quietly laughing and joking about life in Oklahoma and Massachusetts when we heard a truck coming. With Everett crouched in a ditch to cover me, I stood in the road with rifle aimed at the cab to challenge the driver. The area was still infiltrated by German paratrooper saboteurs posing as Americans, and everyone and everything that moved was being questioned. When I demanded the password, an obviously tired and cranky driver opened the canvas cab door and snarled, "It's none of your fuckin' business." I waved him on. No self-respecting German staring down the barrel of a loaded M-1 would respond that way. The guy could only be an American.

When I told Everett what the driver thought the daily password was, he laughed so hard and loud I felt sure every German in Belgium would hear him.

Our relief finally came, and the quarter-mile hike back to the billet was more like five miles as the pain in my feet swept throughout my body with each step. To lighten my load, Everett shouldered my rifle and no matter how slowly I limped along, he stayed with me.

After drinking a breakfast of soupy, hot oatmeal and black coffee, I started to explore the town but was stopped short by another gruesome example of German savagery.

Outside the town's only church were the frozen, snow-covered bodies of 18 men, women and children, their hands bound behind their backs. As in Manhay, they had been lined up against the church wall and machine gunned. Their partially decomposed, blue, shriveled-up faces, most distorted in agony, stared up at me in mute testimony of the horror that had taken place in the village before our arrival. My mind went numb as I picked my way among the bodies. I stared at them for a few moments before shaking my head in shocked disbelief and walking away. In another section of the town, I found four frozen SS troopers in an open grave, and with rage welling up inside me, I jumped into the grave and smashed their heads with my rifle butt. But with the bodies already frozen into blocks of ice, the blows did little outward damage.

On a sloping hillside overlooking the village, I found a decapitated German SS corpse beside a barbed wire fence separating two pastures. I sat and stared at it for a while and then, totally without reason or provocation, sent the head skimming across the snow with a savage kick. Almost gleefully I started playing soccer with the head, kicking it all over the ice-covered pasture and then chasing it as it skidded and bounced back and forth over the snow. Sometimes, where I found a down slope, I was able to make a 30-foot punt. During the whole episode, I felt nothing but macabre elation. Eventually tiring of the sport, I sat beside the mutilated remains and ate a K-ration.

In Grandmenil, I witnessed the first murder by Americans I had observed since entering combat in Germany. A jeep with two German prisoners perched on the front fenders, their hands clasped behind their heads, came by as I walked limping to the company field kitchen for breakfast. Seeing my limp, the driver stopped and offered me a lift.

As we bounced and swerved along the rutted, mud-slicked road, the driver nodded casually to his front seat passenger and, without a word, they each pulled out their Colt .45s and simultaneously fired single shots into the back of each prisoner's head. The impact of the slugs made them jerk upright convulsively in spasms as chunks of flesh, bone and blood spewed from their skulls. The two lifeless forms slumped off the fenders and bounced onto the mud-slick road. I glanced back at them—the POWs' legs were still twitching. Other GIs walking along the road ignored them.

Still without a word being spoken, the GIs in the jeep holstered their side arms and soon we were at the field kitchen where the driver dropped me off. I thanked them for the lift. Breakfast that morning, I remember, was pancakes instead of oatmeal for a change. I enjoyed them thoroughly.

On my way back to my billet, I noticed the dead POWs still lying face down on the road, but someone had pushed them both off to the side so as not to interfere with traffic.

To many GIs, a German was a German no matter what uniform he wore, but to me there was a vast difference between Wehrmacht Soldaten and SS storm troopers. One took prisoners, the other executed them and perpetrated unspeakable atrocities against defenseless civilians. There had been no acceptable reason to murder these two Wehrmacht soldiers who, like ourselves, were serving their country, right or wrong.

I was torn, on the one hand, between my hatred for the Germans for their atrocities in Belgium and, on the other hand, what I considered the limits of human decency. What I had witnessed went beyond that limit. I was ambiguous about how I should feel about the episode, but I was certain about one thing: I never could have committed such a brutal murder.

One of the thrills of mail call whenever it occurred, besides the flow of mail and food packages from home, was the arrival of *Down Beat*, the music magazine that brought me up to date on all the music news back in the States.

My father was able to get a copy put aside for him before they sold out each month at Walberg and Auge, Worcester's leading music store at the time. In the privacy of many bombed-out buildings in Europe and many cold, lonely foxholes, I read this magazine over and over again, almost memorizing it each month.

One mail call included a snapshot of a window display, complete with pictures and two captured Nazi flags at the bank where my father worked, telling of my Geilenkirchen first-day exploits taking prisoners. I smiled as I reflected on his fatherly pride.

Another diversion during the Bulge was listening to Axis Sally's propaganda programs whenever we could appropriate a battery-operated radio. Her inside knowledge of our troop movements and personnel names was uncanny and her attempts to lower our morale were hilarious. If only she had known this wasn't necessary: Army field chow was already doing it for her.

Other reading materials of the soldiers fighting in Belgium were the propaganda leaflets dropped regularly on our positions by German messenger planes. My favorite, and one I saved for my souvenir collection, showed a handsome 4F civilian fondling a scantily clad wife back home in front of a mirror showing a skeleton (death) choking a soldier. I never saw any concrete evidence that these crudely drawn leaflets had any adverse effect on our troops, but they were excellent for starting fires to heat C-rations.

Newspaper clippings sent from home, instead of filling my letters with interesting readable materials, often infuriated me, for the distortions of the truth as I was observing it were difficult to accept. One clipping lashed out at America's GIs for the high incidence of frozen feet during the Bulge campaign.

Another claimed the Luftwaffe was no longer a viable threat to our troops, while still another newspaper account claimed German casualties were five times those of American troops, which I perceived to be a deliberate lie. I began throwing American newspaper clippings away when one stated the American casualty rate in the Bulge was the lightest of any campaign in Europe so far. I couldn't figure out what war these clippings were referring to, surely not the one in which I was engaged.

We were being visited by the so-called, no longer existent German Luftwaffe every night and day strafing, bombing and harassing us at least four times as often as we saw Allied planes in the air. During the fogged-in early days of the Bulge, American fighters and bombers were grounded for nine days in England. The Luftwaffe, however, managed to get into the air over our heads every one of those days.

As far as casualty rates were concerned, I only knew that in the Siegfried Line fighting we fought for each yard or mile, but in the Ardennes, we were clawing for every inch of gained ground.

And in doing so, I had observed the numbers of American dead in both battles and could offer eyewitness testimony that the newspapers were grossly distorting the truth.

One clipping claimed the Allies had already captured hundreds of thousands of prisoners and tremendous quantities of German equipment and supplies, but during the entire Ardennes Campaign so far, I had never seen more than a few prisoners taken at any one time. During the final stages of the Bulge when remnants of some German divisions had been encircled and cut off, thousands of prisoners were, to be sure, being taken, but the bulk of the remaining German Army had already slipped safely back to the Fatherland to face us again in the Roer Valley and the Rhineland. By the time the Germans were cut off and encircled at Houffalize, only the stragglers and abandoned equipment remained behind. The newspaper clippings had failed to mention that.

One nationally syndicated story criticized GIs for falling victim to trench foot and called them poor soldiers for not following clear-cut Army regulations about proper foot care. GIs in combat, the article stated, should replace their wet socks every day with clean, dry ones. Also, a soldier should remove his boots at least once every hour and massage his feet for 10 minutes. Furthermore, a soldier should never put his feet in water if temperatures were going to drop below freezing. And lastly, he should wear overshoes with no holes in them and buckled at the top at all times.

It was apparent the gullible print media were victimized by the Army propaganda machine, and the American public was being sorely misinformed about the war effort. I wished the letters from home hadn't contained newspaper accounts that my parents thought would be of interest to me but instead had infuriated me.

A company runner came to our billet and told us we were moving out to reinforce another company on the line. Not wanting to reveal our presence or intentions with a noisy truck convoy, we hoofed it from 1600 to 2400 to a densely forested section that, for some unknown strategic reason, had to be defended.

Only absolute stubbornness made it possible for me to complete this march on my pain-wracked feet. The stealth move on foot meant we were moving into this area secretively to surprise the Germans.

We were ordered to dig in, an order that brought hearty laughter from everyone for, at best, we could only scoop out some of the two-foot-deep snow and hope it was enough to protect us from artillery shrapnel.

My luck ran true to form: I was told I had the first two-hour guard duty. Conditions had become so chaotic we no longer were even using daily passwords. "Shoot at anything that moves" was the order of the day. We were told that if it moved, it wasn't an American.

No sooner had I settled into my post than I was asleep. I have no idea how long I slept, but suddenly I heard the soft crunch of a step on snow and felt a hand on my shoulder. It was only my relief. I don't know if he realized I was asleep but if he did, he didn't say anything.

With great effort, I pushed my way back through the heavy snow that, in spite of the thick overhead evergreen cover, had blanketed the earth crotch-deep. About the only advantage of snow like this, most GIs knew, was that it made no sound when men moved through it. I weaved my way through the dense pines and then across a wide open fire break. Exhausted from the exertion, I stopped and flopped over backwards to catch my breath for a moment and to look up at the stars.

The night was still and throat-pinching cold. For a moment, it was as if I had been transported into another world, one where everything was peaceful and there was no death. I allowed my reminiscences to wander back to the happy times I had camped as a Boy Scout in weather like this with my father. But after a few minutes, I snapped back to reality and realized there was no protective cover anywhere near me, so I pushed on to where I could find some concealment from the enemy if needed.

When I arrived back where our squad was more or less dug in, all I could see were bodiless heads protruding from the snowdrifts. Off to one side, a voice whispered, "Hey, Blunt. C'mon over here." It was Danny Driscole of Scranton, Pennsylvania, who had come overseas with me in LOVE Company and who, like myself, had volunteered for mine duty.

He had fashioned a pine bough lean-to over a two-man hole he had somehow been able to excavate. He had also made a soft bed out of more pine branches and had a shielded sterno can burning for warmth. It was one of the happiest surprises of the entire winter campaign so far, for I had someplace to nestle in and, to a small degree, escape the cold. Later we wrapped up in a shared blanket and fell asleep.

Come daylight, a building sign we could read in the distance told us we were outside the town of Odeigne. After a search-and-seize patrol determined the town was abandoned, we moved cautiously into the nearest buildings to seek shelter. Soon word was received we would be there only a day and a night. But that was enough—the town, which had been reduced to rubble, would at least get us out of foxholes and the snow for a few hours.

Almost as soon as I started out on my normal reconnaissance of each new town the squad entered, I was confronted with another grisly sight: more murdered civilians in the local churchyard, an almost identical repeat of those in every village through which we had passed so far. These unspeakable atrocities were seemingly a ritual for German SS troops pulling back from each village.

I tried to eat a can of cold, greasy C-ration pork and beans, but the water in my canteen needed to wash it all down was frozen solid. I threw the can away and went hungry.

A bearded GI pushed his way into our lean-to-like billet and asked, "Anyone here know somebody named Blunt?"

"I'm Blunt," I answered. He motioned for me to follow him. As I tagged along behind, I asked him where we were going. He merely grumbled, "C'mon. Cap'n wants ya."

I knew I had met the company commander when my escort said to another bearded GI, "Here he is." The captain wore no insignia and his overall appearance was as grubby as ours.

"You the one from the mine platoon who speaks German?"

"Yes, sir. Some," I answered.

"Where did ya learn it?"

"High school and college back home."

"Ya understand it too?"

"Some," I said.

He told me one of his men had brought in a prisoner during the night and he wanted me to interrogate him.

"Can ya do it?" he asked.

"I'll try," I said, nodding.

To his company messenger slumped against the CP wall he grumbled, "Get the gawdamned Kraut prisoner."

The black-uniformed German was SS and personification of Hitler's perfect Aryan type with shoulder-length blonde hair, blue eyes, in his mid-20s and with a sullen, arrogant countenance about him. He glared at me and I stared right back at him. I had nothing to fear; I was armed and he wasn't. He was the first German to whom I had ever spoken directly.

I asked him his name and he told me. I took his Soldat Buch, verified the name and gave it to the company commander.

"I don't want to know his gawdamned name. I want to know how many fuckin' Germans there are out there and if they have any armor," the captain almost screamed.

"Panzerkraftwagon?" I inquired.

"Nein," he answered without blinking an eye.

"Wie viele Soldaten ist da?" (How many soldiers are there?) I asked.

"Sechs und Sie sind hungrig" (Six and they are hungry), he retorted, still glaring at me.

"Haben Sie Artillerie?" (Do you have artillery?)

"Nein," he said, shaking his head.

I relayed all this to the captain, who just grunted with each answer. The sum total of what we learned from the Aryan trooper was that there were no tanks or artillery, just six hungry soldiers who wanted to surrender.

"You believe the son-of-a-bitch?" The company commander cursed.

I shrugged my shoulders. "As far as I'm concerned, they're all a bunch of lying bastards," I told him. He nodded in agreement.

As I left the company CP, I heard him say out loud to no one in particular, "I'll have to take a chance, I suppose."

Back at the lean-to, I told the others why I had been called. About an hour later, we heard a violent exchange of burp-gun and M-1 fire. Moments later, a GI came crashing through the trees near us, gasping for breath. When he saw all our rifles aimed at him, he collapsed on the ground unable to get the words out. When he finally calmed down, he told us he was the platoon sergeant who had taken a squad out to bring in the reported six hungry Germans the SS trooper had told me about.

Instead, they were confronted by several tanks and what he described as a "whole fuckin' company" of infantry.

"We tried to fight but we didn't have a chance. Some guys didn't even get a shot off," he sobbed. They had been slaughtered because the SS prisoner I interrogated had deceived us.

After reporting back to the company commander, the sergeant returned and grabbed me by the arm snarling, "I'll show you what I do to gawdammed lying bastards." I had never seen such rage in a man's face before.

Furiously, we walked, almost ran, about a half mile to a POW enclosure where a few hundred shabby, expressionless, defeated prisoners were sitting in the snow inside a barbed wire enclosure. We told the guards who let us enter the compound that we were looking for one prisoner in particular.

We wandered among the prisoners until I spotted the one we wanted. The sergeant stared at him for a moment and then smashed him in the face with the Thompson submachine gun he was carrying. Then he yanked him bodily up off the ground and mashed him again.

Blood spurted out from the German's nose and mouth and spattered all over his black uniform. The other prisoners, perhaps thinking their turn was next, started to murmur and grumble. They were getting uneasy.

"You better do this outside," I cautioned the enraged non-com. "The POWs are getting edgy." We were two against more than 200. From somewhere in the ranks, a German soldier cried out "Heil Hitler!"

"Hell Hitler!" the now almost-hysterical sergeant screamed back before viciously bashing the SS trooper again. I looked outside the barbed wire fence and saw that MPs had their weapons at the ready.

"Tell them why this bastard is going to die," the sergeant screamed at me. As best I could in my limited German, I informed the large group of prisoners, many of whom were now on their feet and milling about, that the SS storm trooper had lied to us and a squad of Americans had died as a result. The SS trooper was now unconscious on the ground, his face crushed beyond recognition and bleeding profusely from massive face and head injuries.

"Take a shot at him if you want," the sergeant half ordered. Remembering all the murdered civilians, the disemboweled woman and the dead babies, I kicked the prostrate SS trooper with all my might in the groin. He curled up in a ball on the ground writhing in pain. At this, the sergeant actually laughed.

We dragged the prisoner outside, rubbed snow on his face to revive him and then pulled him to his feet.

"I want them to see this," the sergeant said, the rage still erupting from inside him. The SS trooper never said a word throughout the beating or changed his expression of arrogance.

"I'll show you, you son-of-a-bitch. Die, you bastard," the sergeant yelled and with that he emptied a whole clip of .45-caliber slugs into the German. Then, he casually rammed another 20-round clip into his Thompson and fired that one too.

The German's body humped up and down and tumbled back and forth in the snow as 40 slugs slammed like sledgehammers into it. When the sergeant's Thompson was emptied for the second time, the SS trooper's badly shredded and disfigured body twitched slightly once or twice as the last nerves finally died. Then there were just the multiple rivulets of blood forming a large crimson stain on the snow.

Only then did we turn, glare defiantly at the other prisoners in the pen, and walk away. As we did so, I glanced back at the other prisoners to make sure none were coming after us. To a man, they stood silently watching us, apparently aware that in war, this was an act of justifiable retaliation.

Back at the company area, the squad was preparing to move out again, but our packing was interrupted by a series of high-pitched, terrifying roars close by, a sound none of us had heard before. We could see flames streaking upwards from the tree tops about 100 feet away for several seconds, and then as suddenly as the sound had started, it was silence again.

We looked at one another and wondered if Hitler was unleashing another of his secret weapons that he had promised the people of Germany would win the war for them. Some of us worked our way cautiously through the trees, rifles and pistols at the ready, to investigate the racket and the fire.

In a clearing a few yards away, we found an American rocket launcher with a rack of about two dozen tubes on it mounted on a jeep. As each rocket was fired, those stacked above it in the rack dropped lower into place for firing. The entire battery was expended in a matter of several seconds. It was a most impressive sight that none of us had ever witnessed before.

We waited until the launcher was reloaded and watched in awe as it was fired again with ear-shattering volume and velocity.

Back at Driscole's lean-to, the call to fall back came about midnight. We were all issued crates of M-1 ammunition and mortar rounds to carry. Each crate weighed about 65 pounds and it was all I could do to lift one onto my shoulder.

In single file we tried to plow through the snow but soon, hitting waist-deep drifts, we were forced to push our way bodily a few feet at a time. It was a silent move through the forest under a black, moonless sky—no cigarettes, no talking.

Every few steps I stumbled and fell, for the load was just too heavy for my frozen feet to support. One GI, seeing my predicament, came over and swapped his carton of K-rations for my ammo crate, but if the ration crate was lighter, I couldn't differentiate between the two.

I continued stumbling every few feet until a burly non-com came by and told me to leave the rations there and rejoin the column. In an hour, we had been able to cover about a mile to where a convoy of trucks was waiting for us. I was helped into one of them and I crowded into a corner. I had not felt this bad since the 50-mile march in from the French coastline.

A sign told us we were pulling into the town of Oppagne and when the column stopped, I dragged myself into the nearest shattered building and collapsed on the rubble-strewn floor. In the morning, Joe Everett was tugging at my shoulder to awaken me. An early riser, he had already found a field kitchen with hot food. Breakfast in the field was always the same: black coffee, butterless dry bread and hot oatmeal. You learned fast not to complain about the food for if you did, you got nothing and anything was better than C-rations, even army slop.

Together, we explored a bombed-out church in the town. As we entered the courtyard, we found about 30 more civilian bodies slumped against the church walls. As in the previous three towns, their hands had been tied behind them and they had been bowled over like tenpins. Their haunting, staring eyes and their distorted faces mirrored their last moments of life while facing their executioners.

As we passed by the church, we glanced inside where a solitary GI, his head bowed reverently and with a Thompson submachine gun cradled across his knee, was praying before what had once been an altar. I can only presume he was praying for the souls of those he had seen piled up in death outside in the courtyard, or perhaps he prayed for his own. Quietly, we left him alone with his God.

As Everett and I walked back to our billet, we discussed the future of Europe, agreeing it would take decades to restore what once had been. The war was leaving countless millions of people in upwards of a dozen countries dead or homeless. The soil and many of the rivers had been poisoned and polluted, forests had been decimated, 80 percent of the homes, commercial buildings and industry had been destroyed. Bridges and railroads would have to be rebuilt, farming would be difficult for many years, and entire networks of roads had been made practically impassable. It would indeed be a long rebuilding road back for the peoples of Europe.

Across from our billet, mine fields had been taped off and left intact, for to attempt to disarm or remove them while they were frozen to the ground was not feasible. If the frozen mines were in the way of a strategic move, they were detonated by rifle fire or by a quarter pound of explosives; and if they were in the road, we tied ropes to them, crouched in ditches and yanked at them until they exploded. Slow and noisy, but safe. When we moved on, and we did almost constantly, we left most of the mines behind to become someone else's problem during the spring thaw.

The next morning, I awakened to find a strange woman bedded down beside me in the bombed-out building that served as a one-nighter home for the squad. She had squeezed in between Everett and me during the night, hungry and frightened. The rationale behind her moving in with us, she said, was we would perhaps give her food (we did), close to us she would be protected from death (she wasn't), and if we got to know her, we wouldn't kill her (we didn't). We fed her and the next day, she was gone again.

A company runner came by and told me Captain Bowen wanted me at the company CP. I reported in and was informed there was an opening available for me at the Officer Candidate School in Paris. My army records, stating I had been chosen for OCS at Fort Benning, Georgia, while a cadreman at Fort McClellan six months earlier, had finally caught up with me.

The previous June, I had been deprived of a commission because of a clerical foul-up. A corporal and I, after our transfer orders had already been cut, were found to be in excess of the quota allowed for that OCS cycle. As a result, both of us were assigned to the 84th and sent to Camp Claiborne, Louisiana, and told to wait for the next cycle openings.

Having witnessed the high mortality rate for junior officers during the Battle of the Bulge and having built up a healthy dislike for the brass, I declined the offer without reservation. Bowen tried to convince me of what an opportunity I was passing up but my decision was firm.

By war's end, 26 junior officers in the regiment—practically all of them platoon leaders—had been killed. In LOVE Company that I had left behind when I transferred to Anti-Tank Company for mine duty, 32 of the 401 men on the continuing company roster were killed during the six months the division was on the line—almost one in every 13. In Anti-Tank Company, only three man had been killed. I knew I had made the right decision back in England to volunteer to become an "anti-tanker."

My feet were showing no signs of improvement. When the pain got to the point where I could no longer walk and could, in fact, barely stand, I removed my overshoes and unwrapped the rags and newspaper from around my feet and ankles. The sight that greeted me was frightening. My feet had turned almost black and the skin was peeling much worse. I tried to massage my feet, but even touching them brought on searing pain.

Taking one look at my feet, Everett advised, "You're a damn fool if you don't go to a hospital and have those feet taken care of."

I vetoed that advice immediately and loudly. I filled a compress full of snow and applied it to my swollen feet to reduce the swelling. Then I left my overshoes off for a couple of hours and warmed my bare feet near the stove before finding some oversized dry socks and putting them on.

One of the squad members suggested I try to wear combat boots again to support the feet better and restrict the swelling. A supply sergeant came up with a pair of oversized combat boots. With much effort, I got them on and tried to stand. A wild pain shot from my feet to my head but I was standing, and I found I could walk better than I had been able to do since Christmas. I was foolishly confident I could lick this malady by myself.

At 0500 on January 6, we were told me were moving out again. The convoy stopped at a crossroads and we were ordered to dig in and defend it, if needed. From the attitudes of the company officers, this crossroads was of extreme strategic value, for I was assigned to a machine gun team and I could see a network of other automatic weapon emplacements around me. It was the main link between Houffalize and La Roche on the Ourthe River.

A short distance behind the intersection was a patch of woods. For some unknown reason, probably just youthful curiosity, I decided to check it out. Assured by the other machine gunners that I wasn't needed for a while, I took off.

I wasn't afraid of mines, for the Germans seldom placed mine fields in wooded areas. Several hundred feet into the woods, I came across a string of bunkers. I'd stumbled onto something big, I thought, but I was committed. It was too late and I'd come too far to expect any help.

Dodging furtively from tree to tree, I approached the first snow-covered bunker. When I hit the entrance, I threw a grenade inside and flopped in the snow. With the explosion, I jumped inside. I felt rather foolish when I found all three emplacements were deserted. I scoured them for souvenirs and was rewarded with a beautiful, hand-carved, staghorn knife.

Relaxed after finding the woods deserted, I carelessly started plowing my way back through the snow to my assigned machine gun position. As I circled around a large pine tree, I came face to face with a Wehrmacht soldier. From instinct, I whipped my M-1 around and fired blindly while falling backwards. Without looking, I fired off another round, this one hitting him in the shoulder. Had I looked first, I wouldn't have fired; he had already thrown his rifle down and had his hands in the air in surrender. The bullet had knocked him down, and as he lay in the snow, he raised an arm, stammering in English, "Kamerad. I surrender." All the fight was gone out of him.

"Sind Sie allein?" (Are you alone?) I asked.

Hearing my German, he started jabbering at me in his mother tongue so fast I couldn't understand him. I slowed him down and tried to figure out one sentence at a time.

When I showed regret for having shot him and wondered what to do with him, he said there were about 65 others hidden in the woods, all of whom also wanted to give themselves up. As I dressed his wound, he said their officers had been SS but they had abandoned their command when the Americans were getting close. These whipped Wehrmacht soldiers had not eaten in three days, he said, and they wanted to surrender to get hot American food. He also said they also had admitted to themselves for weeks that Germany's war was lost.

Tears filled his eyes with the realization I was not going to kill him and he quickly pulled out pictures of his wife and children. I assured him he and the others wouldn't be killed, that unlike the SS, Americans didn't do this to prisoners of war. He said they'd been told that German prisoners would be machine gunned by Negro American soldiers.

Suddenly, without warning, he let out a yell, "Kommen Sie hierher" (Come here). Wehrmacht soldiers poured out of the woods from every direction. I felt completely intimidated for they were still armed and all around me. When I threw my rifle up to my shoulder, they dropped theirs and, almost in unison, clamped their hands over their heads, but it was several minutes before my heart stopped thumping and I could regain my composure.

I sat the motley bunch of prisoners down, away from their weapons, and wondered what to do with them. I told them they would be fed as soon as they got to the POW camp, even though I had no idea where one was. Some said they had been in the army for only a few weeks, that they had been conscripted from their homes and sent into the front lines without any formal training.

My wounded prisoner said he was a 56-year-old "Unteroffizier" (master sergeant) and then he pointed to a young-looking soldier in the group who he said was only 15.

Finally, I marched my ragtag German army back to the crossroads and sat them in a group until some brass showed up and told me where the POW enclosure was. When we arrived there, the prisoners were being fed a supper of hot food. I told the POW camp commander my 65 prisoners had not eaten for three days and he promised me they would be taken care of.

As I walked past the barbed wire fence, the wounded "Unteroffizier" called out "Gott beglucken Sie (God bless you)."

These Wehrmacht "soldaten" were a far cry from the SS troops we had been facing all through Belgium, for these bedraggled soldiers were the beginning of the Volkssturm (people's assault force), a civilian army of children and the elderly that Hitler pressed desperately into service during the final months of the war.

As I walked back to the crossroads, I found it ironic: the prisoners were getting hot chow that day and I was going back to cold C- and K-rations.

The GIs back at the machine gun dugout started kidding me: "Hey, the war will be over next week with this guy around." I took the good-natured kidding but inwardly I felt proud. "At least that's 65 we don't have to shoot at any more," I kidded back.

Later, a captain whom I didn't know came over and congratulated me on a job well done. I let him believe what he wanted to believe, for I neglected to tell it had all been an accident that happened while I was goofing off instead of being in the machine gun emplacement where I was supposed to be.

I was told we were still in a section near Odeigne—Oppagne, Odeigne—they all sounded and looked the same to me. I sat in the snow, ate some crackers and candy from home and escaped from the horrors of war for a few minutes.

Nights in the foxholes were still bitter and lonely and daylight was always welcomed, for with it the loneliness usually disappeared. One particular dawn in early January broke bright and extremely sunny as I stared at the surrounding beauty of the Ardennes Forest. After several hours, my head started to ache, my eyes became blurry and images started to shimmer. I thought my concussion was acting up but soon afterwards, I was sightless.

I panicked and yelled for Joe Everett. He and several others, one of them a medic, came running. The medic put a hand on my head and told me not to worry, that it was only temporary snow blindness and that I would be OK in a day or two. He reassured me he had treated many such cases before. Then he placed an ice pack on my eyes and left.

I kept taking it off every few minutes to see if my eyesight had returned, but everything was gray and I was scared, real scared. Only a short time before I had been terrified by the prospect of losing both my feet and now I feared I was blind. But, several hours later, I could make out dim images and I relaxed a little. Full vision returned the next day.

A company lieutenant came by to personally inspect the condition of everyone's feet. Everett had, for my own good, he said, told company officers about me. The lieutenant, after seeing the ugly sight that had once been my feet, told me I would be evacuated immediately. He had known about my feet since Christmas but in no way had offered to restrict or limit my duties. Now suddenly, he was making a big deal about being concerned for my welfare. I refused to be evacuated and he threatened me with disciplinary action: a court-martial.

I pointed out to him that the anti-mine squad was already down to only seven men. How much lower did he want it to go? We were the only ones around who had been trained to handle mines and booby traps.

Finally he said pompously, "Fine. If you want your feet to rot off it's OK with me." With that, he waived all responsibility for what might happen to me medically for not seeking treatment. That was the extent of his concern.

Two others in the squad were found to have mild cases of trench foot and agreed readily to be sent to the rear for treatment and perhaps a little rest and rehabilitation. Now, the squad was down to five.

In what I considered punishment for refusing his evacuation order, the lieutenant ordered me and another squad member to clear an area of mines at a proposed 155 howitzer battery location. I grabbed my cumbersome mine detector and headed out. We were taken by truck to the battery site where we swept about an acre of three-foot-deep snow before declaring it cleared.

The "six-by" taking us back to the crossroads suddenly veered off the road and started plowing through a wooded area, the driver saying he knew a short cut. A few minutes later, the truck was stuck, the wheels spinning furiously and throwing snow and chunks of wood in every direction. We unloaded to try pushing it out as wooden boxes were being hurled past our heads and into the air behind us by the spinning wheels.

"Hold it!" I screamed. "Stop! Shut off the motor!"

"What are those things?" the driver asked.

I looked closer and then did a double take. They were German "holtz minen," wooden anti-tank, anti-personnel mines and they were everywhere in the snow. We had driven over dozens of them, and not one had exploded. In their haste to retreat, the Germans had failed to remove safety pins from the firing devices needed to arm them. The troops that had thrown them here obviously had never handled such mines before.

Not wanting to be killed by some idiotic truck driver taking short cuts, I removed my mine detector from the truck and hiked back to my company. I left the driver to get himself out of the mine field without my help. The episode, another of so many close brushes with death that happened during combat, made good telling back at Anti-Tank Company.

A lieutenant whom I hadn't seen before wandered by and asked if anyone wanted to accompany him on a reconnoitering trip around the countryside. You guessed it. I piled into his jeep and swung down the road toward Houffalize before branching off onto a narrow side road. As the snow on the path through the woods got deeper, the jeep began to labor. We were almost stuck and the lieutenant was struggling to back the vehicle back onto the main road when firing erupted all around us.

We had stumbled into a hornet's nest of German troops and armor. Bullets splattered everywhere. Two squads of German soldiers sprinted toward us from all sides. A tank .88 also blew a round past us that exploded against a tree behind the jeep. Burp-gun slugs were throwing up snow geysers all around us as the lieutenant desperately swung the jeep around so violently through the underbrush, I was almost thrown out.

Deep ruts bounced us from side to side. Only when we hit the main road and screeched back toward the crossroads did we resume breathing again. After passing the word on to higher authorities that a large buildup of Germans was deployed in the adjacent woods, the lieutenant looked at me and I looked back at him. We examined the jeep and found nearly 30 shrapnel and bullet holes in the vehicle. From the expression in his eyes, he realized that I now knew he too was capable of stupidity. Officers didn't like enlisted men finding out they were fallible.

At chow time that night, I couldn't eat; the jeep incident had scared the appetite out of me. While I sat crunched down and hungry in the snow back at the machine gun nest, I promised myself I would never ever volunteer again for anything, no matter what the reason. I tossed and turned all that cold, sleepless night.

Come morning, I stood up and, for some unexplained reason, my feet felt much better. I was able to hobble around with only a barely noticeable limp. I celebrated with a candy bar from home as I waited for the field kitchen to open up.

German Army Routed: Regroups Again in Deutschland

When word came down we would be on the move again, we loaded onto a convoy of trucks concealed nearby in the woods. We were only a few minutes into the move when voices started yelling, "Hit the ditches! Hit the ditches!" En masse, we dove overboard.

An ME-109 at treetop level was strafing the road, but he was upon us and gone again before most of us could react. One of the trucks in front of us burst into flames. I dug my face into the snow, as the plane made another pass over us. Before the pilot broke off the attack, two trucks were burning and two men killed, one of whom, someone said, was slow bailing out of his truck.

As I climbed back aboard, I thought again of the adage about combat GIs—the quick and the dead. This axiom, as true as it may have been, came back to haunt us, for we experienced too many instances where as quick as a GI was, it was not enough. Fate and luck also played major parts in the game of survival.

The rest of the trip was uneventful and we arrived soon afterward in Grandhan, a small town left largely intact by the war. The civilian population was walking busily on the streets, appearing, for the most part, totally unconcerned about the German-American conflict devastating the cities and towns all around them. Only three artillery shells had landed in their pastures, all some distance from the village. I hoped that I could find a little peace in this quaint, isolated Belgian village nestled in broad expanses of snowy meadows and thin tree lines.

But there would be no peace—in fact, no sleep, at least not for a while. During the Battle of the Bulge, shortages were constant—food, ammunition, gasoline, weapons, equipment, vehicles, but primarily men. It was not uncommon for GIs to be abruptly transferred from one outfit to another, from one duty to another, without orders or notice, often for a few days or even a few hours. Bodies were shuffled around to fill vacant slots in the table of organization and usually, the first available body would suffice. Because there were a preponderance of foot soldiers in evidence, they were chosen most often.

Apparently picked at random, I was told one day to report to Graves Registration for temporary duty. When I arrived at a building designated as a field mortuary, I was briefed on what I would be doing: picking up American dead in the field. I didn't fully comprehend what was involved in the new assignment until after we started. Another GI and I were chauffeured around the area in a troop carrier truck, and every time we located a dead American, we jumped off, picked up the remains and slung them any way we could, usually by the arms and legs, onto the back of the truck.

As we hefted each twisted, frozen corpse, I invariably turned away, averting my eyes from the frosted, blue, bloated faces of the dead, each grotesquely etched with the filth of war, many with open eyes reflecting the violence and pain of their last moment on earth. It was almost as if by not seeing these lifeless eyes, I could reject death, push it aside and not let it intrude deeper into my life, as fragile as that was hour by hour.

The bodies, frozen stiff in every imaginable position, were stacked haphazardly like cord wood until we couldn't hoist them any higher. Then it was back to the field morgue where we emptied our load before the process started all over again. We found corpses everywhere, bloated in rivers, trampled on roads, crumpled in ditches, rotting in bunkers, pretzeled into foxholes, cooked in tanks, dismembered in mine fields, buried in snow, sprawled in doorways, splattered in gutters.

We didn't try to identify them; that was someone else's responsibility back at the mortuary. We just found them, picked them up, piled them as high as we could and then dumped them off. Since the bodies were scattered everywhere, it didn't take long to get a load.

While working this detail, I began considering American and German dead with the same lack of emotion. A corpse was a corpse regardless of what color the uniform was, and war was war. When I returned to my platoon two days later, I wondered what was happening to me that I could become so blasé, so indifferent to death, especially those involving our own people. Oddly, no thought was given to the families of the dead or even to the dead themselves. Mental sensitivities had been totally extinguished as we numbly went about our job—find them, load them, get rid of them.

It was not an assignment that I relished, but in the Army you numbly say "yes, sir" and do as you're told without thought or emotion no matter how revolting the order might be.

During my absence, my squad, while looking for shelter, came across a centuries-old, castle-like chateau perched on the side of a sloping hill and totally unmarked by the war. The chateau reminded me of the grandeur I had seen in the Scotch and English countrysides. When I entered, an elegant fireplace, ornate windows, marbled stone floors and rustic, hunting-lodge decor greeted me. I was greeted warmly by two rather plump, wholesome Belgian girls who welcomed me with feminine enthusiasm and hospitality.

I immediately headed for a roaring fire in the fireplace to warm myself. It was the first time in many months I actually sat quietly beside a fire without worrying about some German seeing the smoke or the glow of the flames. Realizing I was severely chilled, one girl disappeared and moments later returned with a large mug of piping hot chocolate. Not believing my eyes, and slightly apprehensive about this unexpected friendliness, I sampled it cautiously. As I sipped it slowly, retaining it in my mouth as long as I could, I reveled in my glorious newfound good fortune.

Remembering a quote I had learned in school, I asked a French-speaking member of the squad to tell our Belgian hostesses the cocoa was "nectar for the gods." They smiled appreciatively.

To forge more American-Belgian goodwill, I went outside and had my picture taken with the girls. Somehow, the picture was published in *Stars & Stripes*. I wondered what my mother's reaction to it would be, if she really believed I was fighting a war, for the snapshot showed me being kissed on the cheek by one girl while the other held my M-1.

The squad was told it would remain in Grandhan for several days, that it was, in fact, a brief rest period for us. Counting the time in Holland, northern Germany, the Roer basin and the Ardennes, we had been on the line nearly two months.

Unofficial word was passed along that the Bulge campaign, for all practical purposes, was over. Instinctively, we couldn't relax our vigilance for, even though we were pushing the German Army back into Luxembourg and Germany, the war was very much still on. Actually, the fact that the end was near was just a gut feeling, an instinct that we all shared. The Germans, who had been stopped at Marche, had been forced to split their armies and improvise their sputtering campaign along alternate routes. This allowed Allied forces to dissect these fragmented enemy divisions into small, disorganized groups. Our 9th Army, under Lieutenant General W. H. Simpson, had pushed southward from the north and Lieutenant General George S. Patton, Jr.'s 3rd Army had linked up with it from the south.

In the case of the 84th Infantry Division, the linkup came January 16 near the small village of Engreux near the Ourthe River when a 33-man patrol from the 334th Regiment met a tanker from the 41st Cavalry, 11th Armored Division, Third U.S. Army.

Although thousands of German troops and hundreds of vehicles were being encircled and captured, the bulk of the German forces managed to escape to Germany with their weapons, tanks and equipment intact. We would meet them again later in Germany.

Naively, I thought of peace, of returning home alive, of hot food, a soft bed with sheets and perhaps even a real toilet to sit on rather than the slit-trenches we had used since early November on Omaha Beach. But all these thoughts were for naught. I was soon to find out the war was far from over.

I pulled a supply detail one afternoon late in January and was told I was needed as one of nine spare truck drivers picking up rations at a supply depot 20 miles away. I was assured the depot was within Allied lines and I wouldn't have to load the truck, just drive it if need be, despite the fact I'd never driven one before.

As the convoy traveled toward our destination, I admired the beauty of the Ardennes Forest. For miles there was little evidence of war, just the majesty of towering pines, craggy mountains and swift-flowing rivers. I didn't realize I was being mesmerized into a sense of false security by our surroundings. It also didn't occur to me we hadn't passed any American units in quite a while. But after all, there was nothing to worry about, for the lead truck had a map and we were barreling right along.

A loud explosion somewhere in front of us made our driver slam on his brakes. On the ice-slicked road, he was not quick enough and we slammed into the rear of the truck in front of us a split second before the truck behind us rammed into us in a chain-reaction pileup, throwing me violently against the windshield and then snapping me back against the seat.

I slumped to the floor stunned. "Jump! Jump!" I heard a voice bellowing. In somewhat of a daze I fumbled for the cab door handle and fell headlong into a ditch. Out from behind practically every tree in the forest German soldiers appeared firing at 18 truck drivers cowering in a roadside ditch. None in the group were wounded so I assumed the Germans were not trying to kill us but rather firing over our heads to intimidate us.

So overwhelming were the odds, there was no realistic thought of resisting. Quickly I buried my P-38 in the snow, for to be found with it meant instant execution. Then we stood up meekly as a group with our hands over our heads and surrendered.

You can imagine our fright when, after a few minutes, the situation settled down and we recognized the SS black tank corps uniforms with the small silver skulls on the lapels and recalled that they had a reputation for not taking prisoners. The first terrifying thought that entered my mind was a mental picture of Malmédy, where a mass slaughter of American prisoners by SS troops had occurred only days earlier. We were lined up roughly and searched for weapons. Quickly, our watches and other valuables were snatched from us. While being herded into the woods for what I was certain would be our mass execution, I estimated nearly 100 of them: the remnants of a company. In the woods, I saw what had caused our lead truck to explode: huge, neatly camouflaged Mark V and Mark VI Tiger tanks.

I was ashamed and dejected in these last moments of my life for surrendering without a fight. I was about to die without my family ever knowing what happened to me. And surrendering without a shot, regardless of the odds, surely was not a brave warrior's way out.

The tanks started to grind their way toward us through the trees and I instantly realized this would be how we were to die, crushed under the treads of a German tank or machine gunned where we stood. It was easy to figure out that 18 American truck drivers would only be in the tankers' way, slowing them up.

But instead, we were forced at bayonet point to watch as the tanks swung into position and their .88s destroyed the convoy, one truck after another at point-blank range. The dense, acrid stench of burning trucks added to the deafening and frightening scene exploding all around us. Never before had I felt such hopelessness and despair.

After the German elation subsided, we were prodded forcibly with bayonets onto the German tanks where we sat watching the tank crews prepare to move out. An SS trooper with a Schmeisser burp gun slung around his neck guarded us. The commander of the tank I was perched on poked his head from the turret, looked at us with contempt and then burst out laughing. He yelled a remark at the foot soldiers, something loosely translated as "Take a look at these sad sack Amis."

Looking around at the sorry-looking bunch, I saw the truth in his insult. What once had been cheerful, reasonably well-groomed GIs had now been reduced now to a bunch of forlorn prisoners in baggy, dirty uniforms. This was the Germans' hour and they made the most of it.

Our helmets were taken from us and discarded, but we were allowed to keep our wool caps. The pungent exhaust fumes blown into our faces brought on instant nausea and near asphyxiation while low-hanging tree branches slapped painfully at us trying to sweep us from the tanks as we moved through the forest.

Flames shooting from exhaust vents scorched bushes along the way, leaving a trail a blind man could follow. I hoped someone would come across this trail and rescue us, but I knew within me the chances of that happening were almost nil. We wouldn't be missed, for I had seen no sign of American positions or entrenchments anywhere for many miles.

After crashing through the forests for about an hour and carefully avoiding roads where they might be spotted by observation planes, the tank column halted and we were ordered to sit in a circle in a small clearing. One soldier who spoke guttural English ordered us to dig foxholes for the tank officers and crews, which we did after considerable effort. When we started to dig some for ourselves, he instantly stopped us and yelled, "Keiner Hohlen" (No holes), and then with arm motions told us that we could stretch out on the ground for the night.

Blowing snow started to fall and as it whipped against our faces during the night, I began to think perhaps the odds were improving that we might not be executed after all but rather relegated to a prisoner Stalag for American POWs. Simple logic dictated that the longer they kept us alive, the better our chances were. I didn't tell any of the other prisoners what my feelings were for fear of raising their hopes and then being wrong.

Sickened by hunger, I couldn't even find a K-ration dog biscuit in my pocket to munch on. After dark, one of the SS troopers approached our huddled, shivering group and shoved a pot of Kartoffel Suppe (potato soup) at us.

"Essen!" (eat) he snapped, motioning toward the kettle. "Trinken!" (drink).

We each sipped some of the soup and then passed it around. When the guard threw a piece of black bread at us, indicating it was for all of us, we each broke off a small chunk. The soup was potato-flavored hot water, for what potatoes there had been had been skimmed off and obviously eaten by the Germans. When we finished, the same trooper retrieved the kettle and disappeared again into the darkness.

The bitterness of night made my feet throb again with pain. When I awakened, the other prisoners were huddled together murmuring amongst themselves, a welcome sound, for during the night no one had spoken. We knew that at least some of the Germans spoke a little English, but our captors still didn't know that I spoke and understood elementary German.

Breakfast consisted of more ersatz potato soup and a piece of hardened cheese that a German threw in the snow before us. He wanted us to grovel.

I took a bite and passed it on. My sense of taste had abandoned me, but I knew that anything I could put in my stomach would stave off starvation.

Trying to pick up any of their conversation to give me a hint as to what they had planned for us, I watched the Germans eating around a fire nearby and I noticed their food was the same as that given us. At least what little they had they were sharing. I took this as a good sign—they might not be planning to execute us and maybe we'd be liberated after all.

Shortly after daybreak, the column started pushing forward again through the trees, this time for nearly two hours. From the erratic course being followed, it appeared the tank commander was probing first one way and then another trying to find an escape route. When the column finally stopped again, some of the SS troops began taunting us in a game of psychological warfare. They formed a circle around us with burp guns and rifles pointed in our direction and then kicked snow in our faces or shoved rifles and pistols in our faces yelling, "Toten!" or "Schlachten!" (Kill, kill), and then laughing boisterously. If their intent was to terrify us, they succeeded.

One time when this charade ended, a slightly built German in his late teens lagged behind the others. When he was sure he was not seen, he took a partial loaf of bread from underneath his coat and threw it to us. In English, he said, "Maybe this will help. I once lived in New York." Soon afterward, a commotion broke out near the tanks and the young German was marched back to our group.

"They found out about the bread and I'm to be shot. Remember, there are good Germans." These were his last words before a volley of firing squad rifle fire cut him down. Then the execution squad pivoted smartly on their heels and walked away without even a backward glance, leaving their former comrade lying dead in the snow beside our group. I had seen countless men die but never one murdered so methodically by his own people. I overheard a group of officers discussing us. Some wanted to kill us, while others felt that if we were murdered, they too would be if captured. The latter group was overruled and the decision was to eliminate us for there was no valid reason to keep us alive.

Hearing this, I was numb with fear. I told the others, who were already on the verge of fleeing in panic. Some wanted to run, hoping they might make it to safety, while others wanted to fight the Germans with bare hands until they were shot. As we deliberated amongst ourselves, three officers walked toward us with pistols drawn.

One barked out, "Auf Stehen" (stand up).

In an act of desperation, I stammered, "Ich wollen zu sprechen" (I want to speak). Surprised, the officer, a major, held up his hand and nodded to me. "Sprechen," he ordered. I told him they were surrounded by the 2nd

Armored Division and that they, like the SS, took no prisoners. I asked him if they had heard of the "Hell on Wheels" division and then I told him I could guarantee them they wouldn't be killed and would, in fact, be fed hot food if we were not executed.

With my heart pounding wildly and a lump in my throat so big I could hardly swallow, I reminded them it was 18 Americans for 100 Germans. "Achtzehn fur ein hundert," I repeated.

After a short discussion, the major came back and said they would surrender if I could assure them they would not be shot.

"But how do we know we won't be killed for destroying your trucks?" he persisted.

"Das ist krieg" (That's war), I answered quickly, trying to think of answers in anticipation of the questions.

He asked how I knew we were surrounded by the 2nd Armored Division. I pointed to two hills near us and told him they were artillery observation points. Nervously, he looked first at one, then the other.

As if my desperate spiel had been heard by the Lord Almighty and had produced divine intervention, an American artillery shell whistled into the woods behind us, then another in front of us. An observer somewhere had spotted the Germans and was bracketing our position. The next round, I knew, would be on top of us.

Ignoring the Germans, their guns and everything else, I sprinted to the nearest tank and threw myself beneath it to escape the shrapnel that was flying everywhere. I figured the tanks offered a safer umbrella than lying out in the open. The Germans had already scattered, finding whatever instant shelter they could from the shelling.

When the barrage stopped, the 17 other American truck drivers, all of whom had remained exposed on the open field, had not suffered a single scratch nor were there German casualties, tanks nor men. The "Red Legs" (artillerymen) expended a lot of shells but, by the fortunes of war, hadn't hit anything of military value. The artillery coming precisely when it did, when it was most needed to save the lives of 18 GIs, remains one of the great unexplained coincidences of the war for me.

The German major stood in front of me, unbuckled his chrome-plated Luger and handed it to me. The surrender was official. The SS troopers and tank crewmen lined up and stacked their rifles militarily into tripods in the snow beside each tank.

When I told the group of frightened truck drivers that we were being freed, one dropped to his knees and blessed himself while the others jumped around, slapping each other on the back. As soon as the last German had relinquished his weapon, we reclaimed the possessions that had been taken from us and, at the same time, liberated a few additional ones of our own.

We took as many weapons as we could carry and destroyed the rest. I told the major to prepare food for us but he informed me there was none. This, I'm sure, had weighed heavily in their decision to surrender. The next problem was how to reach the American lines, for we had no idea where they were. The German major pulled out a map and pointed to a coordinate.

"Vielleicht dorthin" (Perhaps there), he suggested the American positions might be. But, like us, he couldn't be certain. His guess was as good as ours, we figured, so we started out on foot leaving the four tanks behind.

The vexing problem of finding our way back to the American lines was solved after a couple of hours when someone yelled, "Shut up!" We all stopped and listened. We could hear tanks. Around a bend in the road appeared advance units of the 5th Armored Division moments later. Instantly, seeing the large number of Germans in the road, they fired at them. I screamed and jumped around in the road waving my arms until they stopped, but the commotion of the tank fire brought dozens of olive drab uniforms emerging from the nearby woods. I glanced at the SS major and he nodded.

Some of us climbed onto the tanks that were headed for the 84th's sector and as I rode along, looking at the German SS POWs marching smartly in front of us, I thought back to Sherman Allen, the high school teacher who had taught me the language that had saved 18 American lives. (As an aside, Allen beamed with satisfaction when I looked him up after the war and related how we had been captured, held prisoner and then released when one of the biggest con jobs of the war had been pulled off.)

When the captain in charge of the tank column asked how we had been treated, I told him that I had promised the SS major safe passage to a POW pen in exchange for our lives. He assured me no harm would come to them while under his protection.

For a moment, I considered telling him about the incident where the SS officers had executed one of their own whose only crime was to offer us bread. But then I thought better of it. No matter how brutal and senseless the punishment had been, it was still an internal decision committed by a duly appointed superior officer in a foreign army, not ours.

I relayed the captain's promise to the Nazi SS major and gave him a note with my name, unit designation and signature saying we had been humanely treated while his prisoners. He smiled, clicked his heels to attention and gave me a "Heil Hitler" salute. I ignored it for he was still an SS officer who I was sure had committed his share of atrocities in Belgium. But, with the

① MOST LIKELY (JAN 15 to BETWEEN FEB · MARCH 1945)

note, I carried out my promise. He too seemed satisfied when I read it to him in German.

When the armored detachment arrived at Grandhan, the first one to greet us was Joe Everett with "Where the hell've you been, Blunt? Shackin' up somewhere?"

"Yeah," I answered. "Shacking up with Krauts and have I got some stories to tell ya when I wake up."

With that, I collapsed onto my sleeping bag and slept beside the fire. News of our escapade had spread by now and no one disturbed my sleep. When I awakened, my stomach ached and only then did I remember we had not eaten anything for two days but potato-flavored hot water, some dry, moldy black bread and a small chunk of hard cheese. I remember clearly the first hot meal I ate after being released from German captivity. It was plain hot macaroni, slices of dry cheese, hard-crusted white bread, pineapple slices in sugary syrup, cold sliced beets and coffee sprinkled with powdered milk—a king's feast. An understanding mess sergeant insisted that I eat a second helping. I devoured it without argument.

Then I opened a late Christmas package from home and gorged myself on candy, Cracker Jack from Thomas's store in Shrewsbury, animal crackers, fruit, dried meat, popcorn and gum.

Because of the slight interruption in my life by the German tankers, it was time to catch up on my letter writing home. Still governed by what I perceived my parents' emotions to be, I glossed over the hardships of my life and painted rosy images of life in Europe while traveling on the Continent. I touched on the subject of my various exploits but I seldom went into details. I knew my parents suffered every time they listened to a news broadcast or picked up a paper, so I hesitated to alarm them further. Some day I would write about it all, I thought, and release the memories that already were disturbing me deeply. With that eventual goal in mind, I continued to accumulate a daily chronicle, a veritable barracks bag full of impressions and recollections written on any foolscap I could find.

I attempted another nap but soon Everett was tugging at me. "C'mon, Blunt. It's time to wake up and die right." As usual, that was his signal that it was time again for more Army chow.

After the meal, word came we would be on the move again shortly. It seemed as though that was all we ever heard, that we would be moving out again. Before being drafted and sent on this exciting European vacation, I had never realized how desirable it was in life to settle into one location and become acclimated to one's surroundings.

The trucks rolled slowly through the Ardennes Forest closer to where the Germans were being bottled up. Rumor had it we were going back on the line, but this time the rumor proved false. We were just not being allowed to lag very far behind. That was OK with me; I had had about as much action as I wanted for a while.

We entered the town of Regne, where I quickly staked out a mostly intact, two-story house for a temporary billet. The best accommodations—a couch, chair, perhaps a bed or even some rubble-free floor—went to those who claimed them first. It was almost comedic to see hordes of heavily burdened GIs scrambling frantically from the back ends of trucks to the nearest houses—or any building, for that matter—all trying to be first to find a place to sleep.

I climbed to the second floor and found a stove and kerosene lamp. After warming the room, I delved again into my seemingly bottomless food packages from home before dozing off.

Combat GIs, it was said, always sleep with one ear and one eye open. I don't know how long I had been asleep when I was awakened by a strange squalling sound. I bolted upright, rifle in hand, listened again and then, flattening myself against a wall, moved cautiously into another room.

There I found a Belgian woman had just given birth to a yowling baby boy and I hadn't even known she was in the house. At the sight of my menacing rifle and grubby countenance her eyes widened in terror. I quickly called for a medic and then gave the new mother a candy bar. Relieved, she asked my name and said she would name the baby after me.

I mentally scolded myself for becoming so careless, so militarily sloppy, that I hadn't even checked out the house for possible other occupants before relaxing and sleeping. This inattentiveness could well cost me my life someday.

I went back to sleep and dreamt that I was being suffocated by a blinding light that was burning me with its heat. Fighting to wake up, I opened my eyes and found the nightmare was real: the whole room was ablaze. Somehow, the lamp had fallen off the bureau where I had placed it for the night and the burning kerosene had turned the room into sheets of fire.

I scrambled out of my sleeping bag, grabbed my rifle and gear and threw them out a window. Then I dove out after them, landing with a jarring thud in a snow bank. I gathered up my gear and stumbled away from the building as other GIs in the building came flying out the doors.

In all the confusion, it took me a moment to remember that a woman and her newborn baby were still inside. Several of us ran back into the building by a back door away from the flames, made our way through the smoke-filled darkness to the upper floor where we wrapped the mother and her newborn in a blanket and took them out safely, just before the flames reached their bedroom.

For the remainder of the night, we moved in with another squad, where I kept everyone awake coughing most of the night from lungs badly irritated by smoke. Medics took the woman and her infant son somewhere for shelter and we never saw them again.

Our unit was alerted we would be moving out again at 0400. It was getting to be that we spent only a few hours, sometimes only a few minutes, in each town as the division relentlessly pushed eastward toward the German border, now only a short distance away, we were told.

Minutes before the departure time, I propped myself up against the wall of a nearby building and went back to sleep to wait for the convoy. The 0400 jump-off dragged on to 0500 and, after a hour's nap, I awoke somewhat rejuvenated.

During the short motorized trip, I dozed off again and slid off the wooden bench seat without waking up. The rest of the way I slept doubled up on the floor. When the convoy finally stopped, I lowered myself off the tailgate with legs numbed by cutoff circulation and promptly fell on my hind quarters in the snow, my rifle and gear flying every which way.

This brought roaring laughter from the squad, and the gloom of the night move was broken by another example of Army humor. In the military, especially during combat or other trying periods, tension and frustration were kept in check by laughing at others and their misfortunes. It was accepted behavior. You either laughed or were laughed at, and to take offense wasn't allowed.

As always, we raced into the nearest building and claimed it as ours. We were told hot food was available at a farmhouse field kitchen about a quarter mile away. I got my mess kit and joined a stream of men heading for the kitchen. On the way, I passed a sign saying Bovigny. At least I now knew where I was, as if it really mattered.

I could see a building with white smoke spiraling from its chimney, and a long line of standing GIs snaked around a corner toward us. Falling in at the end of the line, we were moving up one by one closer to the promised land of chow when we heard someone shouting for a medic.

We all bunched around a man sprawled in the snow, his head cocked to the side at an unnatural angle. It was one of the anti-mine squad members.

A medic came running and even without touching him, called for an ambulance. It was obvious the man's neck had been painfully injured when a six-foot icicle, nearly a foot in diameter, had fallen off the mess hall building and hit him on the head as he waited in the chow line.

We tried to comfort him with meaningless words until the ambulance arrived and took him away, He had survived months of hard fighting, surrounded by death in practically every form imaginable, and he had been put down by a damned icicle. One by one, the squad was being decimated by the war. I wondered when it would be my turn. Most of us felt it was only a matter of time.

On the way back to my billet, I passed a church and with ghoulish curiosity I looked behind it for the inevitable atrocity scene I had witnessed in previous villages. This time, there were no slaughtered civilians but, instead, the neatly stacked, frozen bodies of about 30 German soldiers two rows high. Some appeared peacefully asleep while others had been horribly mutilated.

Apparently, we stacked our dead like cordwood on trucks while the Germans piled theirs against churches for eventual burial. I felt a strange pleasure in gazing at them, and wondered about divine retaliation for the murdered civilians I had seen.

On a side street, I discovered a German field ambulance tipped over, its body pockmarked with shrapnel and bullet holes. The vehicle, prominently marked with Red Cross insignia, had obviously been machine gunned. The body of the driver was slumped awkwardly over the wheel, and hanging out a rear door was the body of another German soldier, his head buried in the snow, his legs still inside the compartment. The ambulance also contained three more uniformed bodies, killed while apparently being transported to a field hospital.

I was posted for guard duty that night, and as my normal luck would have it, I pulled the 0200 to 0400 relief, the coldest, loneliest shift possible. This relief meant getting a couple of hours sleep, then standing guard duty for a couple more before ambling back to a cold sleeping bag for possibly two more hours before being told to "shag butt" if you wanted breakfast.

As I walked my post, my mind was captivated by thoughts of home. I took a pipe and some crushed apple leaves (a tobacco substitute) that I had found on a dead German, and in the shelter of a doorway, I lighted it up. I thought it would make me feel older, that smoking a pipe was something that men did. After punishing my lungs for a few minutes with foul, rancid tasting smoke, I decided to wait awhile longer to grow up. I threw the pipe away and never tried it again.

Totally preoccupied with my thoughts, I didn't hear, until the sound was almost upon me, running feet approaching. I pointed my rifle at the sound and was confronted by a panting company runner living up to his title. We were moving out again within five minutes. It seemed like there was no end to the on-and-off-again routine of chasing and then trying to keep up with the German in his embattled flight homeward.

Again, as I had done so many times before, I grabbed my gear and propped myself against a wall outside the billet to wait for the trucks. But when they didn't arrive, we were ordered out on foot at 0700, having gained three more hours of bone-chilled, but still sorely needed, sleep. The trucks were supposed to be concealed in woods nearby waiting for us, but in typical Army SNAFU fashion, they never materialized and we were forced to march until about noon through the forest.

Soon after the march began, we fell in behind a detachment of Sherman tanks and I found I could warm myself slightly by walking in the heat radiated by the motor. I tagged along like this for several miles, limping with each step, but the warmth felt good, if you could hold your breath against the acrid fumes.

In the distance was a town almost obliterated by war's violence: Houffalize tucked in a deep valley on the Ourthe River, about 30 miles southeast of Marche where segments of the 84th had initially stopped one salient of Hitler's advance. We were less than 10 miles from Luxembourg and only 20 from the German border.

In Houffalize, we joined other elements of the 84th and the 2nd and 5th Armored Divisions. GIs wearing unfamiliar shoulder patches filled the town. They were from General Patton's Third Army that had fought its way up from the south to intercept General Simpson's Ninth Army pushing down from the north.

It was a time for celebration. The German in his desperate push to the sea had been repulsed and finally routed. Proudly, we had been partially responsible. With the linking of the two armies came the realization that perhaps we had fired our last shot in Belgium, agonized through our last snow-filled foxholes, limped the last frozen miles in the Ardennes and gone hungry for the last time. And hopefully, we had also been subjected to our last civilian atrocity.

Told we could take a 10-minute break, I slumped into a nearby snowdrift and pushed all thoughts out of my mind. The missing truck convoy finally arrived, loaded us up again and brought us to our last stop in Belgium— Werbomont, where we remained long enough to clean up and rest before returning to Germany.

In the billet I was assigned, I found a large mirror and looked at the strangest face I had ever seen: mine. My sunken eyes were bloodshot and ringed with dark lines. Covering my cheeks and jaw was a six-week-old scraggly black beard matted with mud and encrusted with fatigue. Deep furrows crisscrossed my forehead and I stood there wondering whether I would ever again look like the person I once remembered.

Clean uniforms were issued and hot water was available for bathing and shaving. The eventual transformation was remarkable.

I removed the filthy rag dressings and gently but thoroughly massaged my feet with soap and water. Clean for the first time since being evaluated in the field hospital at Marienberg, I was able to obtain some bandages from a medic and rewrap them.

Some of the festering sores had broken open again and were bleeding from the march from Bovigny to Houffalize, but in general, my feet appeared slightly improved.

Once I was clean again, it was time for the last alteration to my appearance, a haircut. Incredibly, amid the carnage of war, I found a barbershop with a red-headed, buxom, middle-aged woman barber dressed in an all-revealing, skin-tight orange sweater. To say she was amply endowed would be a gross understatement. As she leaned over me to trim my hair and shave me, she almost smothered me by pushing her immense breasts against my face. Unfortunately, I was too young then to appreciate my predicament.

In Werbomont, I met cordial 18-year-old Maria, in whose home some of us were temporarily billeted. She waited on us hand and foot: nothing was too good for the American liberators who had driven the hated Germans from her town. She made me promise to return to Belgium someday to visit Werbomont again after the war.

But thoughts that the war was practically over were premature, for the shattering sounds of buzz bombs continued overhead almost every hour. The dreaded truck-like sounds instinctively made us head for the cellars; these robot bombs were as unpredictable and indiscriminate as enemy artillery.

A notice was posted on a tree near the temporary company CP that a band concert by the division band would be held that night in an abandoned brewery at the edge of town. I ran down the street, past the line of GIs heading for the brewery. Sore feet be damned, I wanted a front seat.

When I entered the building, I was nearly bowled over by the sound of full-sectioned band arrangements. I sat there enthralled, jiggling up and down to the beat and envying the musicians who appeared so neat and clean and who, without doubt, had one of the most desirable jobs in the army.

Suddenly, in the middle of the concert, a chant started from the audience: "We want Blunt. Get Blunt up there." The leader stopped the band and asked who Blunt was. Everyone pointed at me. I should have been deeply embarrassed by this interruption of the concert but, instead, I felt sort of special, maybe even honored.

The leader asked if I wanted to sit in. Foolish question. I was given a pair of sticks and told to go to work. I adjusted the drum set and kicked off a tempo for Woody Herman's "Woodchoppers' Ball." The band arrangement culminated in an extended drum solo for the last chorus. In the parlance of the music world, I was "knocking myself out of this world."

When the concert ended, I left the brewery beside myself with excitement and I couldn't wait to write home about my musical experience. My January 26, 1945, letter home was simple and to the point. Boldly across the V mail letter form, I scrawled, "FLASH, FLASH, FLASH, I PLAYED, I PLAYED, I PLAYED. More details when I come back down to earth. I played with a band tonight, that's all I can say. Love, Your Son, Bud."

I'm sure my parents shared my excitement, especially my father, when he read my letter, for he would know that somewhere in Belgium his son had flown high—at least for a few minutes. For it was he who had always been able to come up with enough money for two admissions for the name band presentations each week at the Plymouth Theater when money was so tight during the Great Depression. And it was he who had accompanied me so many times to jam sessions at the Saxtrum Club in the Harlem district back home. I'm sure my father took my letter, closed his eyes and was there beside me, as always when I sat in with bands.

Our rest and rehabilitation period continued for eight days before word was received February 3 we were headed back to the Roer River in Germany to prepare for the push to the Rhine. It was pouring rain when we loaded onto the trucks for the long haul back north. I claimed the pile of duffle bags and stretched out trying to sleep. About 12 hours into the trip, the convoy passed through Aachen, the first major German city on the Siegfried Line that had been taken by American forces.

As the column of trucks continued northward, the weather improved slightly. After several hours, the convoy stopped in a small settlement largely undamaged by the war: Terwinselen, near Heerlen in Holland, where we had bivouacked briefly before jumping off into combat 11 weeks earlier.

My squad was ushered into a dance hall containing pool and ping pong tables, electric lights and a radio. We were told we would be billeted there until we were called forward again. I grabbed a pool table as a bed and piled my gear on it.

The Bulge was behind us. All that remained were the tortured memories of civilian atrocities and a winter that had been almost beyond human endurance. I couldn't know at the time that the emotional and psychological scars branded into my memory by my experiences during the Belgian Campaign would remain with me the remainder of my life.

Author, at age 18, on a weekend pass in Worcester, Massachusetts, in June 1944.

Joseph Winston "Joe Loot" Everett.

"Tophatters" bandleader Fred Barnette cools off "hot" drummer Rockie Blunt with a block of ice in Leutershausen, Germany, after the war.

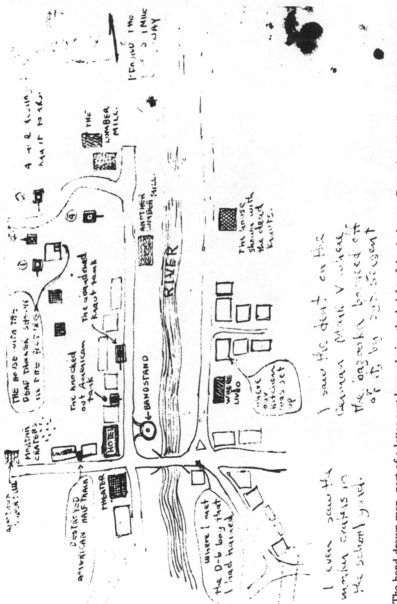

The hand-drawn map, part of a letter sent home during the height of the Ardennes Campaign, details the Belgian town of Hotton, the scene of furious fighting by the 84th "Railsplitter" Infantry Division. The map shows the Ourthe River dissecting the town; the German tanks destroyed by explosives after the battle (upper right); and the wooded area (upper far right) where the author and "Joe Loot" rescued two downed B-17 crew members.

A display of war souvenirs sent home by the author during the war.

Geilenkircken, November 19, 1944.

NATTERDEN

HISCHDEN

NIEDERHEIDE

TRIPS

SUGGERATH →

IMMENDORF →

Sgt Chapman
Geilenkirchen
19 November 1944

The site of the Roer crossing, looking east to Linnich.

Author Roscoe C. "Rockie" Blunt Jr.

Operation Grenade: The Roer Basin Breakthrough

In war, one learns something new every day, sometimes every hour.

Orders were received February 5, 1945, that our push eastward toward Berlin, which had been briefly interrupted by the Ardennes breakthrough, was about to continue. We had been given a few days' rest to catch our collective breaths, but now it was time to get back to work again.

The squad assembled in front of the pool hall and boarded a convoy of freshly washed trucks, this time driven by black soldiers from the Red Ball Express, a supply-line truck network that kept us supplied with the implements of war brought in from the French ports of Cherbourg and Le Havre.

I had been treated cordially by people in the past when they learned I was a combat-tested infantryman, considered by many as a venerated group, but the reception and respect offered us by these drivers was something special and unexpected.

A foot soldier's role is the rottenest job in the Army. He lives, eats, fights and dies in filth. At the same time, however, he is generally looked upon as the toughest, bravest, fiercest bulldog in the entire Army, although airborne paratroopers might take exception to that premise. Out of respect, General Patton once called infantrymen "The Queens of Battle, The Old Footsloggers," and he was a tanker.

The biggest drawback the combat infantryman had was his self-deprecating image. When someone treated him with respect and courtesy, his gratitude overflowed.

Through the dark, the trucks rumbled along the narrow, winding streets of Terwinselen and out into the battle-ravaged countryside. In the distance could be heard the faint, familiar thudding of artillery. The road was so scarred by previous artillery fire, the convoy could barely navigate without driving across the adjoining fields. We jostled our way along mud-slicked roads, kilometer after kilometer, wondering within ourselves what the campaign ahead would be like. One thing was for sure: it surely couldn't be any worse than the Bulge had been.

The undercurrent of artillery became a constant roar and we knew we had arrived at the front. Normally, in these cases, the truck drivers stopped the convoys in some rear echelon area and the troops hiked the remaining three or four miles to the battle area, but not this time. The black drivers wheeled their rigs past the .155-mm Long Tom emplacements and eventually even past the shorter-range .105-mm howitzers.

It was past midnight and the roads were nearly impassable quagmires of Dutch and German mud. Several times, we were compelled to push mired trucks out of water-filled craters. Every German before us must have heard the whining of our wheels, but our drivers stubbornly persisted in taking us as close to the front lines as the roads allowed.

"This is as far as we go," our driver finally yelled back at us. As if to emphasize his remark, artillery shells were swishing one after another over our heads.

I jumped off the tailgate and landed in mud almost up to our boot tops. I was approaching the breaking point of futility and frustration trying to cope with mud in France and Holland, snow in Belgium and now, mud again in Germany. I had only had the newly pressed, clean uniform a few hours and already it was covered with muck. It became obvious dogfaces were not supposed to look like the rest of the Army.

I asked the first GI I saw wandering around where the front line was.

"You're standing on it," he replied as he continued on his way. "The outposts are over there," he said pointing to foxholes about 50 feet away.

"Where are we?" I persisted.

"Lindern, on the Roer River," he shouted back.

There wasn't much left of it after the fanatical resistance the 335th Regiment had met there before the division was deployed to Belgium. The taking of Lindern on November 29, 1944, had been one of the fiercest, hand-to-hand battles the 84th had encountered up to that time.

Even though the Germans had been driven from the town seven weeks earlier, it was still considered hot and the entire area west of the river would have to be contested again, for in many areas, the Germans had moved back in and reoccupied it while we were away.

I was impressed with the black drivers' bravery when I realized they had taken us all the way to where the bullets were actually flying. Some drivers, in fact, tried to wangle ways to remain with us for a few days to join the actual ground fighting. But it was still a strictly segregated Army in those days and their opportunities to fight were limited. Instead, black GIs were mostly relegated to serving in non-combative or supportive capacities.

In the rubble of a nearby demolished building, I was able to clear a space large enough to curl up and allow sleep to blot out some of the exhaustion of constantly being on the move and the mental anguish in which we lived each day.

As I dozed off, I hoped I would get a package from home, that my feet would finally heal, that I could find some hot food somewhere and maybe even some new souvenirs to add to my collection. When I hoped, I always hoped big.

Someone rolled the guard duty roster dice the right way and I was able to get about six hours of uninterrupted sleep my first night in Lindern. Nonetheless, my rest was eventually terminated abruptly by the same reveille call the Germans had invented during the Bulge: wakeup artillery.

To escape the shelling, I headed through a doorless opening leading to the cellar and plunged headfirst about eight feet, landing with a bone-jarring thud on the cellar floor. As I picked myself up, I looked at the door opening and found the cellar stairs were missing. I yelled a warning to the others and one by one they lowered themselves to the protection of the building's two-foot-thick concrete foundation.

Luckily, choosing the cellar for protection was the prudent option, for minutes later the building sustained a direct hit. In the language of later years, someone was sure rattling our cage. The intense barrage, which lasted about 20 minutes, belied the reports the Germans were suffering from ammunition shortages.

I ventured a peek outside and the GI I had talked to the day before was back again. "See what I mean?" he yelled. "You don't walk around much here. Lindern's the hottest town on the Roer. You jump from house to house if you want to stay alive long."

I got the point right away.

"Get back inside," he yelled. With that, another artillery shell exploded in the street. "It's a favorite trick of the Germans to lay in some more rounds after it's all clear and we start walking around again. You play your cards close here."

He said the town was under direct German observation, and whenever they saw anything move, they cut loose with an .88. Later, I learned the chow tent was on the other side of "Screaming Mimmie Alley," a narrow street zeroed in by the Germans. Again, it was a matter of the quick and the dead. During our brief stay in Lindern, we all became accomplished short-distance sprinters.

German troops, only a short distance away in a row of pillbox bunkers, also had the town in their field of harassing machine-gun cross fire. When the 84th was called upon to abandon the Roer Basin sector in order to reinforce the troops being overrun in the Ardennes Forest, units of the German Army had moved back into the previously American-held towns. Now these troops were fighting a delaying action to slow down the American advance toward the Roer River.

"What else do we have to look out for?" I asked the Lindern veteran.

"Mines. They're all over the fuckin' place. The fields are covered with them."

I passed all this information on to the others in my squad, and we quickly accepted the fact that if we wanted hot food three times a day, we would have to run the gauntlet across "The Alley."

I made it across OK for breakfast my first day and then returned to the billet to catnap for a couple hours. When I awoke, I knew it would be a good day, for another package and a couple of letters from home had arrived.

Mail call was a very special event for a GI. It allowed him a few minutes to withdraw into his private shell and close out the sordidness of the war around him. These few private moments were a precious link to the sanity and stability of our civilian lives.

In the combat zones, mail call was different from that back in the States, where the company clustered around a mail clerk standing on a box and yelling out each name as he came to it in the mail sack. Then he scaled letters or threw packages in the general direction of someone screaming "Here" back at him.

On the other hand, in combat where bunching up was unwise because of possible mortar or artillery attack, the company mail clerk generally hand-delivered all mail to the billets where he knew each soldier was living. He even knew each man's bedroll. If he found a man sleeping, he placed the mail quietly beside him. If the recipient was not there, the clerk left his mail on the man's sleeping bag. Often, you awakened to find these most cherished surprises beside you. These packages of love from home were like receiving Christmas presents every few days and served as my inspiration and strength to endure all hardships.

Actually, after bolting across the alley a few times, it became sort of a sport, us against them. Each time we made it safely across, and as far as I know, everyone always did, it brought on laughter for we knew we were driving the German gunners crazy trying to get one of us. Every footrace with death brought a Mauser bullet whacking against a building close to your head, usually chipping off chunks of masonry or splintering wood. It became an exciting game we played with the German each mealtime.

Bored with always being on the receiving end of enemy fire, I legged it at full speed one day to a building on the outskirts of town facing a row of pillboxes on the far side of a broad meadow. I figured if I was lucky, I could get a few shots off at the snipers. Killing had become a challenge, even a need, and I found myself constantly seeking fulfillment.

As I threw myself into the building, I literally bumped into a badly decomposed German corpse. Startled, I recoiled in horror. I had forgotten just how jumpy my nerves had become.

I located a small hole blasted in the wall at ground level. To snipe, you lay on your belly instead of standing at windows and doors as the Germans usually did, for these were the first two targets on which an enemy zeroed in when returning fire.

I waited and watched, hoping to spot a walking target. When after an hour there were no signs of life across the sugar beet fields and, satisfied it was safe, I foolishly walked fully exposed in a low crouch out to the nearest orchard away from German pillbox range. There, I found a foxhole containing two rotted German bodies. Holding my breath against the smell, I searched them for souvenirs but found nothing more than a few worthless Reichsmarks, a fountain pen, some black bread and cheese, pictures of their families and their Soldat Buchs.

While I was gazing at the pictures of their women, parents and children, I felt a strange sadness and for those few moments in a Lindern orchard, I remembered that these unrecognizable, bloated chunks of rotted meat had once been human beings with loved ones, not just the German enemy. I wondered whether their families knew yet they were fatherless or husbandless. Somehow that particular day, I could not subject these soldiers to the final indignity of stealing their personal, cherished belongings. I respectfully put them back in their uniform pockets and walked on. As I walked, I felt a twinge of remorse for the families I had destroyed with bullets. The men I had slain had been only targets to me, not people, and for a few moments, I worried about the killing lust that I knew had built up inside me. I tried to convince myself that I was only impartially doing the job I had been trained to do, but still, I was experiencing troubled emotions. For some unexplained reason, at that moment I identified with the two rotted corpses after I had pictorially met their families.

I was well aware my moral conscience was constantly in conflict with my familial and religious upbringing, but I seemed powerless to resolve the differences. Circumstances had forced me into a life over which I had no control, but still I was concerned that I wasn't even trying to control it, just going along with it—and even, distressingly, sometimes enjoying it.

I looked up. The sun suddenly seemed to have lost its warmth for me. I headed back toward Lindern, unfulfilled.

In a hedgerow near the edge of town, I found another decaying German soldier, his head hanging from his neck by a few shreds of skin. He was holding a Panzerfaustwaffe, a German tank grenade launcher that apparently had misfired and blown up in his face. The utter gruesomeness, the constant variety of death in war again held me spellbound.

I had been in combat a little too long and was becoming dangerously careless in my behavior, for I had wandered around in the orchard aimlessly looking for souvenirs and now found myself in the middle of a mine field. I had been warned but had not paid attention, and I mentally chastised myself, knowing full well that soldiers who ignored warnings didn't live long in combat.

The mines were Schu Minen, small, square, wooden anti-personnel concussion devices with a half-pound of explosive and a detonator. The top telescoped over the explosive charge when stepped on, thereby activating the firing pin and setting off the mine. To avoid detection, the mine contained no metal.

I froze and looked around. There appeared to be hundreds of them, and at first glance, I couldn't figure out a route by which I could retrace my steps. I wondered whether I had pressed my luck too far this time. On hands and knees, I probed for mines with my fingers for I hadn't even brought a bayonet with me. I managed to remove a few mines but most of them were frozen to the ground. Cautiously, I retreated backwards, probing gently as I went. One by one, I carefully lifted the covers and removed the firing devices of about 30 mines, eventually clearing a narrow path back to the company area in Lindern.

One of the mines appeared almost new with no signs of being weather-beaten, so I removed the detonator and fired it harmlessly into the ground. After unwrapping the paraffined paper around the charge, I discarded the now-harmless block of explosive and shoved the deactivated mine in my jacket pocket as a souvenir to send home.

Back at the company area, I borrowed a bar of brown laundry soap from the company kitchen, cut it to the size of the mine charge and replaced the detonating pin. You couldn't tell it from the real thing. I walked over to the CP, found Captain Bowen and shoved the Schu mine under his nose.

"OK if I mail this home, Capt'n?" I asked casually as I "accidentally" dropped it on the floor. Some officers simply didn't have any sense of humor whatsoever during World War II.

The next day, I decided to expand my souvenir search area even farther, so I followed railroad tracks that led to a cluster of small buildings including a rail station, burlap bag factory, garage, machine shop, gristmill and several houses. But I didn't find much; obviously other loot hunters before me had stripped the village clean.

Climbing a nearby banking to look around the countryside, I found the wreckage of an American A-20 light bomber in a field several hundred yards away. After taking a picture of the plane with a cheap German camera I had taken from a prisoner, I headed back to Lindern.

Along the way, an uneasiness, sort of an unnatural feeling came over me, as if my instinct was warning me again. I hit the dirt and looked around warily. Stretched out before me was a row of the most expertly camouflaged pillboxes I had ever seen. Armed with only a carbine, a couple of clips of ammo, a pistol, trench knife, two grenades, some nitro-starch and a candy bar, I began to sweat. I was, for the first time, seeing the real German Siegfried Line. The pillboxes extended into the distance.

Alone in the face of such awesome defenses, I ran panting and puffing, crouched over, all the way back to Lindern. When I told the others about what I had found, they informed me the 102nd Infantry Division had captured 92 already abandoned pillboxes while we were fighting in Belgium. I felt foolish for being so jumpy and letting abandoned fortifications spook me so. The Germans, having evacuated the whole network of boxes when faced with the advancing Allied forces, had pulled back across the Roer, where they were now contented to sit back and take potshots at us while waiting for our next move.

A rough hand on my shoulder was the alarm clock that told me it was my turn for guard duty. I draped an overcoat over my shoulders and stumbled out into the cold stillness of the murky night. I leaned against a door casing and stared into the fog. After a few minutes of staring at nothing, I began to realize the rest in Holland had affected me. I was alone and getting jumpier by the minute. As my nervousness increased, I wondered if I was actually becoming afraid of the dark. Such feelings usually weren't admitted to one's self in combat, but in my case it was becoming quite apparent to me.

To be totally immersed in the horror of war for months and then to be suddenly transplanted temporarily to the relative tranquility of a rear area, only to be abruptly returned without any mental preparation to combat again, strained the nervous system's ability to compensate for the upheaval, and the man could easily become paralyzed with fear. The bravery born of necessity often deserted him.

In combat, a man, in time, becomes immune to the all-consuming fear that envelops him almost constantly; responses to crises become automatic. The mind becomes dulled by the physical and emotional stresses of war and regresses to the primal instinct of survival at all cost.

This, I was afraid, was happening to me. The proof of this was apparent when I recoiled upon abruptly encountering German bodies, by my growing revulsion for mines, my increasing preoccupation with death and now by the gnawing apprehension about what was possibly lurking in the fog that embraced me.

I began to worry, for the one thing I didn't need at this time was a breakdown of my nerves. I had controlled my emotions so far and I didn't want to unravel this close to the end of hostilities.

As I stood at my guard post, the throaty, pulsating truck-like rumble of a buzz bomb overhead heightened my nervousness. The walls of the building I was leaning against quivered from the vibrations. The fog made the rockets, which I had dubbed "messengers of death," sound as if they were only a few feet over my head. One after another they came, their flames tinting the fog a faint, eerie red and then droning off in the distance, leaving me alone again in the darkness with my thoughts.

I ducked into the doorway and lighted a match to check the time. The watch showed 10 minutes to go before my relief was due.

I walked back to my billet to awaken the 0400 guard. After he shuffled grumbling out the door, I put my head on my helmet and figured if I slept double time, I could perhaps get a couple of hours of sack time before morning.

With hot oatmeal in my gut, all uncertainties about my mental state disappeared and soon afterwards, with my confidence restored, I was off again exploring. In what was apparently a last ditch maneuver by Hitler's commanding generals, the V-2 firings intensified as they rumbled overhead throughout the day.

No matter how many of them I saw, I still stopped and watched each one with morbid fascination. They were ugly and fearsome, and they personified a crude but awesome power not seen before in conventional warfare. Even though I feared them for the devastating damage they caused upon detonation, I begrudgingly admired the scientists who had developed them, one of whom I would interview 15 years later as a newspaper reporter.

The toll of dead Germans in Lindern, lying all over the town in every grotesque position imaginable, was reminiscent of Matthew Brady's pictorial history of Civil War battlefields. Any combat veteran might say that one war is the same as any other, that only the uniforms and the armament change.

Another sound that quickly became part of a combat infantryman's life was the whine of approaching German fighter planes, especially the ME-109s on a strafing run. These planes had a sound all their own and GIs learned to recognize that sound and react to it fast. In Lindern one afternoon, I heard that all-too-familiar sound and looked up quickly to see from which direction they were coming. Two of them, the lead plane and his playmate, were already swooped downward from the east and headed straight at me. I dove at the closest house and hid under some fallen rafters, the closest mantle of protection I could find. The pilots, flying with reckless abandon at treetop level, pulled out of their dives a split-second before slamming into the earth.

Their approach was through an almost impenetrable curtain of ack-ack and .50-caliber machine-gun tracers. Thousands of bullets arced through the sky searching for their targets, but when they couldn't find them, they gracefully fell back to earth defeated.

I watched through a shell hole in the wall of the house as the planes' wing guns spat a stream of slugs into the ground and ricocheted off buildings all over town. Violently, patches of earth erupted along a nearby street where several jeeps were parked. Almost in a blur, the planes disappeared in a swooping arc beyond the town as they climbed with a roar back to altitude. The pilots, it seemed, had no specific target that I could determine; we had no tanks in the town or ammo dumps, just a couple of companies of bewildered GIs.

A few GIs had jumped onto trucks with .50-caliber machine guns mounted on their cabs and tried to return the planes' fire, but the Messerschmitts were out of range before any ground fire could be brought to bear.

"Medic! Medic!" someone was hollering down the street. Once the planes disappeared back toward their airfields and the all-clear had been sounded, I ran toward the shouting. A sergeant was lying in the mud near 3rd Battalion CP.

"The medics can't help him now," I heard someone murmur. The sergeant had remained on the street to watch the fireworks display and, by another freakish accident of war, had been hit in the chest by a spent bullet falling from the sky.

The next day I decided to explore more closely the abandoned pillboxes I had seen previously. I entered one and was instantly miniaturized by its mammoth size. The boxes easily covered three acres and had been built into a series of small hills almost totally hidden from aerial observation or detection. On the ground, the boxes couldn't be seen until one was practically upon them and by then, if they were occupied, it was usually too late. Trees grew from their roofs and tall pasture grass almost covered the artillery and machine-gun firing apertures.

I tugged at the two-foot-thick concrete slab that had served as an entry door. Inside was a huge, dank room, empty except for row upon row of steel cots suspended in tiers from the walls. I counted 40 cots in each room.

Hundreds of artillery shells and concussion grenades were still stacked there and I knew our demolition engineers would eventually move in and destroy them. The main chamber where the .88s were located contained empty racks for hundreds of rifles and machine guns; there were facilities for enough supplies to sustain an extended defense had the occupants wanted to. I felt strangely out of place standing in that enormous abandoned enemy fortification, one that only weeks earlier had been filled with German defenders trying to destroy us.

I peered out of the firing ports and saw what their eyes must have seen: the American occupation of Lindern. I stood beside an .88 and peeked through machine-gun slots fantasizing what it must have been like to be a German soldier there.

I scratched around for souvenirs but there were none that weren't readily available on any battlefield. With that, I left the damp, stagnant air of the pillbox and walked back out into the sunshine. I wondered why they had retreated without a fight from this strategically important section of Hitler's vaunted Siegfried Line that had been two decades in the making—unless it was as the Unteroffizier prisoner in Belgium had told me: they already knew their war was lost and wanted to avoid further needless sacrifice of life.

Still wanting to explore farther, I continued walking slowly toward a town I could see in the distance right on the banks of the river and directly across from the German positions. The last few hundred yards were spent repeatedly watching the town with field glasses I had taken off a dead German officer in Belgium. Each time I checked, I detected no signs of life so I stood up and started to close in, somewhat warily, on the nearest buildings in this seemingly abandoned town.

After brazenly walking down the main street, I climbed to the attic of a bombed-out school, a great observation post from which to see across the Roer. The attic was strewn with shattered slate roof tiles, splintered wooden rafters, old textbooks and pre-Nazi German flags.

On the east bank of the river, German soldiers were out in the open on a knoll, apparently unconcerned about our interest in them. It didn't occur to me that my wandering around alone in unoccupied territories was unacceptably foolhardy. I had been captured once, and I probably wouldn't be so lucky a second time. But for some reason, that thought hadn't occurred to me before I started to explore this nameless riverfront town.

Our division intelligence knew from prisoner interrogation that the troops waiting for us on the other side of the river were from the First Battalions of the 59th and 1034th Volksgrenadiers Divisions. At least they were Wehrmacht; perhaps they wouldn't fight with the ferocity of the SS troops we had opposed throughout much of the Ardennes campaign.

Through binoculars, I could see that the entire area beyond the river had been flooded. The fast-flowing Roer River normally was about five feet deep, but the Germans on February 10 had opened the Henbach Dam to the north of our position and the depth had risen to 11 feet. The usual 60- to 85-foot-wide river now looked like a flood plain stretching to the eastern horizon.

At an estimated range of about 300 yards, I fired off an M-1 clip at the figures on the east bank of the river. I might as well have been shooting a pop gun at them, however, for they ignored my rifle fire. They probably hadn't even heard it.

It wasn't long before I found out just how wrong I was about their ignoring me. A couple of minutes later, they laid two .88 rounds into the town, a block away from the school in which I was concealed. I stopped the sniper foolishness right away.

When I returned to Lindern, I learned that two platoons of LOVE Company had been overrun when the Germans counter-attacked in nearby Mullendorf. I was concerned about the fate of those whom I knew in those platoons. Hitler's supermen, as battered as they were, weren't about to give up their homeland that easily.

The company runner came by, informing us a movie was being shown that night in one of the rear-area towns. I grabbed my gear and jumped onto the nearest truck headed that way. *Saratoga Trunk*, starring Gary Cooper and Ingrid Bergman, was a great morale booster, for it took our minds off the war and transferred us into a fantasy world for a couple of hours.

I awakened the next day to more of the sameness that punctuates war, the sameness that insidiously eats away at a man's spirit until he is existing, not living—Screaming Mimmies, mud, cellar habitation, .88 barrages, greasy chow, lonely guard duty, the smell of death, mines, machine guns, mortar attacks, strafings, buzz bombs . . . just another normal day of infantry ground combat.

In Lindern, the Germans added a new psychological weapon to their arsenal: Panzerfaust rockets that whined like .88s. The rocket launcher, a crude variation of the American bazooka, was of limited value as a weapon. Used primarily against tanks, the rockets seldom caused any casualties and we normally ignored them. They more or less amounted to a bark rather than a bite.

Orders came down to strip all divisional ID from our uniforms, patches, rank designation—everything. For no plausible reason (the Army seldom had persuasive reasons for anything it did), divisional brass didn't want the Germans to know who we were. I never determined who our top-echelon brain trust officers wanted the Germans to think we were, the French Foreign Legion?

This strict secrecy, I figured, meant we were heading across the Roer soon—and I was right. Pontoon bridges were being built at Linnich to span the Roer, but whenever the engineers stretched them across the river, the Germans blew them up. The enemy already knew who we were and that we were coming after them for they had moved in heavy mortar, artillery and infantry reinforcements to greet us. The only thing they didn't know was when, but then again, that mattered little for we had given them plenty of time to prepare for us, whenever we decided to appear.

Propaganda leaflet artillery shells showered down on Lindern welcoming us back to the Roer region after having done such a "splendid job" in Belgium. The leaflets said that superior forces were waiting for us. So much for keeping our identity secret.

With all the waiting, I was getting itchy and bitchy, a GI's prerogative. There's an old saying in the Army that a bitching GI is a happy GI, but I never believed that old military saw. When I was bitching, I was far from happy. But I quit my bellyaching fast when Joe Everett reminded me that each day we didn't have to cross the river was another day we lived to see the sun come up.

The only diversion I could come up with to fend off this boredom born of waiting for something to happen was to correlate into booklet form the dozens of pages of journal notes I had scribbled since shipping overseas. The diary of daily events, observations, opinions, impressions and emotions, coupled with a detailed written map of the division's route across the Continent, would enable me to better interpret and relive my experiences in the event that I survived—and the chances seemed to be getting better every day that I would.

On February 21, we were told the crossing—Operation Grenade—would be in two days. It was our first major river assault. On the 23rd, a softening-up artillery barrage commenced at midnight and continued until we jumped off at 0400.

Strategy dictated that we had two minutes to sprint across a two-foot-wide, bouncing, swaying pontoon bridge and secure a position on the other side while other assault troops paddled across in 12-man, squad-sized pontoon boats. Fortifications across the river were known to be strong and armament well concentrated. Looking at my watch, I realized that in six hours I would be across the river or dead.

I tried to grab some sleep but thoughts jumbling around in my head prevented it. The Red Legs had cannonaded the Germans entrenched on the far shore of the Roer for three nights to simulate a river crossing but each barrage was a diversionary sham. This time it was for real and shells were being shoveled past gun breechblocks as fast as the loaders could handle them. We only hoped the Germans would think it was just another routine night barrage and stay huddled in their holes.

For an hour before the river crossing, the ground we stood on reverberated from the intensity of the artillery bombardment. As the jump-off hour approached, we moved through the town and across nearby fields toward the riverbank in mob formation.

The night was foggy and ominous, which helped to conceal the troop movement and perhaps offered us some slight element of surprise. But it did little to alleviate our feeling of impending doom.

Slogging through the mud, I lost all conception of time and distance, but eventually I became aware through the blackness that we were filing between two rows of ruins. There was little left of Linnich that we could see. When the ground sloped downward I knew we were nearing the river. Tentatively, we probed in the darkness for the footbridges that were still under construction.

When we finally halted, the column became a crowd and we milled about aimlessly, resting whenever we could and awaiting further orders. Our job as mine-removal specialists was to cross the river with Anti-Tank Company to clear the landing area of mines for foot troops coming afterwards. The Corps of Engineers, we could make out, mostly from the sound, was feverishly trying to finish the footbridge across the river for us. Strangely, I felt little fear as I waited for orders to cross, just an apprehensive desire to get it over with. The first rays of daylight revealed geysers of mud and debris being thrown into the air on the far bank of the river by our exploding artillery shells. During the American bombardment, the German artillery batteries that had harassed us so much back in Lindern were not returning the fire. Minutes later we learned they were conserving their ammunition for our actual crossing.

German bunkers and breastworks were being destroyed and timbers could be seen being tossed like matchsticks into the air. Shells landed in the river, sending up fountains of spray that, for a moment, shielded our view of the German entrenchments. The orange flashes of exploding shells buried themselves in the earth, making the ground erupt violently as if rebelling at being disturbed. Suddenly, without warning, the dawn was silent.

"Move out! Move out! Move out! This is it!" a muffled voice was yelling. I wiped mud from my carbine and ran blindly toward the bridge. When the solid footing of land gave way to exaggerated swaying and bouncing, I knew I was on the river.

I quickly slung my rifle and grabbed for the rope handrail with both hands as water gushed into my boots. Crouching and running as fast as my tottering equilibrium would allow, I felt as if I were running in slow motion. The other bank of the Roer seemed so unobtainably far.

Midway across, I came to a hurdle in my path. It was a GI, head hung submerged in the swirling water, whose war had ended on the footbridge. I skidded to a stop, hopped gingerly over the corpse and then kept going. Another body was in the water wedged against the bridge by the swift current.

The bucking footbridge did its best to throw me into the river but I clung hard to the rope. German .88 shells and mortars were now exploding in the water all around us, but I was scarcely aware of them for I was trying to contend with a buckling bridge that was fighting me every step of the way.

Behind us I could hear anti-aircraft guns pounding away at waves of Messerschmitt 109s and Focke Wulf 190s approaching from the east to strafe and bomb us before we could secure a beachhead. The Germans were throwing everything they had at us. The banshee-like whine of diving planes, together with the body-battering concussion of shells and mortars exploding only yards away all around us, blanked out all thoughts, all emotions, all reflexes. It was as if we were functioning in a time void where reality ceased and eternity took over.

On the other side of the river, I could make out GIs already engaged in hand-to-hand combat with the Germans. I reached the other shore, sprinted a few yards to the right and threw myself into the mud.

With a resounding thud, a German mortar shell landed on the bridge behind me. Several GIs blown into the water desperately tried to swim the last few yards to shore. Those of us already across lobbed grenades into trenches along the riverbank. A burp gun almost within touching distance cut loose, spewing out a hail of bullets over my head. I threw a grenade at the sound of the chattering gun and was rewarded with a shower of mud by the explosion, but the gun was silenced as up and down the line American grenades and rifle fire were driving the German forces stubbornly back.

I crab-like crawled rapidly to a nearby bunker and lobbed a grenade inside, but it was a waste of taxpayers' money—the Germans inside were already dead. In all the frenzy, I encountered another German and pumped several shots into him before realizing he too was already dead. When the trench appeared to be empty of enemy soldiers, I peered over the parapet and could see a town a few hundreds yards inland with Germans scurrying around.

I cautiously looked around. GIs were running and crawling everywhere. A tenuous beachhead had been established and we were clinging to it by our fingernails, waiting for the inevitable German counter-attack. Behind me, the bridge had been repaired and American troops were pouring across, a most reassuring sight. A Sherman tank and a jeep hove into view from a treadway bridge a few yards downstream.

The devastation around me was total; not a tree had been left standing. As far as I could see in every direction, artillery had laid barren the entire countryside. I rifled through the pockets of the German burp gunner my grenade had silenced and took his Soldat Buch and a grenade, which I tucked inside my jacket.

Orders were passed along to dig in and hold the position while the infantry advanced. Finding a ready-made hole with a dead German in it, I pushed him to one side and squeezed in beside him to wait, for it was easier than digging a foxhole for myself. In the hole I found a badly rusted .32-caliber pistol that was so old it wouldn't even fire, so I thought. I pointed it at the bottom of the hole and pulled the trigger, jumping a foot when it blasted a hole in the mud inches from my right boot. Again feeling stupid for such unmilitary-like disregard for firearms, I tossed the gun into the river in disgust.

During a slight lull in the fighting, I disarmed the German concussion grenade by removing the powder head, punctured the seal with my trench knife and poured out the charge. Then I unscrewed the cap on the other end, pulled the activating string and placed the grenade outside the hole until the detonator cap went off with a harmless pop.

Our platoon had crossed the river without a casualty and now we were securing our positions while the foot troops pushed forward toward the town I had seen in the distance. Fortunately, we were not needed to sweep for mines in front of the advance troops as we had been expected to do. The best way to secure a position, militarily speaking, was to catch a short nap.

By mid-day, the main body of troops was pushing inland and we slogged along behind through the mud to the nearby town of Rurich, where I had observed the Germans earlier. Already the massive Allied assault toward the Rhine River was forming to grind forward. Advance units spread through the town without slowing down and kept going.

Anti-Tank Company's mission was to mop up any bypassed pockets of resistance and clear the area of possible snipers and stragglers. Squad by squad, we worked our way through the shattered Rurich rubble and our only reward was six artillery-stunned Wehrmacht soldiers, all battered into near-speechlessness.

We herded them together and pointed them in the direction of the bridges back to Linnich while telling them that as long as their hands were folded over their heads, they wouldn't be molested by American troops. Without GI guards, the small band of prisoners trudged to the rear, arms dutifully over their heads. But not before we stripped them of all valuable prizes of war.

They were the sorriest looking bunch we had seen in any battle engagement. After we checked their unit identifications, it became obvious they were not Wehrmacht soldiers at all, but rather, more of the disorganized Volkssturm troops we encountered often during the Roer Basin breakthrough. These Volkssturmers were merely untrained civilians in military uniforms but many were still fanatically loyal to Adolf Hitler and, as such, still had to be considered dangerous.

As we caught our breaths in Rurich, we knew that Operation Grenade had been a success. If the American Army could sustain its momentum, the war could surely wind down in a matter of months, perhaps even weeks.

If only we could have anticipated that the push eastward would accelerate greatly in the next fortnight, our exhausted morale would have shot skyward. But in war the future can't be forecast and we had to content ourselves with punching out the kilometers one at a time, as foot soldiers were expected to do.

The Rhineland: The End in Sight

Before pushing inland, I took pictures of the footbridge over which I had crossed the Roer River and of a column of about 50 German prisoners carrying their dead and wounded on crude wooden stretchers on their shoulders. Their numbers reinforced my hope that German resistance in northern Germany would be lighter than that encountered in Belgium.

It was simple logic: the weaker the resistance, the farther we could penetrate into the heart of Germany each day; the more ground we gained, the closer we would be to Berlin, the end of the conflict and the sparing of both American and German lives.

But I'd already learned in war that no river crossing is ever truly secure. There is always the imminent threat of enemy counter-attack. The Bulge—where often for every kilometer we gained, we were pushed back two—was ample proof of that.

In Rurich, we were ordered to remain indoors. We were still within sight of the Roer, and the closer we pushed toward Berlin, the harder the German would resist. Since blind obedience is the best course of action in the army—at least when it's convenient— I obeyed and grabbed a rubble-free corner of a building where I could get a few minutes of precious sleep.

A bellowed "Let's go!" brought me back to my senses. I climbed into a three-quarter-ton weapons carrier waiting for us on the street and this time was lucky in getting the much sought after tailgate seat that offered fresh air and fast escape. When I wanted out, I wanted out in a hurry. I remembered the GI killed during a convoy strafing when he hesitated when bailing out.

We were fighting, for the most part, on the flat sugar beet fields of northern Germany and we soon realized that the hills that disturbed these plains were put there by Hitler, not nature: the hills were cleverly concealed pillboxes.

As the weapons carrier lurched along the road, a shell burst behind us. Before we could yell a warning to the driver, another .88 hit, this time closer. We were in an exposed field of fire and were being tracked by German artillery or a tank.

Ignoring the shell craters in the road, the driver rammed the accelerator to the floorboard while we grabbed anything we could to hang on in the back. The next shell landed almost beneath us, lurching the truck sharply into a field. But despite a shredded tire, the driver kept the vehicle under control as he sped toward a village to escape the German gunner tracking us. We won the race and eventually skidded to a stop behind a building on the outer perimeter of the town. Spasmodic machine gun and rifle fire told us the town still hadn't been taken. We remained in the truck, ready for anything, watching and listening. For a half hour the battle seesawed back and forth. Both American and German tanks could be heard grinding through the village before us, taking potshots at each other. Occasionally, GIs could be seen leaping from one rubble pile to another as they darted through the streets. It was house-to-house combat, the final resort of the infantryman when all other assault methods failed. Eventually, our troops were pulled back, artillery called in and the issue was quickly resolved.

Intrigued by the action, I jumped out of the truck and worked my way forward a short distance to get a better view of the fight. "Get back here, Blunt, where you belong," a platoon lieutenant cursed. "I'm tired of always having to look for you." I glared at him and obeyed, climbing back onto the truck almost defiantly as he continued to fume and ream me out.

If the good lieutenant was finding me recalcitrant at times, it was because he couldn't accept the fact that I possessed an adventurous imagination, a flair for the dramatic and an independence that bordered on disobedience of all laws, natural or otherwise, not to mention a single-mindedness best described as all-consuming. He and I were never in the same Army—or same world, for that matter.

Once the fighting in the town died down and we were able to enter, we found that billets had already been designated for our squad. In ours, we found a table of hot food, including a platter of steak, in the kitchen. The Germans had pulled out so quickly, they hadn't had time to finish their meal, so we, always trying to be helpful, finished it for them like a bunch of scavengers.

Beside the kitchen stove, we found a pair of highly polished boots. Somewhere there was a barefoot German soldier running around probably cursing us.

"They're coming back!" someone hollered from the street. We ran from the building, "advancing to the rear," as it was called, and didn't stop to regroup until we reached the edge of town where we waited to see what would happen next. Several hours later, when the firing subsided again, we returned to our billet to find the Germans had reoccupied it, cooked more food and taken it with them. And the barefoot soldier was no longer barefoot, for the boots were gone.

"Where are we, anyway?" I asked one of the men in BAKER Company, some of whom were also sharing our building.

"Doveren, or something like that."

By daylight, we were better able to survey conditions in the town, and like every other city or town we had seen in Germany, it had been leveled. A few snipers remained and occasional artillery continued to shower us with death, but these were more a nuisance than a danger. The Germans had relinquished Doveren, but they had made sure we paid a dear price for it.

To move around in the town necessitated a series of duck-and-run maneuvers, for short, uninterrupted sprints out in the open invariably invited sniper bullets. Timing a run was not a safe answer because the Jerry was also timing them and he already had his rifle sighted in and his finger on the trigger.

When it came time to head for the chow tent, you took a deep breath and literally ran full tilt for your life. Whenever we tried it, a sniper bullet smacked into a building behind us. Then we crawled to the next open space where it was the same routine all over again: pause, take a deep breath, jump up, and run, usually with another bullet whistling past us. One time, after making it back safely to my billet, I brazenly and foolishly stuck my head around a corner and thumbed my nose at the sniper.

Eventually, our tormenter was located, captured and sent to a rear-area POW pen. He was not harmed, for as far as we knew, he had never hit anyone, just played his deadly game with us.

From the attic of our billet, I could see more than a mile into German territory, an ideal location for an artillery observer . . . or an American sniper. At the crack of dawn each day, I climbed to the attic and began scanning the enemy territory, watching for any movement by the German troops. Every day the hunt continued. It became a game. Then I spotted him, a Wehrmacht soldier at a distance of about 500 yards hiding behind a large tree. Occasionally, he peeked around the tree before ducking back behind it again. Several times he kept this up as I watched, not daring to move a muscle for fear he would see me.

Without warning, an .88 slammed into the building from which I was watching. The explosion almost tore my head and ears apart; I was showered with roof slate, mortar and splintered roof rafters. The observer had picked up a reflection off my field glasses and called up a single artillery round to say "hello."

Figuring my observation post was no longer a good place to be, I crawled backwards to leave. A sharp pain shot through my leg and my pants were stained with blood. I had been hit by shrapnel. Feeling a lump on my leg, I dropped my pants to examine the wound and found a jagged fragment imbedded in my leg. I dug it out with my trench knife and put it in my jacket pocket as a bloody souvenir. I poured some sulfanilamide from my first aid kit on the wound and bandaged it.

As I limped back to my billet, I became determined. The war had just become personal and strictly between the German artillery observer behind the tree and me. He had won the skirmish that day but there would always be another time, and that one, I vowed, would be mine.

Again, as in Belgium, I didn't put in for a Purple Heart for I didn't want to upset my parents, and I didn't want to cheapen the medal by accepting it for a minor wound.

I told one of the squad members, a zoology student from Brooklyn, what had happened and he became interested in my sniper scheme. The next day, before the sun was up fully, we were in the attic with rifle and field glasses. For almost an hour we watched for targets of opportunity even though the chances of hitting one at that range were minimal.

Just about the time we were going to call the venture off, the German was there again concealing himself behind the same tree, his green Wehrmacht uniform blending almost perfectly against the background. Now I was certain he was a forward observer and he would be the perfect target, but again, I knew the distance made it an almost impossible shot.

Each time his head appeared, I cut loose with a round with my buddy correcting my windage and elevation. But I couldn't see the point of impact, so after a couple of clips, I resorted to an all tracer cartridge load. I watched each red streak ricochet off the tree or dig into the ground, but each time I was missing. Finally, I held my breath and squeezed the trigger slowly.

"You got him. You got him," my observer started singing. Then he went into an animated account of how the German had been thrown backwards when the bullet struck him and had then plopped face-first to the ground.

We watched as other German soldiers scattered away from the tree but they too blended into the background and made for poor targets. I really wasn't interested in them very much for I had finished what my German adversary had started.

Doveren became quiet, and for as long as we remained there, we were subjected to no more artillery shellings.

The next day, after a breakfast of canned cheese, hard biscuits and cold lemonade, I sought out the artillery observer to get his Soldat Buch. This would be a real trophy but it meant penetrating deeply into enemy-held territory. After about a hundred yards, I found it would also mean crossing a mine field laced with barbed wire. To worsen matters, the route was across wide open territory.

Not knowing any better and motivated by the desire for the identification book, I picked my way past dozens of anti-tank Teller mines that had been scattered across the beet field. They had, for the most part, been sloppily covered with straw to conceal them, an indication they had been put down with extreme haste as the German troops pulled back.

It is said that God protects the innocent. Apparently he also protects the stupid for I made it safely across the field, and when I eventually arrived at the tree line, the Germans had pulled back for there was no one there. They hadn't bothered to remove their dead from the battlefield for there he was, the observer, still lying face down. I rolled him over and found my bullet had hit him in the forehead and had taken most of the back of his head off. His shattered face was matted with dried blood and it wasn't until I looked as his Soldat Buch that I knew what he had once looked like. He was in his teens. After relieving him of the book, I left him there to rest in the silence of death.

When I returned to the company area, the lieutenant was looking for me. Word had already circulated about my sniper shot and he congratulated me on my marksmanship. Odd duck, that officer. One minute he chastised me, the next minute praised me. I didn't have the nerve to tell him I couldn't duplicate that shot again in a hundred years. I showed him the Soldat Buch picture. He shook his head, irked at my bloodthirsty enthusiasm.

Later that afternoon, the company runner began yelling we were pulling out again. The only redeeming factor of constantly being on the move was that each time we climbed back into the damn trucks it was to get closer to Berlin and this fact alone became our sustaining strength.

The convoy proceeded along a flat highway flanked by tall poplar trees until we passed a roadside sign designating the group of shattered building we were approaching as Baal. As quickly as I could, I found a remote building and settled in to sack out for a few more minutes of sleep. I was always careful to notify the company runner where my billet was in each city or town, especially if I was living alone, for if he couldn't locate me and the company pulled out without me, leaving me alone and vulnerable in a German town, it could really spoil my day.

It was obvious the tempo of the war was picking up, for our stays in each town were becoming more and more brief. This meant we were pushing ahead harder and faster and meeting dwindling German resistance. For every kilometer pushed behind us, chances escalated that more American GIs would return home alive.

During the next troop movement, the truck stopped after about an hour to give us a break, and while stretching my legs around the convoy, I noticed a World War I–type trench that extended outwards into a field. It was close to the road so I jumped into it and landed almost in the laps of three dead GIs, all victims of German artillery. There had been no indication they were there. One of them had been disemboweled. Another had a leg practically blown off and the third had an arm hanging only by threads of skin.

They had attempted to dress their wounds in the few moments before they bled to death for I found bloody compress bandages and empty sulfur drug packets scattered about the trench. It had been a losing battle to stem the bleeding; the mud in the bottom of the trench was tinted a dark brownish red.

I quickly lost my appetite for souvenir hunting and returned to the convoy. My optimism about the war's duration faded in that second I leapt into the trench. The war, as long as one shot or one artillery shell was fired, was far from over, regardless of how fast the convoys moved forward or how close we got to Berlin.

On February 27 we rolled into the city of Erkelenz, where we met our first large masses of German civilians. A major breakthrough was in the making and the 84th was leading the way for the whole Allied effort in the dash for the Rhine. The division had covered 30 miles in six days, taking nearly 3000 prisoners. Before the division reached the Rhine, another 20 miles ahead, the prisoner total climbed to more than 9000.

In Erkelenz, I stopped a woman on the street and asked where we were. She replied we were in the Rhineland and that the river was close. But that was as far as we were going, she stated pompously, for "Der Fuhrer's" new secret weapons would drive us back to France and we would never reach Berlin.

This was the first time I had heard Nazi propaganda being spewed at me firsthand other than from Axis Sally. Disgusted, I prodded her angrily in the stomach with my carbine to join other refugees evacuating the city and fleeing west. As she walked away, she glared back at me over her shoulder. I smiled back and then, as a sarcastic parting shot, I blew her a kiss.

I searched several nearby homes for weapons and returned just as the trucks were pulling out again. We were told the 84th had swung north after crossing the Roer instead of concentrating its effort due east, the shortest route to the Rhine. The strategic reasoning was twofold: to confuse the German high command into committing its troop concentration where the most logical push was expected, and second, to probe for weak spots in the German defenses where the reinforcement troops had vacated. The strategy apparently worked. We were really putting the kilometers behind us each day.

No sooner had the convoy gotten on the road again than our truck was violently thrown into the air with a deafening roar. Duffle bags smothered us and men fell on top of each other like jack straws. I was knocked over the tailgate and onto the ground by the blast. I couldn't focus my eyes. Someone lifted me up and said, "This one's OK." After several minutes, my vision cleared and I learned the truck had hit a Riegal mine. The truck was demolished and was lying on its side. The only casualty was one GI whose ear drums had been damaged. A field ambulance took him away but the injury was not permanent for he rejoined us later in Rheinhausen. After reclaiming our gear, we doubled up with another Anti-Tank Company truck to continue on.

The close call with the mine made me realize that I wasn't the only one who was careless at times. The convoy commander had put hundreds of GIs in peril by barreling over roads that had not been first cleared of explosives. In officer manuals, that was called taking a calculated risk, an acceptable strategy as long as the determination was made by an officer.

Now the squad was down to only a handful.

Later, a few miles down the highway, our driver screamed "Hit it! Hit it!" through the cab's rear window. We dove for the ditches just as an ME-109 screamed past us on the first of several strafing runs.

Furious at having to bury my face in the mud, I jumped up onto the truck cab, swung a .50-caliber machine gun mounted there around and yanked back on the bolt. When the fighter made another run, just above the tree line, I started firing. Another GI down the line was doing the same.

The plane was coming in dead on and I could see I had a perfect field of fire so I held the gun steady and let the pilot fly into my stream of tracers. The striped fighter shuddered and started to trail a plume of black smoke as it peeled off to the right before we heard it slam into a nearby field.

Several of us bolted from the convoy toward the burning plane and found the pilot lying unconscious near the wreckage. Even before he came to, I grabbed his Mauser pistol from its holster, his helmet off his head, his fleece-lined leather gloves off his hands and was tugging on his flying boots.

When he opened his eyes, he was surrounded by a ring of rifles, and other GIs had relieved him of his goggles, leather jacket and flight suit pants. He didn't appear so invincible sitting barefoot and half naked in the mud and snow. I tried to speak to him but received only a torrent of arrogant insults in return. Mixed into his tirade, I could make out the words, "Amerikanische Schwein Hund" (American pig dog).

When we all laughed at this denuded Aryan Luftwaffe warrior, his glowering expression darkened into absolute contempt for us. Jubilantly, we ran back to the convoy with our prizes of war knowing that this "superman" would never threaten us again. We hadn't even deemed him worth taking prisoner.

I don't know whose bullets actually knocked the fighter out of the sky but I had seen some of mine hit home and I knew I had helped. Later, one of the GIs in my platoon gave me a picture he had taken of me atop the truck firing the machine gun.

The convoy rolled on, destination, as always, unknown. After an hour, it stopped so we could relieve ourselves, this time beside a graveyard offering us a rather macabre sight.

A 500-pound blockbuster bomb had landed in the middle of a cemetery beside the road leaving a mammoth crater. Scattered throughout the sides and bottom of the hole were the remains of graves and the buried dead from apparently many generations, for there were skeletons of the ancient, the taut-skinned frames of the old, the decomposed remains of the more recent and the almost perfect cadavers of the newly buried.

The smell was overwhelming. I felt as if I had stumbled upon the tombs of Egypt. I had never seen death in this form before; all over the sides of this enormous crater were scattered bones. It made me wonder about subjects I hadn't thought about before—like, what happens to us after we die. I was now seeing the answer firsthand for myself.

It sobered me and I walked away, leaving these German souls to their now disinterred and disturbed sleep. As we rode along, I began wondering about heaven and eternity. There were so many questions to which I didn't have answers and I realized now that, even after death, there is sometimes no peace. What I had witnessed, I supposed, was all part of growing up.

Suddenly, thinking back to the Luftwaffe strafing a few miles back, I started laughing, drawing quizzical expressions from the others. "We're towing a whole bunch of flak wagons. Where the hell were they when the ME-109 strafed us?" I asked. The whole truck had a good laugh.

The bone-rattling ride continued but no one complained, for it was still better than walking. During one highway break, I spotted a farm on the far side of a field. Turning to Everett, I said, "C'mon, Loot. Food." We hopped off the truck and away we went to forage for something to eat. As we cautiously entered the farmhouse courtyard, rifles at the ready, we faced a scowling German farmer.

"Lebensmittel?" (food) I asked him. "Eier?" (eggs).

"Ich habe gar nichts. Gehen Sie weg" (I have nothing. Go away), he protested.

I shoved my M-1 against his gut and yelled back just as loud, "Sei ruhig!" (Be quiet). He glowered viciously at us.

Everett and I searched the barn and the farmer's vegetable cellar, returning with arms and pockets full of eggs, pickled beets, flour, potatoes, pilfered German army chocolate, smoked ham and other staples from the farmer's well-stocked larder. Everett milked a cow and filled his steel helmet and our canteens with warm milk.

I yelled to the convoy. The farmer became apoplectic as a horde of men came running and soon picked his remaining food shelves bare. One of the GIs fired a shot in the air to intimidate the old farmer, but he stood his ground screaming curses at us.

When the mob from the truck convoy finished looting the farm, the farmer might be a little hungrier that winter but the conquering forces wouldn't be. To the victor went the spoils. A few minutes later, we moved on. But this time we were chomping happily on anything edible we had liberated from the farm.

I felt little sympathy for the farmer. My stomach had seldom been truly filled since leaving England, and satiating my persistent hunger was important to me. Having their countryside and homes ravaged was a price the vanquished paid in wartime.

At each break along the way, I jumped off the truck, kindled a fire and tried to boil eggs in my helmet beside the road, but each stop was too brief even to heat the helmet up slightly. This was the same helmet that a few days earlier had served as a toilet in a Belgian foxhole but, when truly hungry, you don't worry about small details like that. I had, after all, washed it out with snow. A steel helmet was a wonderful piece of multi-purpose combat field equipment. It was perfect as a portable toilet, a cooking pot, a shaving basin and even, on occasion, as protection from bullets and artillery shrapnel for your head.

Before bedding down for the night in the village of Wegburg, I was finally able to cook some of my liberated ham and eggs on a stove and enjoy a memorable meal.

In the morning, I found an abandoned bicycle and went for a ride, which was a major accomplishment on Wegburg's mud-filled streets. Everett found a horse wandering around a nearby pasture and promptly went for a bareback ride. What a strange sight we were, Everett on a plow horse, me on a wobbly bicycle.

Together, we went to a nearby farmhouse where the occupants stood silently by the door waiting for us to start looting. I told them we meant them no harm. At this, they started jabbering between themselves, both scattering in different directions. She came back moments later with an apron filled with eggs and he reappeared around a corner of the house with a bottle of schnapps.

I went for the eggs, Everett for the liquor. When I hesitated momentarily before accepting the eggs, the woman understood and ran back into the house to fry some up for me. To say they were delicious is an understatement for they had a woman's touch, something that can't be duplicated any other way.

Then in a strange twist of war, the couple insisted we stay for the night. Fearing a trap, we declined. But they persisted and we finally agreed. Tempted by real beds, neither of us worried about the consequences of being left behind by the convoy. The wife made up the beds, complete with linens, in the attic, but since this was too much for us to accept at face value, we set up a flimsy system of standing guard. The wife warned us to stay alert; a few German soldiers were still active nearby.

In shifts, we slept soundly and were awakened at 0530 by the woman asking whether we planned to sleep all day. Her day had already begun. She had breakfast, a wash basin and razor waiting for us in the kitchen.

We ventured outside and could hear rifle and machine-gun fire in the distance. As I gazed around this peaceful farm, I realized we were once again caught between the worlds of war and tranquility. I'd heard the Rhinelanders were friendly, outgoing, hospitable people and now I believed it.

I asked the farmer if he knew what was going on with the distant firing. Just some "Amis" fighting with German soldiers, he replied, disinterested with it all. His world was his farm, and his attitude was a striking example of German isolationism.

After eating and shaving, Everett and I headed toward the fighting, Everett saying he was tagging along only to protect me from myself. Cutting across a pasture, we were joined by another anti-tanker who, like ourselves, was goofing off.

Crouching low in a ditch as we ran, I stumbled upon a mortally wounded Wehrmacht soldier lying on his back. Half of his face and skull had been blown away. Only one eye remained and it was watching me. I drew down on him with my carbine, but realizing instantly he was no threat to me, I lowered it again.

That one eye held me in its grip and I couldn't move. The German kept looking at me deplorably. Like so many others I had seen, this man had also been disemboweled by a massive gut wound.

The one remaining eye blinked at me repeatedly. From the bloody foam drooling from what had once been a mouth, I could make out only one barely discernible, whispered word over and over: "Schieszen. Schieszen." (Shoot. Shoot.)

I again put my carbine to his head, but no matter how hard I tried I could not put him out of his misery. Some unknown force prevented my finger from squeezing the trigger.

I remained transfixed on this man's pleading eye for several minutes before lowering my rifle and running along the ditch to the town.

We sprinted to the closest building and crouched in a front room where we could see the street. Suddenly a Schmeisser machine gun erupted from beneath us at some unseen target. There were Germans in the building where we had sought refuge, but for some unknown reason, they had not heard us yet. We tiptoed across the floor and waited for the next burst of fire. When it came, Everett quickly opened the cellar door as I pulled the pins on two grenades and rolled them down the cellar stairs.

When they exploded and the smoke billowed up the stairs, the other anti-tanker leaped into the cellar and cut loose with his submachine "grease" gun.

"C'mon down. These guys are loaded with loot down here," he hollered up at us. On two machine gunners and a lieutenant we found a pair of Lugers, three P-38s, a grenade launcher, a Leica camera, field glasses, jewelry, knives and a Nazi armband. It was a lucrative day for loot collectors. We divvied up as much as we could carry and started back to the company area. I never found out who the Germans in the cellar were firing at, and why we weren't subjected to return fire.

When we retraced our steps back to the convoy an hour later, the wounded German in the ditch was dead. Troubled by my inability to put him out of his misery, I asked a chaplain whether it would have been right to commit a mercy killing. "No. If God had wanted him, He would have taken him," was his answer. That was the only answer I ever got, but somehow it seemed totally unsatisfactory.

In the meantime, we returned to the company area to face the music for being AWOL. We knew the punishment would probably be severe, but the farmer's meal and a good night's sleep had been worth it, and, we had all that good loot to ease the pain.

When we arrived, we found that no one had missed us even though we had been gone for two days. We bartered some of our loot with others in the platoon and then settled back in as if nothing had happened. Everett and I loved to take chances, but if we kept it up much longer, we were sure to get caught eventually.

On March 1, orders came through that troops were needed to reinforce EASY Company in an attack on the nearby city of Dülken. It had gotten to the point that when such orders came down, the lieutenant looked at me first. In my youthful enthusiasm and ignorance, I was constantly doing foolish things, like volunteering for practically every detail that came along.

Word was received that booby traps had been found in the city so at least we were going to work in an area where allegedly we had some expertise.

The approach to the city was a 400-foot-wide open field offering no concealment whatsoever. In the distance, factory chimneys were still smoking. Tanks lumbering toward the city offered the only protection we had. With my new binoculars, I could see white sheets and flags hanging from practically every window indicating that at least the civilian population wouldn't be a problem. But since I also knew Germans had in the past offered to surrender under a white flag and then had come out shooting, I remained somewhat skeptical of surrender flags.

A truck-mounted public address system rolled up to the edge of the city and blared out in German, "People of the city of Dülken. You have 10 minutes to surrender yourselves. Those who remain behind may be killed for in 10 minutes we will start an artillery barrage that will destroy your city. When we attack, those found behind will be treated as soldiers. This is your last chance. All civilians must leave the city. Take whatever possessions you can carry and come this way. You will not be harmed."

The announcement was repeated over and over again. As the minutes ticked away, a handful of bewildered civilians straggled toward us. Then the numbers swelled. When they reached our position, they were directed to the rear by German-speaking GIs. We were the first Americans they had seen and most of them appeared frightened. More and more came through our ranks carrying battered suitcases or sheets and blankets filled with their meager belongings.

Many had the appearance of Wehrmacht soldiers taking the easy way out, for they were of conscriptable ages between 18 and 50. Hitler was scraping the bottom of the barrel and Volkssturm troops were becoming more evident each day. But we didn't challenge those who may have been active-duty soldiers because this was just another form of surrender—only this way without bloodshed, and without the civilian population realizing that they were capitulating.

Refugees were methodically searched for weapons and then motioned to the rear. Occasionally, a weapon was found and that person, man or woman, was diverted to a POW pen.

Eventually, the flow of refugees stopped and the loudspeaker gave the last warning before an intense howitzer barrage pounded the city for about 20 minutes.

When it stopped, a solitary German soldier crawled out of the rubble and limped toward us, one arm held feebly up in the air. The stump of his other arm, badly shattered, hung limp at his side.

I started in his direction but the commander of the tank I had been walking behind waved me away. Then, without hesitation, he deliberately veered the tank toward the soldier and ran over him with the treads. The severely wounded German soldier appeared to be a teenager. It was as barbaric an act of war as any I had ever seen committed by the Germans, and I was finding out that cold-blooded murder was also well within the realm of American warfare.

The tanks pounded away with their .76-mm cannons. Every GI in sight was hammering away with M-1s at every door and window. I did the same, even though I never actually saw any targets at which to shoot. The sounds of battle were deafening and powder smoke enveloped us, making it difficult to breath or even see, for that matter.

The ground in front of the tank erupted in a showering fountain of dirt. The tankers spotted the German Nebelwurfer before we did in a bunker off to our right. The tank turrets traversed slowly and the duel began.

I had already hightailed it for cover—the tank suddenly became no place to be just then. The Shermans won after several rounds were fired and a squad of GIs moved in to mop up what was left of the hastily erected bunker.

The American fire on Dülken was far heavier than the return fire we received from the Germans left behind as a delaying action. The American rationale, I presume, was that this close to the end of the war, ammunition was far more expendable than soldiers' lives. Pound the city into submission first and eliminate the opposition before sending in the troops, was the theory, one I hoped the Army would continue to use.

As isolated sniper fire lessened, I started a house-to-house search for booby traps, the job I had been sent there to do. I came across a sidewalk air raid shelter and was preparing to throw a grenade into it when I heard a woman's voice.

"Kommen Sie heraus" (come out), I commanded. First a hand appeared in the opening, followed by a terrified elderly woman holding her arms in the air. I asked her if any German soldiers were in there.

She assured me there were only "Alte Frauen und kinder" (old women and children). She told them to come out but no one appeared. Cautiously, I entered the shelter and found the occupants huddled in a corner trembling and crying. I looked at their wrinkled faces and I felt a little ashamed for doing what I had been contracted to do back in September 1943: soldiering.

I softened my voice and told them there was hot food behind the American lines or, if they wanted to, they could stay in the city for the Americans had already passed through and they were no longer in any danger. The old woman's tears came when she realized she and the others would not be harmed. I think she was also greatly relieved to hear an American speaking German, even though haltingly.

Before walking away, I threw a candy bar to the small children still crying in the shelter. I had more and they had nothing.

"Gott sei Danke. Gott sei Danke" (Thank God. Thank God), she kept murmuring as she tried to kiss my hand. In a gesture of youthful chivalry, I let her.

I kept up my search but found no booby traps. The city was mostly deserted, at least where I was looking. I worked my way down one of the streets as other GIs continued mopping up.

As one of them in front of me walked past a house, an old woman leaned out a second-floor window and poured a tub of scalding hot water on him. As he screamed in pain, his buddy across the street, in a lightning move, shot her. She tumbled to the street with a sickening thump. I just stepped over her and kept walking with only a sideways glance. Nazi fanaticism came in all ages and genders. I'd reached the point where even the killing of old women didn't bother me.

In one of the partially demolished buildings, I climbed to the top floor to start working my way down room by room. I heard no sound but still sensed that someone else was there. The instinct, born of months in combat, was warning me again. I inched toward one room and violently kicked the door open, jumping inside as I did so. In a blur, I scanned the room and saw only a blanketed figure in a bed on the far wall. With carbine at the ready, I moved closer.

Under the blanket was a man who appeared to be in his 90s and obviously on his deathbed. His face was wasted, his cheeks hollowed and eyes dimmed with time. The sight of this helpless old man completely took the fight out of me as I envisioned my own grandfather who had died only eight years earlier.

"Entschuldigen Sie mir Mein Herr" (Excuse me, sir), I whispered and walked softly away, leaving him to his oncoming death with dignity. There was nothing else I could say to him; the war raging around him had already said it all for me.

Deep in thought, I stumbled over the rubble to the next house, again to look for possible booby traps. As the saying goes, you never hear the shot that hits you. As I entered the front door, a violent blow punched me in the side, spinning me around and dumping me in a heap on a pile of shattered masonry. A sniper had been following me in his sights and my preoccupation with the dying old man made me careless in a city that had not yet been declared completely safe.

As I lay stunned in the rubble collecting my thoughts, another bullet slammed into the room over my head, throwing splinters of wood about me. This time I reacted fast and rolled inside the building.

Instinctively, I felt for the wound. I couldn't understand why there was no pain, just a dull ache as if I had been walloped hard in the side by someone. There was no wound. The sniper's bullet had severed my cartridge belt and had hit my M-1 ammo pouch. The cartridges had been flattened and twisted but not one had exploded. Another close call with death.

I remained momentarily fascinated with the shattered ammo clip in my hand, then tucked it into my jacket pocket. Foolishly, I ignored the sniper, another careless mistake. I crawled to a window and shot nervous glances out at the street. I even dangled my helmet out the window on a piece of wood as a ruse but the cagey sniper didn't bite. I heard the roar of a Sherman tank approaching and I yelled at the sergeant crouched in the turret. "Sniper, sniper over there," and pointed at the building across the street. He heard me and quickly buttoned up his turret.

I hadn't noticed at first but the tank was equipped as a flamethrower, similar to the British crocodile tanks. The tank turret slowly ground to its right and in the next moment, the building across the street disappeared in massive sheets of fire. I watched the building consume itself to a pile of burning debris. But I also knew that a sniper would most probably move to the cellar and wait the fire out. Then he would resume his deadly game.

When it was safe, I climbed over the rubble and, not finding a charred corpse inside, I tossed a grenade into the cellar but didn't bother to check if anyone was there.

Back into the street, I found other elements of Anti-Tank Company entering the city. They informed me EASY Company had been assigned to occupy Dülken until further orders and I was to rejoin my old outfit.

The squad had taken a billet in the cellar of a former coffee mill where the dampness penetrated our bones and our hand-warming candles were most welcome. Looking around in the flickering candle light at the faces of what remained of our squad, I smiled at what sad sacks we were, but we were buddies, we had shared a lot and that was all that was important. We were now only a few and I again wondered if all of us would see the end of the war. Then I blew out my candle and fell asleep.

In the morning, we found it had snowed and turned quite cold during the night. We were issued K-rations, and as crazy as it might sound, they hit the spot. It is amazing how good dry cheese and cold lemonade tastes on a winter morning when you have nothing else. The Army always went to great lengths to assure we always had a well-balanced, nutritionally correct diet.

In an attempt to bolster our morale and pride, a written commendation was passed on to each of us individually through the chain of command March 15 from Ninth Army Headquarters (Lieutenant General W. H. Simpson), to the XIII Corps Headquarters (Major General A. C. Gillem, Jr.), to 84th Division Headquarters (Major General Alexander R. Bolling), to Regimental Headquarters (Colonel Lloyd H. Gomes), to Battalion Headquarters (Lieutenant Colonel William T. Barrett), to AT Company Headquarters (Captain John C. Bowen), to Anti-Mine Platoon Headquarters (Lieutenant William L. Ray, Jr.) to Blunt's Headquarters.

The citation, in part, read: "The 84th succeeded in the course of a very few days in making a name for itself by reducing the enemy strongpoint of Geilenkirchen, thereby facilitating the advance of the Army to the Roer River and the speedy installation of bridges and expeditious seizure of key towns east of the Roer River . . . during Operation Grenade, thereafter the rapid advance despite an extraordinarily exposed left flank . . . and never losing its momentum from the Roer to the Rhine rivers . . . and superior performance," on and on ad infinitum. Like the old Army saying of that era, the unit commendation and ten cents would buy a cup of coffee back in the States.

I tried to catch up on my correspondence home and my daily diary notes but my hands were too numb to hold my German fountain pen and scratch paper, so I put them away for another day and tried to sleep.

The Wehrmacht on the Run

With only a few minutes' warning, we were on the move again, this time haphazardly, as if we didn't know where we were going. And as it turned out we didn't—we had inadvertently intruded into territory that had not yet been wrested from the Germans.

During the breakthrough from the Roer to the Rhine, the situation, as it was so often during the Bulge fighting, was not clearly defined. We seldom knew where the enemy was, or even where we were. In essence, the Germans were in full retreat but during this rout they kept stopping and confounding us with pockets of token resistance.

We were moving eastward so fast and with so many salients that on numerous occasions, we were penetrating the enemy's rear areas and leaving our flanks dangerously exposed. Had the Germans at this phase of the war had more organization, military strength and equipment, they might well have reversed the momentum in this 50-mile stretch of their homeland between the two rivers. But they didn't, and the American forces were fanning out helter-skelter on a wide front in every direction wherever they faced the slightest resistance.

The cold, penetrating March dampness, the constantly wet uniforms and the lack of proper rest and food were gradually wearing me down. One exhausting truck convoy after another, one rubble pile bed after another on top of weeks of cold food were too much for my system. There were times I went into uncontrolled fits of shivering that lasted for hours.

During one of these episodes I lapsed into unconsciousness, for I remembered nothing until I came to some time later wrapped in blankets on the floor of an ambulance with a medic sitting on the rear compartment wooden bench above me.

I tried to sit up but couldn't. I hurt all over, but at least I was warm for the first time in days.

"What's the matter with me? I'm OK, I just don't feel well. Just warm me up a little," I protested.

"You've got a touch of pneumonia, buddy," the medic said. "We took you out of the truck when you passed out."

"How bad is it?"

"Not too. It's just coming on. I've got you all doped up. You'll be OK."

I don't know how long I remained in the ambulance but one time I looked out it was light, another time it was dark.

"How long have I been out?" I mumbled.

"Two days," he answered.

"Where are we?"

"Beats the hell out of me."

"Have I eaten?"

"Nope. Feel like a K-ration? It's all I've got."

I tried to eat it but my arms were too heavy to open it and my jaws ached too much to chew.

"How long will I have to stay here?" I kept on.

" 'Til you're all better. Maybe a couple more days."

The ambulance was a limousine compared to the six-by-six trucks in which I had covered half of Europe. I drifted off again.

When I woke up, the ambulance had stopped and the sun was shining brightly outside. A head popped in the back door, asking cheerily, "How ya feeling, Bluntie?" It was my ever-faithful companion, good old Joe Everett again.

He told me the convoy had advanced almost 20 miles while I was out of action. I struggled to sit up and found myself in a motor pool with smoke coming from a kitchen a few feet away. With Everett helping me, I made it to the chow line.

"Sick man coming through," Everett bellowed. The chain of GIs parted respectfully for us up at the front of the line. The menu of the day was plopped into our mess kits and we wandered off to find a quiet place, away from the others, to slop down our slop. Bucking an Army chow line is a well-defined, time-tested science that takes great talent honed by years of experience. Everett and I were two of the best in the European Theater of Operations.

The 84th had taken 1,461 Germans prisoner during the Battle of the Bulge. In this dash for the Rhine River, the division was credited with taking 7,306 prisoners, a sign of the vastly different type of warfare we were facing here in the Rhineland.

Hitler's defenses were falling like dominoes, and the resolve of his troops weakened with each day we kept them from regrouping. Apparently convinced of the futility of further effort and resistance, some officers surrendered entire commands. But, as Germany's Lebensraum (living space) shrank, the resistance, in direct proportion, became more fanatical in some areas. Many German units, usually the SS, continued to resist fiercely as they were pushed deeper into the heartland of Germany toward Berlin . . . and the Russians.

The German Army was being squeezed unmercifully by American, British, Canadian and Australian forces from the west and the Russians from the east. They were literally in a geographic vise with no viable avenue of escape. The fervor and fanatical loyalty to Hitler's leadership were rapidly being extinguished and many German commanders were merely trying to save their skins, and those of what remnants of their troops remained.

One of the positive by-products of our sprint to the Rhine was that most of the villages we passed were left mainly intact and the roads were largely undamaged. Forests were not being decimated and the beet fields would grow bumper crops again.

Also absent were the heavy toll of dead bodies and the carnage of burned-out German or American tanks and vehicles along the roads, sure signs the German army was still completely disorganized. A war was being lost, an entire nation's military might was being literally obliterated, but thankfully, hundreds, perhaps even thousands of lives were being spared. It was already too late to salvage an entire generation of Germany's male population, but at least there was still time to prepare for the next one.

The convoy coursed its way along a cobblestoned street in another typical German town when suddenly it halted, backed up fast, hung a U-turn and sped back from whence it had come. When I suspected we had taken a wrong turn and wound up in an enemy-held village, I was correct. When everyone was able to breathe easier again, the teasing of the driver began.

"I was only following the other guy," he alibied with a big grin.

We continued on. After two more grueling hours we pulled into Monchen-gladbach, just west of Düsseldorf. From the degree of destruction, it was easy to tell that a fierce battle had taken place there. From all the bullet-pocked buildings, we knew there had been heavy street fighting before the town was taken.

Mess personnel handed out more K-rations to us as we emptied out of the trucks. I was so famished, the rations went down easy. I was, after all these months, becoming hooked on them, for this was the fourth time in as many days that these abominable rations tasted good to me. Continuous hunger over a long period of time does funny things to someone's digestion.

While walking along one of the city's deserted demolished streets, I came across what to me was a sad sight, a music store that had sustained a direct bomb or artillery hit. Drum sets, violins, horns and pianos were scattered everywhere. I picked through the rubble, found two Zildian high-hat cymbals from Constantinople, stashed them in my barracks bag and moved on.

After the war ended, I used them during my months of occupation duty in southern Germany and eventually brought them home, where I played them for many years in civilian life.

White flags and bed sheets were draped in capitulation from practically every window in the city, not unlike those we would see in every city and town in our path from the Roer to the Rhine and Elbe rivers, where the Germans finally abandoned their weapons and will to fight and the killing ceased. Civilian resolve, it became obvious, was collapsing as fast as that of the Wehrmacht.

When dealing with civilians, I never once met a Nazi the whole time I was in Germany, either during the war or after. Strangely, the Nazi was universally some other guy.

Monchen-gladbach was only a rest stop for us. Soon we were rolling again, only this time I was in a jeep with a lieutenant on billeting detail again. My basic knowledge of German made me handy to have around when it became necessary in each city or town to locate and secure adequate quarters for the platoon.

My job was to evict the occupants from their homes once we found what we wanted. It was considered a choice detail, for it meant I invariably wound up staking out the prime billeting quarters, and the souvenirs.

On March 3, 1945, we drove across a broad field and approached the major industrial center of Krefeld, practically on the Rhine River. It was considerably larger than Geilenkirchen, the largest city the 84th had taken so far.

I asked a civilian whether there were still German soldiers there and was told, "Nein. Nur Amis" (No. Only Americans).

As our jeep probed its way cautiously along a major boulevard into the city, we were practically swallowed up by a blinding flash. German artillery was still shelling the city.

The jeep was riddled with shrapnel; only the windshield saved us from serious wounds. With the lieutenant screaming for the driver to take evasive action, we zigzagged and careened around corners until we found a side street not under the direct observation of the .88 batteries. I reminded the lieutenant that he too had assured me earlier that Krefeld had been cleared of Germans and was secure. If looks could kill, his expression would have done the job.

After the ringing in our ears stopped and our heads cleared, we realized this shelling was an isolated incident. This was confirmed by civilians crowding the sidewalks in business suits, women bicycling with shopping bags hanging from their arms and even a few cars driving on the streets. Just your everyday, normal German city.

Without realizing it, I was seeing for the first time the carefree attitudes of the German Rhinelanders. They laughed a lot, loved to party and were even somewhat receptive to Americans. As in Dülken and Monchen-glad-bach, white surrender sheets hung from most windows.

The lieutenant and I entered an ornate apartment building and started knocking on first-floor doors, each time being greeted by civilians who couldn't comprehend that we were Americans, the first they claimed to have seen.

We told them to evacuate, that we were taking temporary possession of their homes. They didn't seem to mind too much and reappeared a few minutes later with their paltry belongings over their shoulders. We told them they would probably be allowed to return to their homes in a few days when we moved on.

One woman, however, shook her fist at me and hurled invectives at both of us. In other words, she was swearing up a storm. A hard slap on the ass with my rifle stopped her yapping. Out on the street she started up again. When I put my rifle to my shoulder and pointed it in her direction, she took off down the street as fast as her fat little bandy legs would carry her. The other residents thought this was quite funny. I figured the irate woman with the disturbed attitude was an "auslander" (foreigner). I was learning to appreciate the Rhinelander sense of humor.

I informed the lieutenant of what the residents had said, that we were the first Americans they had seen. This disturbed him. We both hoped the Germans had, in fact, retreated to the river. If not, the enraged woman's cursing would summon them from five miles around.

We found the empty apartments suited us well, and decided to take over the entire building for Anti-Tank Company. I was ordered to find the most elaborate room for the company CP. It was on the second floor—but I claimed it for Everett and myself. A much smaller, more ordinary room on the first floor was set aside for Bowen and the other officers.

When Everett first saw his luxurious new accommodations, complete with soft beds, sheets, radio, drapes, electricity, bathtub, working toilet, paintings, ornate pastel tiling and carpeting, his mouth fell open. The first thing he did was bounce on the bed to make sure it was for real.

"Not bad, Bluntie old boy, not bad. You're finally learning," Everett commented. For him, this was high praise.

Actually, the best find of all after months of slit trenches, four-holers or behind-the-bush relief, was not the soft bed but rather a real toilet that worked. It was sheer heaven to have some place to sit and meditate.

The whole time we stayed in Krefeld, the company brass never caught onto my "coup de Guerre." Everett said he was proud of me, another glowing compliment.

After a solid night's sleep, I stepped outside to check out the city. An MP came chugging by in a miniature Volkswagon sedan about the size of the English Austins seen in the States. I stuck my hitchhiking thumb out and squeezed in beside him. We cruised the city until the liberated car ran out of gas, after which I hoofed it back to my billet.

Fortunately for us, German resistance in Krefeld had been light and the fury of war passed the city by quickly, leaving most of it undamaged. The streets were now filled with American soldiers, but for the most part, they were ignored or tolerated by the German populace.

I pulled billeting detail again, for as quickly as our luxurious respite began, it was over and the company was heading for the town of Mörs. As in Dülken, Monchen-gladbach and Krefeld, we found a sea of white cloth hanging everywhere. As usual, I was left alone in each city or town we entered to protect our interests, namely billet sites, until the platoon moved forward. I entered a private home and informed the occupants we were taking possession temporarily. The couple, appearing to be in their 60s, outwardly didn't seem to mind and the husband started questioning me about the progress of the war. As I brought him up to date, he sat shaking his head dejectedly.

He told me he was a retired Wehrmacht soldier and as we talked, it was obvious he had long since resigned himself to Germany's failure to win the war. As a gesture of his acceptance of his fatherland's fate, he confided in me where an SS officer who had committed atrocities against his own people was hiding.

Casting caution aside, I located the house, kicked in the door and leaped inside. The house was abandoned but the officer, in his haste, had left behind an ornate, chrome-plated ceremonial dagger, complete with gold tassel. It was a welcome addition to my collection and well worth the effort of searching the house.

We remained in Mörs for four days, and I had ample opportunity to discuss American and German cultures with the old man who had informed on the SS officer. We both learned much from the stimulating "unterhaltungen" (conversations). We made the world a little smaller, in a manner of speaking.

Before pulling out of Mörs, I gave division MPs the address of the SS officer and I heard later he was arrested.

The order to move out came just in time, for some of the "midnight snack cooks" in the squad managed to blow up a stove and heavily damage the billet. Except for the fact the building had been the home of the old couple, this didn't bother me for it was the third time I had narrowly escaped from burning and exploding sleeping quarters. I hoped the old Wehrmacht soldier and his wife could find other suitable housing.

During this period of our push to the Rhine, the war was being waged by other outfits elsewhere and, frankly, I was relieved that at least temporarily, we weren't involved. I had had enough fighting to hold me for a long time and now I wanted to slack off and watch it from the safety of the sidelines.

Throughout the night of March 8–9, minutes dragged on into hours and as we pulled into a small village, the resignation of those in the back end of the troop-carrier truck was interrupted by the distant rumbling of artillery. As soon as we stopped and unloaded, I yelled to the first civilian I saw, "Wo sind wir?" (Where are we?)

"Rheinhausen Im Rheinland," he shouted back with a smile.

I found a room with a couch in the first building I entered, a one-story stone structure, almost on the banks of the Rhine River. We were warned to be careful for we were under German surveillance from the other side of the river, only 400 yards away.

The first familiar face we saw was the squad's zoologist from Brooklyn, who had rejoined the mine-removal platoon after his ear injuries. No sooner had he seen the river than he was off frog hunting for rare specimens for a New York museum. One afternoon not long after his return, I found him walking blissfully along with a thermos bottle filled with German schnapps and containing two pickled frogs he said were native only to the Rhineland and which he claimed would be valuable additions to the museum's collection.

The squad teased him about his rather unusual hobby. But the laughter stopped when he received an engraved certificate of appreciation from the museum for his contribution. After that, he was treated as a respected, learned student. To each his own.

The chow tent was about 200 yards away and our orders were to stagger eating schedules so only a few men at a time were seen on the street. We didn't want to draw artillery fire or allow the enemy to assess our occupying troop strength. Our first breakfast in Rheinhausen, the first hot meal in weeks, was pancakes, bacon, coffee and bread.

The town was small, with rows of simple one- and two-story homes formed in a square in the middle of a vast flat plain. It was a peaceful village and the occupants accepted us without noticeable malice.

Army life returned fast. Guard duty rosters were posted as soon as we arrived there. I was called to the company CP where the captain asked me to find a civilian woman who could launder his uniforms. I chose a nearby house that had several entryways and inside I found a middle-aged woman and a raven-haired daughter whose beauty instantly riveted my attention.

The mother, who seemed honored to have been chosen as a laundress for the Amis, assured me she was the best in the village. As the mother washed and ironed the captain's uniforms, the daughter, Inga, asked dozens of questions about America.

Figuring that laundering uniforms did not constitute fraternization—which the Army had already declared strictly "verboten"—I brought my uniforms to also be washed and ironed. After several days of this, I was summoned to the company CP and informed I was to face a special court-martial for consorting with the enemy. Placed under house arrest until the trial, I could only think of the shame I was bringing upon my family.

Instead of sympathy and understanding, others in the company kidded me about not being a real soldier until I had at least one court-martial on my record. The way I felt, I would just as soon not be a real soldier if that was what was required to be one.

Bowen admitted he felt partially at fault for sending me into a German civilian's home in the first place to get his uniforms cleaned. He said he would help me any way he could during the trial. He also admitted that a certain second lieutenant, not even a line officer, was pressing the charges in order to get promoted to first lieutenant. Bowen said he had tried to coerce him into dropping the whole matter but this sad excuse for an officer was adamant in using me as a stepping stone to a silver bar.

Before departing the billet for the trial, I shoved a drum stick up my sleeve for moral support. Even feeling it there would offer me strength, I thought. I was scared.

When I entered the makeshift court room, I was faced by two colonels, two majors and two lieutenants. Bowen sat near me. The panel asked my name, rank and serial number. Then I was advised not to testify against myself.

One of the colonels read the accusatory specifications against me: that Private First Class Roscoe C. Blunt Jr., Serial Number 31390582, did on 20 March 1945 and again 21 March 1945 fraternize with German civilians in violation of memorandum, Headquarters, 84th Division dated 23 November 1944, Subject "Fraternization," by visiting the home of Egne Novotne, 6 Fresareder Strasse.

My mind was so befuddled with embarrassment and apprehension, it hardly recorded what was being said. When the voice reading the charges stopped, I pleaded not guilty to both charges.

I was asked why I went there. I looked at Bowen and he nodded. I told the court he had asked me to find a laundress for his uniforms. The presiding judge, a colonel, asked what I did there while the uniforms were being cleaned and I answered, "I talked to the woman's daughter about America."

The court asked why I engaged in conversation with the women. Slightly exasperated by this question, I asked the colonel if I was expected to sit there and stare at the walls while the clothes were being washed. From the expressions on the court panel's faces, I knew my retort had been the wrong one and had not pleased the presiding officers.

The hearing lasted about an hour. Bowen, true to his word, tried to intercede and assume some of the blame for my actions. The intervention was to no avail for a week later, on April 2, I was found guilty on both counts and sentenced to six months hard labor and forfeiture of $40 a month in pay.

Bowen, still feeling that I had gotten a raw deal, appealed my sentence and it was reduced to three months labor, without confinement, and a fine of only $120.

But to someone earning only $50 a month—$1.64 a day—that fine was still a lot of money. But invention is born of necessity. During my subsequent tour of duty in Europe, I found a variety of ways to make up the money taken from me by the Army.

Again, Bowen apologized for the severe penalty and said he would make the labor as light as possible. He suggested KP, for there I would have first crack at the hot food every day and there would be no more C- and K-rations.

It sounded good to me but it was all a big charade. After a couple of days of kitchen duty and a few pots and pans scrubbed, I was back with the mine-removal squad and no one seemed to care. But I also had the added advantage of being able to sneak back to the kitchen looking for food any time I wanted to by just saying I was assigned there. I did it often and it always worked.

The bucking second lieutenant was awarded his silver bar a few weeks later.

Even though I supposedly was on KP punishment, I never was able to escape guard duty. The night was clear and cold, as it usually was after midnight, and the moon on the river was serene. As I casually walked about my duty station, secure in the knowledge that infiltrators or raiding parties would not come back across the river once they had reached the comparative safety of the other side, I gazed at the stars and my thoughts crossed the Atlantic to home. I was convinced I was destined to be a musician—I still harbored ambitions of being one of the best drummers in America some day—but I wondered what else I would do. Hell, the war was practically over and it was time for me to plan ahead. It was a beautiful Rhineland night for quiet reflection.

Word came down from division that the 84th had been the first Allied division to reach the Rhine in northern Germany and had taken more prisoners than any other outfit on the Continent. It made me realize my division was more distinguished than I had given it credit for. I couldn't know it at the time, but the 84th would set many more records in the months to come.

The squad started to horse around. We had been resting and getting stale on the west bank of the Rhine for nearly three weeks while the big brass pondered how to get across it.

Food boxes from home, usually accompanied by a dozen or more wonderful letters, continued to reach me. Animal crackers or Cracker Jack can do wonders for low morale. A can of fruit cocktail is like a lobster dinner. A tin of Spam can be fantasized into steak. The loving thought that deprived my family of much-needed ration points and the tenderness with which these many packages were sent were my sustaining strength.

As I walked a guard post the next night from midnight to 0400, I noticed a shiny object on the ground. It was a four-by-six piece of cardboard with a vial attached. The instructions on the back told German civilians it was a delayed-action incendiary device that could be used to sabotage American vehicles. I looked around and found the ground littered with these potential bombs that were dropped by a recon plane I had ignored a short time earlier.

I notified the sergeant of the guard and then sprinted to the CP where I woke up the captain. Quickly, he ordered the whole company awake to search the village and recover as many of these incendiary chemical vials as we could. Within minutes, men were scurrying everywhere with boxes, sacks and flashlights.

We must have found them all, since no incidents of sabotage occurred while we occupied the town.

Off and on, I did some kitchen time. The company executive officer concurred with Bowen that I had gotten a bum deal at the court-martial and he made sure I had plenty to eat during my imposed sentence. As officers went, he was OK. Anyone who kept my stomach full couldn't be all bad.

I heard the division band was performing back at Krefeld and hoped I would get another opportunity to perform with them. But it wasn't to be. The Army, with its usual inefficiency, didn't find out until after the war ended that I carried a Number 435 (bandsman) classification on my military records.

Promising to return it before we pulled out, I liberated a small shortwave radio from one of the townspeople, which enabled me to listen to Axis Sally broadcasts, always a source of amusement in the company. When atmospheric conditions allowed, I could also faintly pick up BBC in London for the latest war news.

As the squad crowded around the radio, a tank rumbling by brought us to the windows. It was 5th Armored Division reinforcements, an indication that something big was in the wind, like perhaps the river crossing we had all been anticipating.

While this was going on, a German plane came threatening out of the sky at the town and, just as suddenly, banked around and retreated back across the Rhine. As we picked ourselves up off the ground, we were showered by more propaganda leaflets, the same ones showing half-naked wives in the arms of their supposed lovers. The leaflets made excellent tinder for our morning fires.

I swear the Germans across the river heard our laughing, for moments later we were under another artillery bombardment, this time by shells containing more propaganda leaflets extolling the virtues of surrendering to the Third Reich.

The leaflets promised no more cold food, no fear, no more dodging bullets, no more foxholes, no more artillery, no more snow or mud. The leaflets made it all sound so wonderful, we could hardly resist the temptation to defect to the other side.

It was only a matter of days before we were restricted to quarters for what we all hoped would be the unfolding of the final phase of the war. If we crossed the Rhine successfully, Germany's military strength would be smashed once and for all. We were about to attempt what Hitler had convinced his people was impossible: to breach and penetrate the area east of the Germany's largest natural barrier, the formidable Rhine River.

If anyone could make possible the impossible, it was the 84th.

Across the Rhine: The Last Obstacle to Victory

There wasn't much conversation at the "last supper." A pall of uncertainty and apprehension hung over most of us as we counted the hours ticking by. Crossing the Roer had been a bitter, bloody, hand-to-hand fight orchestrated by some of the most intense artillery fire experienced by man. The Rhine was much wider, more strategically important, better defended. It was the do-or-die campaign for the German Army, the last defensible position before Berlin. But how could it be any worse than the Roer had been?

The questions uppermost in our minds were, How often can one go back on the line and still come out again in one piece? When would someone's luck run out? Was this going to be that time for any of us?

As I loaded my gear onto the six-by-sixes, the last remembrance of Rheinhausen was the villagers standing in their doorways watching us pull out. I hoped that some day I could return for, court-martial notwithstanding, these had been interesting days for me there.

Nightfall came quickly and the convoy headed north along the west bank of the river under full combat restrictions: no sound, no lights, no talking. I looked at my watch. It was a little after midnight April 1, 1945.

"Happy Easter," someone on the truck chirped up. The remark came as a surprise. Whether it was Thanksgiving or Christmas, most of us failed to keep track of holidays. In combat, there are no dates. Every day is a continuation of the one before.

The road became rougher and the temperature dropped sharply, causing us all to shiver, partially from the cold, I presume, and partially from the dreaded anticipation of what lay ahead.

I was puzzled that we had received no briefing whatsoever. This was not like the Army, for as lousy a communicator as it was, we were usually told something. All we knew for a fact was that we were part of the 13th Corps on the move again and, according to Axis Sally, heading across the Rhine. The answers we sought were soon forthcoming, for eventually, the convoy slowed to a crawl and we saw for ourselves where we were.

I peeked under the canvas hanging from the rear of the truck and observed another strange sight. As it had been in Geilenkirchen, the whole landscape and sky was lighted up by huge anti-aircraft floodlights casting an unnatural, eerie blue mode everywhere, turning shattered trees into silent sentinels and transforming shadowy buildings into macabre, ghost-like silhouettes of death. These lights surely could be seen forty miles away by the Germans, so why not hire a brass band to announce our arrival?

In the distance I could make out a Corps of Engineers treadway bridge across the river and I realized someone else had already done our dirty work for us. A crossing had already been made, a foothold established, and we were going to ride across the river without a fight, probably to reinforce troops on the other side. I was greatly relieved. For although I never considered myself a shirker, I also knew full well that one's destiny is determined strictly by how far fate is pushed, and I had been pushing mine pretty far, hard and often.

From the heavy concentration of anti-aircraft and artillery batteries on both sides of the river, it was obvious that counter-attacks by German planes, armored units and infantry were expected at any time. For years we had been taught to conceal, deceive, sneak, hide and camouflage and here we were riding down Broadway for all the world to see and hear. This, we hoped, meant the enemy had been pushed some distance inland away from the river.

The convoy swung creaking and groaning onto the bridge and the soft swaying of the river could be felt. MPs were everywhere jabbing arms up and down, flagging us through, urging drivers to "Go! Go! Go!" as fast as they could negotiate the narrow steel treads across the bridge.

Even though we were surrounded by a massive troop buildup, I still felt exposed while crossing the bridge. Our truck lurched up an incline on the east bank of the river and promptly became mired in mud, churned up by the first tank companies to cross.

Off to our right stood a ghost-like monolith: the remains of a huge masonry bridge, its center span collapsed into the water. Its support pillars had been blown away and now what once had been an architect's dream lay in ruins in the swirling brackish waters of the Rhine.

The bridge had been blown by the retreating German troops to thwart our advance, a futile maneuver, for nothing now could effectively stop the American forces powerhousing their way almost recklessly toward Berlin.

Almost as soon as we hit the far bank of the Rhine, the German artillery started. We jumped from the truck and landed in water-filled shell craters. In my haste, I neglected to grab my rifle when I dove off the truck and now, pinned face-down in the mud, I couldn't go back after it.

Somewhere down the line, non-coms were yelling to get back onto the trucks, that we were going to make a run for it. I was so covered with mud and river muck, I kept slipping off every time I tried to climb back on board. Finally, strong hands reached down and lifted me aboard as the truck started to roll.

Weaving and careening around shell holes, we drove toward a glowing red horizon. Before us, a whole city was burning and we were heading directly into the flames. I thought I had seen total devastation in France, Belgium and western Germany, but nothing compared to the city we were approaching. To say every inch of it was burning would be accurate, for there in the city of Wesel man had accomplished the ultimate obliteration.

As we moved slowly through the city, flames seared both sides of the convoy. I titled it "the city of the burning dead" in my diary notes. In the Catholic religion there is reference to "man's hell on earth." As we advanced slowly through Wesel, flames scorching our truck's canvas covers, I had found hell on earth, and I was in it.

I had seen the name Wesel on military maps and I knew we had traveled about 15 miles due north from Rheinhausen. From the same maps, I measured the distance from the Rhine to our next major objectives: the Weser River, slightly more than 100 miles ahead of us, and the Elbe River, only 250 miles east of us. According to the map, it was then only 65 more miles to our ultimate destination: Berlin.

I spent some time studying the map of Germany's northern plains and trying to calculate the remaining distance divided by the 50 miles we had just traversed in the past nine days. If my rudimentary arithmetic was correct, I figured that at the rate we had been pushing forward, we should be able to reach the Weser in 18 days, the Elbe in 45 days and even Berlin in 54 days, give or take a few hours. In my mind, I was projecting that the war would be over in a month and a half. I didn't dare transmit these private thoughts to anyone for fear of being accused of lunacy.

Time proved my calculations incorrect. The 84th actually covered the distance from the Rhine to the Elbe rivers in precisely one month. Math was never my forte.

The 5th Armored Division continued to cut a path into Germany's heartland for us, and the 102nd Division was mopping up behind us eliminating small pockets of resistance we bypassed in out frenetic advance. The 333rd Regiment penetrated almost 10 miles inland to Warendorf before encountering moderate resistance. The following two nights—April 2 and 3—the 333rd and 335th regiments were in a virtual race northeastward almost 60 miles inland to the outskirts of Bielefeld and Telgte, respectively.

The 84th was still advancing on a broad front and in some areas was meeting only token German resistance. Close behind the armor and infantry battalions, we found that whereas we had advanced sometimes as little as 10 miles in a day between the Roer and the Rhine, we were now capable of covering 60 miles in a day. The mighty German war machine was crumbling faster and faster each day the war was prolonged.

Only the battered remnants of the Wehrmacht and a few straggling Volkssturm conscriptees appeared to be in our way. The SS divisions, once Hitler's pride, no longer were in evidence anywhere. What was now facing us were only the dredgings of Hitler's once awesome military might that had struck terror in the hearts of nearly a dozen European nations since 1939. And now they were sharing the same fate, for a similar massive inexorable force of Allied might was striking back at them with the same ferocity they had once displayed.

We were part of a military force that was practically invincible, and growing even more so with each passing day.

The resolve to defend one's homeland is strong and we eventually encountered elderly women with pitchforks, men brandishing rusted-out World War I vintage rifles that would no longer shoot, and children with knives and clubs. We were occasionally confronted by those resorting to werewolf tactics whereby cables were strung across roads to behead anyone riding on motorcycles or in jeeps. Some of these cables were hung higher off the ground to decapitate anyone standing up in a troop carrier. The barbarism of modern warfare continued as we received the repulsive order to shoot these defenders on sight, regardless of their sex or age, if they were armed and threatening us.

In reality, there is no basic difference between a loaded rifle in the hands of a 10-year-old girl or in those of an experienced Wehrmacht soldier. One kills just as expediently as the other.

By dawn, we were driving over flat plains of sugar beet fields interspersed with marshes, lakes, smooth-sided valleys and belts of rounded-off hills. Militarily speaking, the terrain would offer no major obstacles to tanks, walking infantry or the thousands of vehicles needed to sustain our thrust.

During a roadside break, small fires sprang up along the convoy as men tried to warm themselves. During this drive, I tried to stomach C-rations that had been issued to us but they continued to stick in my craw, bringing on almost instant nausea. As I had done so many times before, I dug into my duffle bag for the contents of my most recent package from home to sustain me.

Without stopping, we whizzed through two small villages, both untouched by the fighting, a sure sign the Germans were still in full and uncontrolled flight.

After we had sat 24 hours practically motionless in the rear of a jouncing truck with only a few 10-minute roadside stops all the way from Wesel, the truck finally stopped and 12 muscle-sore men tumbled out.

I pulled the first guard tour and started a slow limping gait for four hours in front of our temporary billet while the others slept or tried to find food. I was kept company by the inevitable V-2 buzz bombs rocketing their way westward toward civilian destinations.

Even before my tour was up, we were ordered back into the trucks for another move, and the only solace was that even though each move totally disrupted our eating and sleeping cycles, they also brought us that much closer to war's end. As we pulled out again, sleet and freezing rain started to fall.

I remembered the spirit-killing march of France, the extreme pain of the Belgian winter and the soul-consuming terror of combat in between. But this truck confinement between the Rhine and the Elbe equalled them all as far as discomfort and exhaustion were concerned. Of course, I could have been walking all these miles instead, and then I would have really had something to complain about.

Company brass distributed copies of *Stars & Stripes* relating an incident in Stuttgart in southern Germany in which 18 GIs had died from allegedly drinking buzz bomb rocket fuel as a substitute for liquor. Amazed at the stupidity of such booze-craving GIs, we all got the message. I had seen men squeeze Sterno heating jelly through a woman's silk stocking to get a few drops to drink, but buzz bomb juice was just too much.

Seventy-two hours elapsed before we were told we could leave the convoy for a much-needed rest. With no town in sight we all flopped to the ground and slept in ditches beside the trucks. What seemed like minutes later, a company non-com came along kicking the feet of each man, telling us to climb back on board. Hours had no meaning, nor did kilometers and scenery. Twelve hours became 24, and 36 became 48, and I have no recollection of them for my mind was, I still believe, mentally unconscious most of the time. The human body gets to a point where it demands rest, and when it doesn't get it, it rebels and collapses.

On April 4, we were in Bielefeld, a small city in the heart of Germany's northern central plains. Here and there we could hear the mopping-up sounds of occasional rifle fire and grenades. We pulled past smouldering German and American tanks beside the road. Resistance obviously was stiffening the closer we got to Berlin—and with it, came the accompanying increase in the number of combat dead.

Without warning, the truck slammed to a stop and we were told to "deploy and form a fire line." We had met a small pocket of resistance that had to be eliminated.

A lieutenant, Everett, another GI and I crawled along a ditch toward a machine gun nest that had been raking the convoy and causing multiple casualties.

The lieutenant handed me two grenades he had been carrying and told us to take out the nest while he supervised from back in the ditch, adhering to the old "delegate and disappear" officer tactic. Machine gun slugs tore up the edge of the defile in which we were hidden, and no matter which way we moved, forward or laterally, the wildly ricocheting bullets chased us.

We were out of effective grenade-throwing range and the stalemate dragged on. Then I felt a hand on my shoulder. It was our black truck driver who had appeared out of nowhere with a Browning Automatic Rifle. He took my grenades and said he would show us how it was done. I tried to tell him he would get his head blasted off if he tried, but he just stared back at me almost in contempt.

Disregarding the bullets spraying all around us, the driver stood up and ran toward the machine gun emplacement, firing the Browning from the hip. Miraculously, he was able to get to within a few feet of the bunker unscathed even though the German gunners were concentrating their fire solely on him.

In almost a single sweeping motion, he threw the grenades into the bunker while hitting the ground. Simultaneously with the explosions, he jumped inside and emptied his 20-round BAR clip into the three German gunners. Then he picked himself up and casually sauntered past us without a word and returned to his vehicle. Whoever this Quartermaster Corps driver was, he had earned the respect of an entire convoy of GIs who were on their bellies observing the caper. He was a true hero, and none of us ever learned his name.

With each short roadside break, fires were started as men continuously tried to get warm. I had been trying to boil an egg the past 100 miles or so and had barely managed to get the water in my steel helmet even lukewarm.

In desperation, I poured the water out and broke some eggs into the helmet to try frying them. A gooier mess one never saw, but when they turned to charcoal, I scraped them off with my trench knife and ate them anyway. Even burned to a crisp, they tasted better than cold C- or K-rations.

We rolled into the only slightly damaged town of Herford. As we milled around stamping our feet for warmth, a fancy horse-drawn carriage came around a corner followed by what appeared to be a whole battalion of German soldiers surrendering themselves to us. At the head of the column was a colonel who stopped and handed his Luger to our company commander.

I was quickly summoned to interpret. His men, he said, had not eaten for two days and they just wanted to return to their homes. He gave the captain a portfolio of military maps and other pertinent data.

He said they were all that remained of the once-proud Hermann Goering Division, and they had recently been redeployed from the eastern front to fight the Americans on the western front after the Russian campaign had been abandoned. He expressed relief that he could surrender to the Amis rather than the hated Ruskies, whom he said he feared.

Bowen instructed me to tell them to walk to the rear to Bielefeld and once there, to disband and find their way home. When I translated this to the colonel, a sudden outburst of emotion swept through the German ranks. Their bitter war in Russia was over and they had survived. Our orders signalled the end of their American war and they had beaten the odds twice and survived. They swarmed over us with pictures of their wives, mothers and children while others tried to embrace us or, at least, shake our hands. This emotional display by hundreds of Wehrmacht soldiers completely unraveled the hatred that had been welling up inside me since witnessing the atrocities of Holland and Belgium.

But, I knew something they probably didn't, that their homes and towns had been reduced to smashed mortar and stone, their loved ones most likely were refugees wandering from city to city all over Germany like nomads seeking loved ones, food or shelter. For most, there would be no home to go to. It could be years before many would be reunited and to reacclimate themselves to postwar Germany.

Liberation

During the next troop movement, the convoy stopped abruptly in the middle of nowhere for no apparent reason. We could hear no firefight nor see any traffic tie up.

As we waited patiently for the column to start up again, a mob of people, without warning, swarmed around the rear of our truck. They were all trying to get at us, babbling in foreign languages I couldn't understand. Some were trying to climb aboard and kiss us. For a moment, not knowing who or what they were, we braced to fight them off.

One of the GIs in the truck was jabbering with them in Polish. The truck was suddenly turned into a cacophony of languages. They were slave laborers from a nearby concentration camp. Over and over they asked whether anyone in the truck spoke Polish, Serbian, Dutch, French, Russian, or Czech. A few spoke limited English. It took a few minutes to sink in that concentration camp prisoners we had seen in newspapers and magazines back in the States were now surging all over us.

As fast as they could talk, they told us of starvation, of working 20-hour days until many collapsed and died, of mass genocide and open graves with corpses covered with lye. All of them were intent on telling their individual stories as fast as they could to the world, or to anyone who would listen to them, for that matter. It was crucially important to them, even before finding food for their withered bodies. They were consumed by a need to talk, and the longer they crowded around us with joy, the more we learned of the limitless German cruelty.

Many of the liberated concentration camp prisoners did not take part in the jubilation, but rather stood respectfully at attention, their hands saluting their liberators silently. The majority merely stood stunned with their heads bowed unable to react at all mentally or physically to their liberation.

Was the war over? Was Poland free? Belgium free? Had Germany surrendered? Was France still occupied? Were we in Germany to stay? Was the Russian Army coming too?

They clamored almost hysterically for any news from the outside world. No matter how fast we tried to answer, to use sign language or to shake or nod our heads, we couldn't keep up with the frenzy of questions. Some of them had been locked up and tortured for years and had no idea what had been going on in the world during that time. As we tried to answer every question, our responses set off groups of prisoners dancing in the muddy road between the trucks.

Not realizing they were holding up the whole war effort, they practically carried us to a nearby pine grove where a mass grave contained the skeletal remains of more than 400 slave workers of all nationalities. The stench of death was overpowering. I cupped my hand over my nose and mouth. The rags hanging from the emaciated concentration camp inmates told only part of the horror story, of the appalling filth, the inhuman cruelty and the starvation that had been perpetrated upon them. Captured by these inmates who were feebly demanding only that the world be told of the horrendous atrocities committed there, we were brought to another grave site in woods behind the camp where the remains of 2000 more slaves had been buried in long, open trenches by bulldozers.

They told us of a guard who had hanged two Russian workers and, on another occasion, had arbitrarily shot an American aviator who had been critically beaten by the people after parachuting into a nearby village.

Next, they took us on a forced tour of a long, one-story wooden barracks in which 60 men and women had lived. Most slept on the earthen floor without blankets and many had died of tuberculosis and pneumonia.

Most of those surrounding us were covered with lice and ugly sores festered on their bodies. Their gaunt faces and sunken eyes told us what their mouths couldn't.

In one of the barracks, I found a practically skeletal woman cowering in a corner, her face to the wall, her arms covering her head. A large tattered rag that served as a blanket was draped over her. Our Polish-speaking squad member ascertained that she was a nun who had been thrown into the SS guard barracks to satisfy the physical needs of an entire company for more than a year. She had been reduced to an insane mute living out her life in tortured memories.

We emptied out every C- and K-ration crate we could find in the convoy and fed them, reasoning that even if we missed the next meal of rations, we never could be as hungry as these wretched souls standing before us.

I spotted a German officer walking briskly away from the camp on the road to Herford. I stopped him, confiscated his .32-caliber Mauser pistol, and turned him over to the prisoners who erupted into a violent mob scene when they saw him. He was the commandant of the camp and had, on one occasion in an act of intimidation, shot a Russian slave five times with his pistol in the face and chest and then threw him from a barn loft. The camp inmates related how they had been forced to take his body by wagon to the woods for disposal.

In an example of instant justice, I left the major to the crowd whom I assumed would beat him to death. At least that was my intent in doing so. I didn't stay around to watch.

As soon as I could I broke away from the crowd. The stench was more than my sensitivities could stand and I was afraid I was going to break down emotionally. I thought I had seen everything in Belgium that war could spawn, but what I was looking at now was almost beyond human comprehension. I was learning fast that there is absolutely no limit to what man is capable of doing to man. The name "Rehren" on the concentration camp entrance sign would stay with me the remainder of my life.

Soon the convoy was on its way again, but over and over it was stopped by mobs of newly freed slave workers wanting only to touch our hands as they passed from truck to truck. It was impossible to move forward without running over them.

Several miles down the road we passed another concentration camp, this one in flames. The freed slaves there were purging their past with fire. Many of the inmates had already started the long foot journey to the west, toward freedom and, for some of them, their homes in Holland, Belgium and France. At the same time, thousands of others were trudging eastward as far as their diminished strength allowed, looking for their futures in Russia, Poland and Czechoslovakia. As we drove past them, we tried to scrounge from our barracks bags even more rations or cigarettes that we could throw to them. These peoples spawned a new terminology to the American vocabulary: DPs (displaced persons).

During our entire campaign eastward from the Rhine River, our division repeatedly was forced to stop, usually for hours, sometimes for days, to wait for British troops lagging behind on both flanks.

A Canadian paratrooper told us the British were meeting almost no resistance on our northern flank, but were nevertheless unable to move forward except at what seemed to us like a snail's pace. Their reluctance in battle left our flanks dangerously exposed and vulnerable, increasing the chances of costly counter-attacks from retreating Germans. This lack of daring, or even aggressiveness in battle, added to a general feeling of resentment and bitterness toward the Brits.

I could readily understand this, for I had seen them stop in the heat of an attack near Geilenkirchen and indulge themselves in a spot of tea. They never demonstrated the boldness or initiative on the battlefields of the American troops. This slowed down our breakthrough for almost a week and, I felt, had been responsible for a needless waste of American lives.

Between the Rhine and the Weser River, the skirmishes with the Germans were mostly hit-and-run affairs, day in and day out. During one such firefight, we were deployed in a field and ordered to advance on a nearby town in full frontal formation.

One GI, passing by a house, found a large jug of schnapps, a potato-based whiskey, and passed it around. Potent stuff. When the attack finally got underway, pie-eyed GIs were weaving and stumbling their way across the field. Mortar rounds dropped among them and machine gun fire raked the meadows, but still the drunks staggered on undaunted. Seeing this incredible invincibility, the Germans pulled back quickly, leaving no American casualties behind.

As part of a support platoon, we were at the rear of the attack when it disintegrated. Without orders to the contrary, we continued on to the edge of a small town where I entered a farm courtyard at the outer perimeter of houses and farms. The firefight was over and it was time to relax my guard a little. I figured the Germans were probably still running. As I walked into the courtyard, a bullet splattered against a wall a few feet away just as I caught a fleeting glimpse of a gray-green uniform disappearing behind a building.

Instinctively, I jumped backwards. I had seen him and he had seen me. Now the standoff began. With my luck, there had to be a diehard in the village. The advantage was mine, however, for he was probably alone and I had dozens of GIs somewhere close by.

We traded shots but it was no contest. He apparently was unaware that American GIs were armed with semi-automatic rifles rather than the clip-loaded, bolt-action Mausers they carried. As I fired a round, I stayed sighted-in on the corner behind which he was hiding. Sure enough, his head and rifle lunged out again after my shot and I quickly finished the duel. As he pitched forward, I fired another round for good measure. Ammunition was plentiful and I didn't believe in taking chances—at least, not at this stage of the game. I relieved him of his Soldat Buch and his watch.

The whole incident had taken only minutes and I continued the house-to-house search at a crouching run. When satisfied my section of the town was cleared, I rejoined the squad.

The sun was warm, so I sat a few minutes against a building to rest and catch my breath. I didn't even know the name of this small village in which I had nearly been shot.

After the maddening stop-and-go travel of the previous day, our next move covered almost as much ground as we had after crossing the Roer River. Every time this happened, our hopes and morale soared. In each small village and town we passed through, we saw groups of unguarded German prisoners sitting propped against buildings beside the streets. I wondered what went through their minds as the almost endless columns of troops and armament roared past them.

On other occasions, we saw long lines of German soldiers who had been captured and then released with instructions to go home. All the fight had been knocked out of them. We realized that any future fighting would be strictly going through the motions for the Wehrmacht ranks. The once-swaggering goose-step marchers with heads held arrogantly high were now bowed and shuffling as the conquered tasted the ignominy of total, unforgiving defeat.

Many of the repatriated German prisoners begged for food along the route in search of their homes. In many instances, they were refused. The German people, as a whole, wasted little forgiveness on losers, men who could not produce the promised victory for the Vaterland. Many of these once-feared fighters were turned away when they merely asked for a place to rest on their long journey home.

But the Volkssturmers still gave us cause to worry. Their hero-worshipping, propagandized loyalty to Hitler made them individually unpredictable. Some merely playacted at putting up a defense while others sought martyrdom.

The exhaustion of war is insidious. It doesn't come on all at once, nor is it quickly relieved by a period of sleep. Its inception is hardly noticeable at first, but then it grows inside, paralyzing first the body and then the mind. It slowly builds and finally becomes solidified like old age, and there is only wisdom, born of tribulation, to take its place.

The convoy continued its buttocks-blistering path toward the Weser and Elbe rivers, stopping only occasionally to keep from killing its GI passengers.

At one stop, Everett and I ran to a nearby farmhouse to liberate some food. The farmer adamantly denied having any, but a carbine in his gut changed his story. Finding several cows and a flock of chickens, we filled our helmets with warm milk and eggs. Then, after raiding the farmer's sub-cellar, we loaded our pockets and overcoats with beets, schnapps, ham and potatoes. More and more, we rejected the Army's contention that C-, D-, and K-rations constituted a nutritionally correct, balanced diet.

The farmer violently tried to restrain us from taking his food, but a rifle round in the ground at his feet gave him pause to reflect. His hate-filled facial expression told it all, and we felt absolutely no qualms about relieving him of his larder.

The eggs were fried in our helmets, the meat was eaten almost raw and the schnapps was passed around. Anything to wash the dust out of our throats and take the edge off our hunger.

The many days in the cold back end of a truck brought the pain from my frozen feet back, intensifying the almost agonizing beating to which I was being subjected.

Kilometer after kilometer, the numbers of prisoners filing westward were increasing. It appeared that entire regiments were giving themselves up and it was evident that Germany's final, complete military collapse was imminent.

During one rest break, a large group of men came running at us across a field, yelling and waving their arms. We figured just another bunch of DPs wanting to vent their emotions at being liberated. But this time, something was different. The men were yelling in English and most were wearing olive drab uniforms instead of the standard, striped concentration camp rags.

They were American prisoners of war, some taken by the Germans as early as the African and Italian campaign. Others had been captured during the Battle of the Bulge. Like the slave laborers, they too were gaunt and undernourished. Some jumped on the trucks with us and demanded to fight the Germans again. Others just wanted to hear the news from the war front and from home. Battalion officers rounded them up fast and informed them there would be no more fighting in their futures, that they were going to be fed, given medical exams and treatment, processed, paid off and then shipped home as fast as the Army could arrange it. Many of the liberated GIs couldn't hold back their tears.

Again, as we had done for the DPs, we emptied out every bit of food we still had left and gave it to them.

When we finally pulled into another of the many nameless villages we had seen, Everett and I tried to bed down in a barn beside the road but aching bodies and the cold prevented it. We decided to look up our old companies for a visit, me to LOVE Company, Joe to EASY Company.

I found my old company and one of the first men I came across was a platoon sergeant, one of the few I still remembered from the old days back in the States. He seemed happy to see me and know that I was still alive.

He told me very few of the originals who had shipped out with me from Camp Claiborne seven months earlier still remained, that 32 had been killed and more than double that number had been wounded. I was saddened when told that one of those killed was someone I had buddied with back in the States. LOVE Company's combat mortality and casualty rates had been extremely high, a condition that was prevalent in most infantry line companies.

When the sergeant invited me on a recon patrol with him for old time's sake, I jumped at the chance to get away from truck travel for a few hours, even though I had not forgotten what had happened to me in my last two recon patrols.

We fanned out and approached a wooded area to determine whether there were snipers there and, if so, how many. Once in the protection of the trees, we started to crawl. As soon as we started, the fatigue that had built up the past week from almost constant truck travel caused me to lag behind. I was out of rifle company shape.

The forward scouts detected a sniper position even before the first shot rang out. The point men were already in a fire fight and we were moving forward to cover them for even though we were the hunters, we were still the hunted.

I spotted a German legging it across a clearing about 100 yards away. I emptied a clip at him, some rounds of which I felt sure had hit him, but he continued running until he disappeared into another clump of trees. Everett, who had rejoined me when he couldn't find his company, also emptied an M-1 clip at the fleeing German. He, too, missed him.

Disgusted with my apparent poor marksmanship, I wondered if I should volunteer for rear echelon duty until I heard Everett muttering to himself, "Jesus Christ, Blunt. This damned defective ammunition from the States is getting worse every day. It doesn't traject straight." Until he explained it I hadn't known what was wrong. He broke me up, and the embarrassment of not being able to hit a running target at a mere 100 yards evaporated in a laugh.

I reminisced a little with the sergeant and then it was time to return to Anti-Tank Company, where the others chided us for glory hunting instead of sleeping when we had had the chance.

I checked the German map I had been carrying and learned we had already crossed the Weser River, apparently during one of the nights without our knowing it. Now we were on the road again, this time our destination being Hannover, Germany's twelfth largest city. I asked around about the Weser River crossing and was told the 335th Regiment's 1st and 3rd Battalions had made a successful crossing April 6 and established a secured position just north of the Weser Gebirge (mountains).

Elements of the 333rd Regiment had gone across in support the next afternoon and immediately pushed inland toward Eisbergen, about eight miles away. I did some fast calculation and determined we had covered 100 miles from the Rhine to the Weser in four days. If we continued at that rate, the war would be over by the weekend and we would be in Berlin.

We continued northward toward Hannover where its inhabitants spoke the "Hoch Deutsch" (High German) I had been taught in high school. People throughout Germany understood High German but most spoke varying dialects and had difficulty understanding those from other geographic provinces.

On April 10 as we approached the city, friendly artillery fire was winging its way over our heads for Hannover was still under siege. From about a quarter mile away, we entered the city on foot as reinforcement troops spaced at 10-foot intervals on both sides of a broad boulevard.

Fires were burning everywhere and more dead littered the streets. Only one thing differed radically from the street scenes in the previous cities and towns. Here, the German equipment, field pieces and supply wagons were all horse-drawn. Burning ammunition carts were exploding and often beside them lay the corpses of the soldiers who had been pulling them.

The Luftwaffe and most mechanized vehicles were less in evidence now. For the most part, men performed the tasks of horses. Each one of these realities buoyed our spirits. What gasoline was available to the German Army was now steadfastly reserved for the remaining few tank divisions.

We found increasing evidence of defective artillery shells. The sabotage efforts of slave workers in the munitions factories were making a difference. The Wehrmacht had abandoned use of the Nebelwurfer (tank grenade launcher) after so many had proven faulty and had blown up, killing the users.

Every day now, American troops were lifting a page from Germany's military manuals and were taking full advantage of the pincer movement strategy: encircle the enemy from two sides and entrap or eliminate him. Hannover was a vast city, and we infiltrated it for more than an hour before we reached what appeared to be the business district. No civilians were seen anywhere; obviously, they had been evacuated earlier. Like every village, town and city before it, Hannover was being methodically destroyed by overwhelming American fire power.

We were told to form a skirmish line and clear the area for several blocks in front of us. When a German burp gun sprayed a building near me, I hit the ground and buried my head in rubble. Each time I lifted my head, machine gun bullets whipped in my direction, ricocheting in every direction. I was exposed and pinned down.

Out of the corner of my eye I caught a glimpse of movement across the street and saw a GI firing a BAR. He purposely revealed himself to the German to divert attention from me momentarily. As he did so, the German's return fire cut him in half with machine gun slugs. In that precious moment the GI with the BAR had given me, I spotted the gunner in a second-story window and pumped a bullet into him. He jackknifed out of the window and fell to the street with his Wehrmacht helmet bouncing away from him. I jumped up, ran to the German and shot him again.

Then I ran to the other GI but there was nothing that could be done for him. His body had been ripped apart and his blood was trickling across a sidewalk and forming a crimson pool in the gutter. I shook with rage and gratitude at the same time. This man had purposely sacrificed his life for mine.

The almost constant death all around me was heavily gnawing away at my sensibilities, for we were so close to the end that I wanted all the killing to stop once and for all. My brain had reached a saturation point of how much carnage and slaughter it could absorb. I realized the Allies would settle for nothing less than unconditional capitulation after the Germans had been totally vanquished, but I wondered why this wasn't possible through negotiations rather than the continued and senseless throwing away of lives on both sides. I didn't realize it at the time but the voluminous massacring of so many lives was converting me from a hawk to a dove. Enough was enough, my mind was screaming. I couldn't take much more of it.

I edged my way around a street corner and was greeted by the sickening sight of two German boys about 10 years old, hanged from a lamp post for refusing to serve as Volkssturm defenders. We quickly cut them down with bayonets and left them to two hysterically wailing mothers who cradled the children in their laps as we continued on. Words wouldn't come: we just walked away silently, leaving them to their private torment. I reflected back on the young German tanker who was executed back in Belgium for feeding hungry American POWs.

The lieutenant told us to bed in for the night in a nearby school. Guards were posted. After pulling my tour, I climbed to the fourth floor seeking a quiet night's sleep. Everett and two others were already settled in. Everett and I stretched out on the floor, the others in bunks along a wall. Sleep came fast as the sounds of the street faded. I don't know how long we had been asleep when the world caved in on us. A mind-shattering explosion knocked me senseless as walls and ceiling caved in, burying us where we slept. I could neither hear nor see. I sensed men probing their way with candles and flashlights through a thick, stifling cloud of gunpowder smoke, all the while yanking debris off us.

I tried to stand but overpowering dizziness knocked me back down again. The room was filled with splintered timbers and masonry. Shadowy figures were stumbling around and yelling everywhere. Gradually, my senses returned and I realized that our room had sustained a direct artillery hit.

Everett and I on the floor had escaped unscathed. One of the GIs had a badly lacerated wrist from shrapnel and the other had disappeared. The shell had come through the wall and exploded in his bunk. All that remained of him were chunks of meat and flesh spattered over all the walls.

Everett tried to pick me up and drag me to a hallway where we met company officers who were unnerved by the incident. Through badly ringing ears I heard their hollow voices asking if I was all right. As I struggled to respond, two men with a blanket removed the dead GI's remains. Their load was light; there was little left of him.

In the kerosene lantern light of the command post, I vomited when I saw my uniform was covered from head to toe with the dead man's blood and flesh. I staggered outside and continued to throw up, crying in total frustration at fate. I had said good night to him only minutes before. I stood there pondering the same question I had asked myself over and over so many times before. Why had I been spared during these months-long series of close calls? These near-misses were becoming almost a daily routine. There had to be a pattern, a reason, but I couldn't figure it out.

I wasn't prepared for what came next. It was one of the most emotionally shattering experiences of the war: we were told the pulverized GI had been killed by a shell from one of our own tank divisions that had not been informed we were occupying this section of Hannover. I never found out if this was true or not. Later, we heard that such accidents of war were referred to as "killed by friendly fire," a cruel misnomer if I ever heard one.

My tormented brain collapsed into despair, followed by a period of deep depression. I couldn't fully comprehend then just how long these memories would haunt me throughout life. There were just too many of them, one piled on top of another. When would they all stop, and how much more insanity could I endure around me?

We had made our contribution to the war effort and now it was time to move on again. As the convoy closed in on the city of Braunschweig, we saw dozens of American, British and German tanks burning on the streets and fields. German and American dead were everywhere, hung out of windows, sprawled over piles of rubble, in doorways and in tank turrets.

It was obvious from the carnage that Braunschweig had been one hell of a battle. I gazed into the faces of the American GIs crumpled in the gutters and thought about how far they had come and how close they had been to the end. I felt deep remorse for these GIs and their families for the senseless deaths at this stage of the war. The ferocity of the fight for Braunschweig meant that German resolve was obviously stiffening.

In the truck the next morning, moving eastward again on April 14, I could only stare with dimmed eyes at the canvas wall of the truck. I withdrew into an emotional shell. Everett, sensing my grief, put his arm around me and we rode in silence the rest of the way.

When the truck column halted, we were told we would remain there about an hour. A nauseating smell permeated the air we breathed. In the distance was a row of wooden barracks, the type we recognized as concentration camp huts. A sign over a barbed wire gate read "Nord Stalag III." Nearby was the town of Ohrdruf.

The genocide of Jews and other foreign nationals was spread out before us everywhere we looked. The barracks were filled with dead and near-dead skeletons staring up at us with sunken eye sockets wherever we walked. These pathetic creatures were too far gone to speak or even move. Just their haunting eyes remained to stare without emotion at us.

A 12-foot-high fence strung with double rows of barbed wire enclosed the camp and beyond it were coils of concertina wire. Inside the primary wire fence stood a six-foot-high electrified fence, and between the two outer fences the ground was littered with shards of broken glass, rusted scrap steel and anti-personnel mines. The mine field, we learned later, was a favorite method of prisoner suicide. The Germans didn't try to foil these attempts for to do so meant more mouths to feed.

A railroad siding ran into the camp, and strings of boxcars were parked with their doors open. As a few of the prisoners stood at the wire fence staring silently at us, most of us lowered our eyes rather than stare back. Many had had their teeth pounded out for their gold fillings by inhumane guards. It was difficult to differentiate between the living and dead skeletons stacked on wooden platforms that served as beds.

At each row of bunks, I tried to tell them softly, "Wir sind Amerikaners" (We are Americans). It seemed so inadequate, for most of these wretched souls would die before our medical teams could help them. We had arrived too late.

I entered the administration building—easy to identify, since it was the only structure in the camp constructed of brick—and found a prisoner seated in the commandant's desk chair. He stuck out his hand. I reluctantly took it in mine for I was squeamishly repulsed by his appearance and hesitant to touch him.

In a hollow whisper, he said, "Hello."

When I realized it was the only English word he knew, I conversed with him in German. He told me the German doctors at the camp had conducted experiments on his throat and he no longer had a voice box. I winced as I listened to his tales.

He showed me large scars on his arms and back where the camp doctors had performed skin grafts for plastic surgery. Extensively scarred areas on his legs and buttocks showed where skin had been surgically removed for other experimentation.

Then, in an attempt at a joke, he said all this had been done while he still had meat on his body.

When I asked about the multiple scars on his shoulders and back, he repeated over and over again, "Das peitschen. Das peitschen" (The whip. The whip). He told of guard dogs ripping inmates to pieces and then eating them. I wanted to believe him but the stories were just too incredible to comprehend.

I asked him his nationality.

"Ich bin Deutscher Jude" (I am German Jew), he answered, a glimmer of pride still showing.

As such, he had been considered an enemy of the Third Reich. I told him that in America, a Jew was treated as freely as any other citizen. He nodded silently in docile resignation.

He took me to a concrete building with a tall chimney at the rear of the camp. As we approached, he slowed his pace and then stopped, obviously still terrified of the building.

"Das crematorium" (the crematory). He insisted I go inside and then tell the world what I had witnessed. While he waited outside, I entered it alone and instantly wished I hadn't.

Skulls, bones and ashes were everywhere; and again, the smell was suffocating. Fingernails had gouged out walls and a deep pit contained the bones of hundreds of prisoners. The walls were a gruesome mural of smeared blood where many, when finally realizing their fate, had bashed their heads against the walls to render themselves unconscious or to attempt suicide.

When I rejoined the Jewish prisoner outside, tears were streaming down my cheeks.

Softly, he said in German, "Now I will show you the others, the more fortunate." They had been frozen solid and then thrown into vats of hot water in what had been primitive cryogenic experimentation. Camp doctors never successfully determined how long the human could be frozen alive: there had been no survivors.

In nearby woods, he showed me cremation pyres of railroad ties and skeletal bodies stacked crisscrossed higher and higher. The concentration camp guards had not had time to light the last pyre before being overrun by American troops.

"This was how they disposed of bodies," my guide told me.

Other skeletons in boxcars were covered with powdered white lye to ward off disease and to hasten deterioration.

Before we pulled out of the area, we watched American MPs, at gunpoint, herding men, women and children, young and old, from all the surrounding towns to tour through every inch of the camp bearing witness to what had transpired there. To a person, every last one of them denied all knowledge of the camp's existence. Some, I was happy to see, were being forced by Army officials to carry the skeletons to graves where they could be interred properly.

I asked my guide about humane guards at the camp. He said there were some but they were weeded out quickly, sent to less desirable details, and replaced by more sadistic SS guards.

I told him American doctors were on the way. "They can't help now," he answered simply. "It's too late for most of us. But you must never forget what you have seen here. The world must be told," he insisted. The date was April 25, 1945, and I can say, in his memory, that I never forgot what I saw and inhaled. As I left to return to the convoy, his echoing last words were, "Vergessen Sie nicht" (Don't forget).

As we moved out, Army Intelligence Units began interrogating the prisoners who were considered prime sources of military information about German troop and armament strengths and locations of enemy fortifications. After all, they had built most of them.

I made a covenant with this nameless Jew and it was a solemn pact I've kept for a half century. I haven't forgotten. I almost wish I could, but I can't, even if I wanted to.

The Elbe River: The Final Shot Is Fired

When the convoy halted in the small village of Weinhausen, I was offered a "good deal" that promised me lots of sleep and good food. Skeptical of the Army's good deals, I eventually agreed. With some reservation, Everett and I were joined by a new replacement to the company whom I didn't know, as we crowded into the back seat of a battalion colonel's jeep and were driven to battalion headquarters. There, our new job was guarding POWs as temporary MPs. It seemed like a good deal and for once, I was pleased that I had volunteered for something non-hazardous and perhaps even enjoyable. We were dropped off at a large farmhouse and told to await further orders.

The first prisoner placed under our protective custody was a frail, bespectacled, sneaky-looking civilian who was principal of a local school and also the local Gestapo Gauleiter. He was one of the most feared and hated Nazi officials in the area.

Instantly I had a vengeful idea of retribution for him. When I told the others, they answered with sly smiles and nods of approval. I walked up to this known Gestapo official, positioned myself inches from his nose, and snarled in my best sinister voice, "Ich habe Ohrdruf gesehen" (I have seen Ohrdruf).

His steely eyes widened for a moment and then narrowed to slits again but his stone-faced expression never faltered. Even when I prodded him to a manure pile and jammed my carbine into his gut, he didn't flinch a muscle. This was one hard-core Nazi. I shoved him again and this time he fell backward into the manure. Still, he just stared at me without a trace of fear. This strengthened my determination to break this heartless bastard. I picked him up by the collar, gave my carbine to Everett, and gave the Gestapo supervisor a roundhouse belt in the face as hard as I could throw a punch.

He lurched backward again, blood from his nose smearing his face. I hit him again but still he didn't utter a word.

"I'll make this son-of-a-bitch crawl and beg," I roared at Everett. I took the German's face and smeared it in the manure until he was in danger of suffocating. His face was cut, his nose was bleeding badly, manure clogged his eyes and mouth and by now his glasses were gone.

I dragged him to a barn wall and stood him up facing us. Then I methodically paced off 10 steps, counting each one out loud. "Ein, zwei, drei, vier. . . ." I pivoted on my heel smartly and rammed a clip into my rifle, all the time glaring at the German. I theatrically elongated each move I made, for I wanted him to suffer maximum mental anguish. It was street theater at its best. Still, he refused to make a sound. I asked him if he had anything to say. He continued to glare at me, his eyes filled with hatred. Without another word, I fired a shot at the wall only inches from his head. He didn't even flinch. In mock-sarcasm, Everett and the replacement teased me about missing my shot. I took careful aim and put another round inches from the other side of his head.

At this, he wavered and almost collapsed. I knew that I had gotten through to him at last. He fell to his knees and I let go another round in the dirt before him.

He staggered to his feet and tried feebly to again assert his Nazi superiority. His pathetic attempt to maintain his dignity made us laugh. His eyes became slits of rage, but now fright could be detected. I hit him again and dragged him back to the manure pile, threw him in it and ordered him to "Bleiben Sie da" (Remain there).

I beckoned the replacement over to the gauleiter and snarled, "Er ist ein Jude und er hat auch Ohrdruf gesehen" (He is a Jew and he has also seen Ohrdruf). "Er willen Sie haben" (He wants you), I added.

The German, hearing this, leaped up and ran. I fired a shot at his fleeing feet and he stopped in his tracks. The bullet, ricocheting off the courtyard cobblestones as he attempted to flee, coupled with the constant screamed threats, reduced the Gestapo prisoner to a comedic, dung-smeared, incoherently babbling spectacle. Roughly, we stood him up again. The guard being passed off as a Jew placed his rifle against the Nazi's head and fired . . . on an empty chamber.

The loud click of the M-1 sent the prisoner to his knees sputtering so incoherently I couldn't make out what he was stammering. Finally, we walked away leaving him on the manure pile. He had groveled and I was satisfied. I wished that my guide at the concentration camp had witnessed my stage performance. He would have enjoyed it immensely.

Fortunately, the colonel didn't witness our treatment of the Gestapo prisoner, for he wouldn't have approved. Officers were funny like that.

By now, the POW count in the area had risen into the hundreds and we spent each day patrolling a barbed wire enclosure that held them. There was little fear of their trying to escape for they were being fed, probably better than they had been in some time.

In probably the easiest and most productive loot haul of the war, I located the town burgermeister (mayor) and told him all weapons in the town must be turned in to me or he would be imprisoned. One character trait about the Germans that worked to our advantage was that they were indoctrinated since birth to obey an order. About an hour later, he returned with a blanket filled with pistols, antiquated rifles, knives, bayonets and swastika flags of all descriptions. I nodded authoritatively and when he left, I delved into the pile, retrieving an engraved chrome-plated, pearl-handled .25-caliber automatic.

Eventually, when the crunch of German prisoners that was mounting every day had been processed, interrogated and then sent home, I was reassigned to Anti-Tank Company in Hildesheim. I tried to rest but the Germans interrupted my sleep by counter-attacking with tanks. Anti-tank units took to the hills behind our billet and formed a skirmish line, climbing until we reached the top where we flopped on our stomachs. I laid out a row of extra grenades and M-1 ammunition bandoliers beside me. The much lighter carbine was the weapon to have when marching, but in a firefight, nothing beat the M-1. Also, I had seen German soldiers take a carbine slug in them and keep coming. This seldom happened when shot with an M-1.

A crashing sound to the rear startled me. It was only a bazooka team coming through to establish forward positions. The tank noise grew as someone shouted, "Here they come!" Two badly scarred and rusted-out Panther tanks emerged from the trees with no infantry accompanying them. The bazooka team fired off a round but it fell far wide of the lead tank, which started spraying the ground around us with machine gun fire.

I prepared to hightail it out but was stopped by the bazooka team barreling past my position. Without realizing what I was doing, I grabbed their abandoned bazooka and put it to my shoulder. Everett loaded me, tapped me on the helmet and I fired. The rocket round hit the side of the closest tank and glanced off before exploding into the ground. The tank kept coming; it was only about 75 feet away. Suddenly the tank exploded in flame and smoke. The tank spun around and tried to pull back, but another round struck true and the tank began to burn. The turrets of both tanks opened up and their crews surrendered.

As Everett and I lay panting for breath on the ground, GIs from Anti-Tank Company appeared out of the woods trailing a .57-mm cannon behind them.

As they danced around celebrating their kill, I wondered if I should confess to Everett I had been on the verge of bugging out in the face of the tanks before the bazooka team did. We brought the weapon back to the company area and gave it to the captain, who figured the team must have been new replacements from some nearby line company. While trying to sleep I wondered why, after all these months, I had almost panicked. I admittedly didn't want to die in a war that was practically over. Disturbed by my thoughts, I couldn't sleep so I went for a walk to indulge in a little self-analysis.

The company field kitchen caught up to us and we enjoyed one of the Army's two standard breakfasts: pancakes and coffee or oatmeal, coffee and bread without butter.

The weather in northern Germany in mid-April was starting to moderate, allowing the canvas sides to be rolled up on the truck as we moved forward again. This offered us an opportunity to drink in what was left of the northern German landscape and the fresh air was invigorating. We marveled at the autobahn highways that Hitler had built years before in anticipation of the war he had planned for so long. The multi-lane highways stretched through Herford, Hannover, Braunschweig and Magdeburg, and all led to Berlin. Other equally direct roadways ran north and south throughout the country, making the autobahns, engineering masterpieces for their times, one of the most efficient highway networks in all Europe. These super highways had been built for the speed that helped assure the success of Hitler's Blitzkrieg (lightning war). They were a welcome relief after being jounced around so roughly on the shell-pocked highways of France, Holland, Belgium and the Rhineland.

I vacated my usual tailgate spot and stood up facing forward behind the cab to let the wind blow in my face. Suddenly, I was jerked backwards abruptly and violently and sent sprawling by Everett. After bouncing off the floor, I came up ready to fight until he pointed out a steel cable stretched across the road that would have beheaded me had I remained standing. I had not even seen it, so much was I enjoying the passing scenery. I sat down again, grateful for Everett's having spotted the cable in time.

He had saved my skin numerous times before in combat and now he had done it again. Officers gave themselves medals in combat for all sorts of things but "Joe Loot" Everett never received one, for I had never had one to award him—just my friendship.

During our move, we began to see launching ramps at the edges of fields and hidden in wooded areas. We assumed they were for the German V-1 rockets and V-2 buzz bombs. The convoy was moving fast and we were able to get only a fleeting glimpse of some of Hitler's secret weapons.

We entered the town of Seehausen, a few kilometers from the west bank of the Elbe River, where we were assigned an abandoned farmhouse as our next temporary billet. I ran to it, grabbed a bed and defended it from all comers. I passed Bowen on the street several hours later and he informed me my billet would also be the company kitchen, and reminded me I still had KP punishment to serve. A month had elapsed and except for washing a few pots and pans back in Rheinhausen, I had ignored the court-martial sentence completely. KP was my guarantee of hot food. I settled back into my bed and slept, secure in the knowledge that my fighting days were over: that is, if I wanted them to be.

After I ate and scrubbed a few pans, my time was my own. That meant more souvenir hunting and countryside exploration. I was beginning to miss the adrenalin surges of combat. There was a reorientation transition going on inside me and I was having some difficulty adjusting to it. Challenge created excitement, I'd found, and boredom stifled enthusiasm.

My punishment in the company kitchen required about an hour's work after each meal, leaving me the rest of the day to explore the river area. On the way back to the company, I became nervous. I was at least a mile and a half into territory that had never been declared clear of German troops. Beside a pathway, I spotted a log structure in the trees—a machine gun dugout.

I hit the ground and crawled to it, damning myself for being so careless this close to war's end. My stomach knotted up when I realized I was scared there alone without Everett's usual backup. The dugout was empty and I reasoned it probably wasn't a bunker after all but merely something put there by some farmer or woodsman.

Getting jumpier by the minute, I looked up and down, left and right, in front of me and behind me as if searching for a sniper. It was a good thing that I did, for through the trees I spotted a uniformed Wehrmacht soldier coming toward me.

Before even determining whether he was armed, I flopped to the ground and started firing. I emptied a whole clip at him. I could see branches being snipped off and bark flying from trees. But no German. He had fled, armed with an intriguing story to tell his family some day about one of his close calls during the war. Like the German, I started to run and didn't stop until I was safely back in the company area.

The Polish-speaking GI in the platoon dropped by to tell me he had found a couple of Polish and Czech DPs in nearby Seehausen and asked if I wanted to do a little fraternizing. Defying the court-martial sentence, I went with him. After all, the DPs were not Germans and the fraternization ban specifically said Germans.

We snuck out after dark and entered the village, where we found a group drinking and partying around a single candle in an abandoned warehouse. The other GI immediately started drinking whatever was in a clay jug being passed around and soon he couldn't stand up.

Some of the women, recently released from a work camp, began pawing us over, while the men in the group urged them on. The men were a surly-looking bunch and I wanted no jealousy problem from them. My buddy simply giggled drunkenly through it all. I tried to get him to leave with me but he was already babbling incoherently in his ethnic tongue and I couldn't get him to speak English to me any more. When the opportunity came, I beat a hasty retreat to the company area, lucky to still be in one piece. The other partying GI made it back to the company a couple of days later after he sobered up.

The sameness of each day was broken up by radio broadcasts telling us that Hitler was dead by his own hand, and Benito Mussolini, Fascist premier of Italy, had been strung up with his mistress in a public square by his own people. I felt that at last, the war was only a formality, but until it ended, it was business as usual.

Almost simultaneously with the news about Hitler and Mussolini, we heard on April 12 that President Franklin D. Roosevelt had died of a cerebral hemorrhage and that Vice President Harry S. Truman had been sworn in as our new president. This tempered the joy of the earlier broadcasts considerably.

Four teenage German girls carrying babies walked into our camp one day asking for food. We fed them and played with the babies. The young mothers were fleeing from the oncoming Russian troops advancing from the east because they had been told that the conquering Ruskies would pillage, loot and rape them. Before continuing their trek westward to safety, the girls told me they had been impregnated for the Vaterland and the babies were illegitimate. One girl wore an ornate blue and gold medal which she gave me. It had been awarded to her for having five "pure Aryan" babies. They told us the national honor of bearing as many babies as possible prompted many wives to put themselves in German Army barracks, at the will of entire companies, to ensure quicker pregnancies. I couldn't help but think how proud their husbands would be upon returning from the war and learning how honorably their wives had also served their country.

I told the company commander I was getting restless working in the kitchen. He told me he never checked the kitchen and as long as he saw an American uniform working there, that was all that mattered. I hurriedly hitched a ride to the nearby town of Trebel, where others from my squad were billeted. The town was graced by a peaceful common not unlike those in New England. I located Everett and learned the Elbe River was only a couple of miles away. He reminded me there were still some minor skirmishes going on and occasional German patrol action along the river.

Just fine, I informed him, for I was looking for a prisoner to replace me in the company dishwater. On foot, we headed for the river. After a half hour, we broke out into the open and found a panorama of activity before us. The fast-flowing river was clogged with small boats and makeshift rafts; people were clinging to them and swimming frantically toward the west bank.

An American machine gun emplacement was dug in near the river bank and the gunners were intermittently firing short bursts across the river at thousands of German troops massed there. We scrambled into a ditch when a few of them returned fire. I asked one of the gunners if I could have a crack at the .30-caliber machine gun. He moved aside with a wave of his hand and I sighted in on a group of Germans already partway across. The stream of bullets spattered little geysers of water all around them. Some turned back, but the others continued on despite being fired upon, ducking beneath the surface when the firing started.

The fear of the Russians closing in on them from behind overruled their judgment. To some the machine gun bullets spitting around them were less of a threat than the hated and feared Russians.

I turned the gun over to Everett, who fired a few bursts at the far riverbank, feeling that he too had made his small contribution to ending the war. They were the last shots of World War II for us.

We watched the growing swarm of humanity crowding both shorelines. Many women, fearful of the treatment they would receive at the lust of the advancing Russian troops, were climbing out of the water naked without noticeable embarrassment.

To one of them, a blonde about 20, I called out, "Wo gehen sie?" (Where are you going?)

"Amerika," she answered without a moment's hesitation. "Vereinige Staaten" (America. United States).

We stashed her into some bushes while I rustled up fatigue pants and a shirt. She dressed herself and dried off. I gave her a K-ration and told her to stay away from the other Americans. She understood immediately.

A high-ranking German officer stepped from a half-swamped rowboat and was immediately taken into custody. Standing beside him was an attractive woman, also dressed in a Wehrmacht uniform. "Offizieren Matratze" (officer's mattress), the blonde girl with us mumbled under her breath.

A small band of German soldiers, their hands already folded over their heads, appeared from a wooded area. I pointed to one and beckoned to him. Wide-eyed, he walked hesitantly toward me. He said he had been a radio repairman in the Wehrmacht. I asked him if he wanted some hot food in return for work. He almost jumped out of his tattered green uniform at the offer.

What a fine-looking parade we made when we walked back to Trebel: a good-looking, water-soaked blonde in sloppy Army fatigues, a disheveled Kraut prisoner and two combat-dirty GIs.

I entered Wegener's Gasthaus in the town and commandeered some clothes for the young girl. Then I claimed a pool table in the bar area as my bed. Herta Wegener, the owner, welcomed us as she would any other guest for the night.

I deposited my prisoner at the company kitchen in Seehausen, dressed him in one of my uniforms and put him to work. The two Louisiana cooks didn't particularly like the idea but they kept their mouths shut. Besides, it was the closest they had been to a German since we landed on the Continent.

The prisoner, who spoke some English, stayed with me, for he would be useful to me later. He slept under my protection for several weeks as we moved throughout Germany after the cessation of hostilities. We argued constantly over who was the better soldier, the American or the German. We were better equipped, he conceded, but they were better trained and smarter.

Well, I argued, if they were smarter, why had we won the war? Equipment, he always retorted, equipment. Despite dozens of spirited discussions, we never resolved the issue to either's satisfaction. One of his favorite boasts was that I could be in a flat field with a machine gun and he could approach me with no concealment whatsoever and take me out. How we argued this point! But no matter how spirited the discussions became, he never forgot he was the prisoner and I was the victor. We often became angry but always wound up laughing in the end.

Partially because of the food he was receiving, he wanted fervently to join the American Army, even if it meant being transferred to the CBI (China-Burma-India) theater of operations as had been rumored for the 84th. He was a professional soldier and fighting was all he knew or wanted.

Every German I spoke to expressed shock and disappointment that the Americans were halting at the Elbe River and giving Berlin to the Russians, but it was a political decision that sentenced the world to more than four decades of cold war and military tension between the two world superpowers. At the rate we had pushed eastward, we could have made it first to Berlin in a day—two at the most. Most Germans emphasized over and over that Germany was not America's real enemy, Russia was. The decision to give Berlin to the Russians after so many men had died fighting so long and hard to reach it didn't sit very well with most of us either.

We had been deprived of the jewel of all Germany, the capital city that had been our dream and goal for so many months, but there were other considerations, namely our lives. Still, the disappointment and resentment of what we considered the gross error of the political decision allowing the Russians to take Berlin was deep and would not be easily forgiven.

The streets of Trebel were becoming clogged with armies of Germans trying to make their way to the west. We were told that at a certain time the next day, American forces would fire a green flare out over the river. If the Russian troops had reached the other side, they would answer with a red flare.

It was May 2 and tension was growing by the hour.

We all journeyed to the river to watch. The hours dragged to 1100 when someone yelled, "There it is," and we all stood silently watching the graceful arc of the Russian Red Army signal.

The war, although not officially over for another six days, had ended. Tears rolled down my cheeks as I dropped to one knee and gave thanks for being spared. Then I sat under a tree to meditate. I wanted to be alone in those final few moments.

Joe Everett joined me and in his Oklahoma drawl, said softly, "God was good to us, Bluntie old boy." I just nodded. Nothing I could say would express my feelings more eloquently.

It was not a time of vigorous backslapping but of quiet reflection during those initial moments when we first fully realized we had fired our last shot at the German and he had fired his final shot at us. Each of us had our own private memories of what we had seen, what we had done and wondered what the future held for us. It took some time to accept the fact that we would go home alive and someday resume a normal life. We would all need, each in our ways, considerable reactivation to civilian life.

I excused myself from Everett and walked away until I found a small stream leading to a wooded area. I followed the brook to a pine grove where I lay down and looked up at the sky as I had done so often in civilian life.

I listened for the songs of birds but the woods were silent. There were so many questions for which I had no answers. Of one thing I was sure: I had to push the horror of the past behind me and rebuild my life. I would have my memories. The notes I had jotted down every day would assure that. But I also knew how difficult it would be to ever relate to anyone what I had seen, felt and done.

But all that mattered, questions not withstanding, was that the war was over and I was still alive.

The End of Hostilities

The ending of hostilities meant I would have to undergo the transformation from violence and fear to peace and security, but I didn't realize on that calm day in May 1945 just how difficult it would be for me, or how long it would take.

First, I would be separated from buddies with whom I had endured so much. Friendships would end abruptly, probably never to be shared again. These wartime relationships were like family love and were nurtured by months of shared deprivation and hunger, of survival-threatening cold and excruciating anguish, of stark terror and sensitivity-shattering horror, crippling exhaustion and personal triumph. And never again would there be the nonsensical hilarity and crazy escapades that had forged bonds among us that would be emotionally difficult to break.

A company notice was posted that we had earned battle stars for the Rhineland, the Ardennes and Central Europe campaigns. The symbolism of the battle stars was significant to all of us. Each star had been earned with considerable suffering.

The 84th had taken more than 70,000 prisoners and captured or destroyed 112 German pillboxes and bunkers. In addition, we had been on the line for 171 continuous days, a noteworthy feat.

On VE Day + 1, a bulletin was posted that henceforth boots would be shined, pants cleaned and pressed, close order drills would commence, hair would be cut, beards would be shaved, neckties would be worn and first bugle call would be at 0615. Also, saluting of officers would resume immediately. The "chicken shit" had begun, as we all knew it would, but we hadn't expected it quite that soon. We had underestimated the Army in thinking it would give us a reasonable period to savor our victory. We had not saluted officers in combat. To do so would have helped snipers decide which of us to shoot.

Late in May, relocation orders came without warning and our departure from Trebel was abrupt. But, before leaving, I applied for a transfer to Anti-Tank Company. I was still carried on LOVE Company rosters and if we were headed for the China-Burma-India theater of operations (CBI)—the persistent rumor confirmed by our brass—I wanted no part of an infantry line company again. The law of averages might smile upon me once, but never twice.

Without delay, the convoy churned westward on northern Germany's modern autobahns and as usual, we had no idea where we were headed. But at least while heading west, we also were moving closer to home.

By the time we finally stopped for the night, the convoy had traveled through Hannover and Braunschweig to the small, untouched village of Wennigsen. The relocation pace quickened and we rolled the next day to Rolfshagen bei Minden where we remained for a week. While there, I decided to put my knowledge of German to practical use. I set up an office in the farmhouse living room, brought in a desk and placed flowers, a Colt .45 pistol, a walkie-talkie and a pile of official-looking books and papers on it.

With all the impressive trappings in place, I declared myself the area's war criminal investigator on May 25, 1945. We spread the word that I wanted to interview DPs about war crimes perpetrated against them by local Nazis. A few slave laborers came singularly and reluctantly at first but eventually, they came in droves to my makeshift courtroom.

I sought the aid of GIs in the company who spoke various languages and then listened to incredible horror stories, each more heartrending than the one before it. One involved a 10-year-old boy who had been taken to Dachau at age seven and then forced to watch his mother and sister raped and murdered. Later, he watched German camp guards execute his father.

The boy stood mute before me, expressionless eyes cast on the floor, unable to retell the memories he held locked up inside him. I tried bribing him with candy and soft words but he never spoke, as others in the room recited his story for him. I was helpless to do anything for him but give him a chocolate bar and dismiss him.

As the boy was led from the room, I had momentary pangs of conscience for this was a game I was playing and this small tyke's world was real. I considered ending the charade as a travesty against human suffering. But I reasoned that even though I might be accused of playacting, I still was in a position to subject war criminals to American justice. I also knew the MPs and war crime tribunals would welcome any assistance available from any source, even me.

Other DPs told of floggings by a local schoolmaster, and some told of cruelties committed by the local burgermeister, a member of the SA, Hitler's Sturm Abteilung brown-shirted storm troops. He was accused of customarily beating foreign women and children and forcing them to work inhumane hours. Then, when they were of no further use to him, he had them deported to Rehren, the concentration camp we had visited during the push to the Elbe some weeks earlier.

I recorded dozens of signed depositions and turned them over to our regimental intelligence corps for further investigation and possible prosecution. My contribution to seeing that justice was served might be considered rather insignificant, I'm sure, but at the time it was something I felt I had to do. I was just supplying more pieces to the puzzle of who committed what crimes and against whom.

After about a week in Rolfshagen, we moved on to Lauenau. where I received word on May 30 that I was being transferred to the division's Special Services unit as a bandsman. Inwardly, I fumed when I realized that some stupid rear-echelon clerk should have noticed my bandsman classification before I was sent into combat and subjected to months of suffering and danger.

I joined a 10-piece group officially designated as the 333rd Regimental Band, but we billed ourselves as The Tophatters. That name had a little more pizzazz, we reasoned.

One day, the band was told to prepare a program for a special event at the noon meal. We set up on a makeshift stage and started to swing for about 200 GIs eating there. While playing, I spotted Major General Bolling and Colonel Louis W. Truman, Bolling's chief of staff, filing into the mess tent. So that was the special event, a visit by Bolling, who by now had his second star. But I was stunned when I saw they were being followed by President Harry S. Truman, General of the Armies Dwight D. Eisenhower and Secretary of State James F. Byrnes. I immediately swung into "Missouri Waltz," upon which Truman left the visiting entourage, came over to the bandstand and thanked us.

Without thinking, I put out my hand. He shook it vigorously with a grin. Bolling and Colonel Truman, the president's cousin, glowered at my breach of etiquette but nothing was said.

We continued playing as the delegation of Army brass and politicians quickly left without sampling the food. Most of the troops appeared totally uninterested in what was going on, for this was the best chow they had had in a long time.

When I returned to my billet, I found that Joe Everett and all my other squad mates had been transferred back to their respective line companies. I knew our paths would never cross again, and in Everett's case that disturbed me, for we had shared so much.

Soon, the band moved out again, this time segueing through the Pied Piper–famous town of Hameln and on to Kassel, Paderborn, Frankfurt, Darmstadt, Lampertheim bei Mannheim, and finally to Leutershausen, where we culminated a grueling 400-kilometer drive. The band remained there for seven months performing in dozens of cities and towns in southern Germany. On one such occasion, we were rousted out of our sacks about 0200 and told that Colonel Gomes, regimental commander, wanted music at his castle quarters immediately. He was throwing an all-night party and by the time we arrived the place was crawling with top brass, most of them quite drunk.

After setting up my makeshift drums, I cornered General Bolling during an intermission and registered a complaint about the runaround I had been getting from a certain major at Special Services command. He had several drum sets but refused to issue one to me. I reminded the general that I couldn't perform very well for officers' parties without decent drums. I showed him the Hitler Jugend snare drums I was using as tom-toms wired to a bass drum and confiscated cymbals wired to makeshift stands. He nodded and walked away. The next day I was notified to pick up a new set. At the next officers' party, I gave Bolling a friendly wave of thanks. He acted as though he had never seen me before.

Secretly one day, we were told every house in the town was to be searched at a prearranged time for illegal weapons or Nazi propaganda materials, all of which would be confiscated.

At 0400 on the designated day, the door-to-door search began. The townspeople were herded onto the streets while the searches were conducted. Dozens of pistols, rifles, bayonets, knives, Nazi flags, propaganda booklets, swastika armbands, ammunition and even hand grenades were seized.

At one house where I was acting as an interpreter for a team of officers, we heard strange sounds from within. Edging with guns drawn closer to a bedroom, we listened to pained groaning sounds. On signal, we burst in and found a girl about 12 wiping an older woman's brow with a wet towel by candlelight. The groans, which sounded like utterances preceding death, were only warnings of impending new life. We were about to assist in the birth of Leutershausen's newest citizen and the closest available doctor was in Weinheim, too far away to help.

I jumped into the officers' jeep and in five minutes, I was standing in the middle of a Weinheim street yelling for a "Doktor." An older man appeared at a window, and when told the situation, he climbed into the jeep and returned with me to Leutershausen. The bloody, wiggling baby boy was beautiful.

On August 15, a flurry of rumors was rampant that Japan had surrendered in the Pacific. If true, the 84th wouldn't be going to the CBI theater of operations after all. But it was not until some time later that we received the word officially in the third stall at the company latrine, where else?

Rotations home continued to deplete the band's ranks and eventually, the Tophatters band was reduced to a sextet.

I wangled a trip to Berlin in a 20-hour ride in an uncomfortable, cold, two-and-a-half-ton troop carrier but I didn't want to go home without first seeing what was left of the German capital. I planned to deliver a letter from a Leutershausen family to relatives in the Hackenfeld Spandau section of the city. Sifting my way through the rubble, I eventually located the address. After I knocked vigorously, the door opened a crack, allowing a woman to peek out before the door was slammed shut again. I knocked more authoritatively and a stern-looking woman stood in the doorway demanding to know that my business was with them. I quickly told her I was an American stationed in Leutershausen and that I had a message from her in-laws there. The door was flung open wide and I was literally yanked into the woman's apartment. After accepting my identity, a beautiful girl about my age cautiously appeared from hiding. Thinking I was a Russian, she had fled, as she always had done when Russians appeared, to a potato bin in the cellar where she had buried herself for fear of being raped. Mass ravaging of women by Russian troops when they entered Berlin had been reported.

When the girl offered to show me around the city, I let her wear my full-length GI overcoat. As we waited for a trolley, I became aware of the scornful looks of Berliners waiting near us who, I was sure, considered my date just another shack-up job. I couldn't stand still for this; she was one of the sweetest, most innocent girls I had met so far in Europe.

"Meine Frau" (My wife), I nodded to the crowd knowingly. Embarrassed, they turned away. We were barely able to stifle our giggles through all this.

When I ventured into the Russian sector on the other side of Brandenburg Tur, I was besieged by Russian soldiers bartering for watches, cigarettes, anything they could bring back to Mother Russia. I set the hands to the correct time on a $2 Ingersall watch that hadn't worked in months, and sold it instantly to a Russian soldier for $75, and then a carton of American cigarettes for another $100. Before I left, he tried to con me into buying one of the 20 or so watches he wore strung up his arm under his army overcoat and which he obviously had lifted from German prisoners or battlefield dead.

Back in Leutershausen, word came down that most of my former outfit had been transferred to the 78th Infantry Division in Kassel, above Frankfurt, for rotation home. Because my name was not on the shipping lists, I could only watch as the trucks loaded and pulled away, happy for those going home but disappointed that I was not among them. I had not built up sufficient rotation points to go home with the others in November, but my time would come.

No sooner had the trucks pulled away than orders came transferring me to the Seventh Army, 12th Armored Division band in Seckenheim, a suburb east of Mannheim on the Mannheim-Heidelberg highway.

The curtain on my odyssey was slowly being lowered. Even before I accepted the fact that I was being left behind by my division, I was sent confusing signals on my next duty station. I had orders to join the 60th Army Ground Forces Band, but before I could determine where they were located, the orders were changed. Instead, I was being transferred from the 9th Army to the 7th Army, from the 84th Infantry Division to the 12th Armored Division, and from a swing band to a music school about 15 kilometers from Leutershausen.

The postwar rotation of troops out of the ETO raised havoc with the forces left behind. Units remaining overseas were decimated as Army logistics coordinators tried to procure available troop deployment ship space while still keeping remaining units up to strength. Transfers were on paper only. The Army was trying to get us all out of Europe as fast as it could—and this would eventually work to my advantage.

Upon arriving in Seckenheim, I found housing was on a catch-as-catch-can basis, so I quickly grabbed an attic room in a building a short distance from the Special Services Music School and cafeteria-style dining room. The room had a potbelly stove to keep me warm during the harsh German winters, a window offering a panoramic view of the town and a built-in bunk bed. No sooner had I settled into Seckenheim than I called my brother-in-law, H. Whitney Parmenter, back in England. I posed as "Colonel Blunt," a ruse I had used before. The call was routed to Frankfurt, then Paris, on to London and several minutes later to Parmenter's Air Corps base at Hanley, Staffordshire. As each operator came on the line, I kept repeating, "military urgent priority."

The ploy worked like a charm and the next voice I heard was, "Pfc. Parmenter speaking." He said afterwards that as soon as he was told a Colonel Blunt was on the phone for him, he started to playact his part on the other end.

All he kept saying over and over on the other end was, "Yes, Colonel. No, Colonel. Yes, Colonel." After five minutes, our luck pressed as far as we dared without risking court-martials, we ended the "military urgent priority call" with military urgent priority haste.

Rumors circulated constantly about rotation home. This kept us on edge, for the number of overseas service points needed to be shipped home was constantly being lowered. Time eventually erased each rumor as we continued our monotonous daily routines—but for most of us, getting home was becoming almost an obsession.

To break up some of the routine at the music school, I began hanging around the military airport at Mannheim, where I met a warrant officer pilot from an artillery unit who took me for a spin in his L-5 observation plane. When he offered to take me along on a 90-mile trip to Frankfurt, I jumped at the chance.

The next day we took off and headed north for Supreme Headquarters Allied Expeditionary Forces (SHAEF), about an hour's flight away. The flight was the first time I had been in the air since 1937 when I flew in an old barnstorming Curtiss Condor tri-motor biplane with pioneer aviator Clarence Chamberlin, who had piloted the monoplane Columbia from New York to Germany a decade earlier.

Partway into the Frankfurt trip, the warrant officer yelled back to me, "Take it!" Without hesitation, I grabbed the joy stick and soon mastered the gentle touch needed to fly these delicate, canvas-covered birds.

I flew the plane back to Mannheim and, following his instructions, managed to settle the aircraft into an approach pattern. Just before we touched down, I took my hands off the controls so he could land the plane. We bumped down rather hard and rolled to a stop.

"That wasn't too bad except for the landing. It was a little rough," he commented. Only when I told him I had given control of the plane over to him at the last moment did I learn he had not taken it and the plane, a slightly larger and heavier version of the Piper Cub, had landed itself.

After several months at the music school, orders came through transferring me to the 278th Engineers, but again, it proved to be a transfer on paper only and I remained in Seckenheim. It appeared that names were still being shunted from roster to roster, trying to keep units filled regardless of whether the name switches were actually ever validated.

Shortly after New Year's, the Army perpetrated one of the great con jobs of the century on me. If offered to swap a week of rest and rehabilitation in Switzerland for a 12-month extension of duty. Like a gullible fool, I accepted the offer. I was eager to ship home but, at the same time, I realized I was getting the opportunity of a lifetime traveling throughout Europe, an opportunity that might never again offer itself to me.

While I waited for my travel orders, word was received that General Patton had been injured in a traffic accident. He died several days later of what had been reported as minor injuries.

The day of his funeral, I stood on a Heidelberg sidewalk and watched Germans weep openly as the procession passed by. Although a former enemy, he had been a great general and if there was anything the German people respected, it was a victorious military officer.

Former German soldiers who had fought against his Third Army saluted a fallen comrade as Patton's body was taken to Heidelberg castle and then later to the train station. Thousands along the route fell silent as the horse-drawn caisson carrying his body passed in review.

Often, I heard Germans remark that if the Fatherland had had Patton and Eisenhower on its side, they would have won the war—after all, they added nationalistically, Eisenhower was German.

My travel orders for the Switzerland furlough arrived in mid-January, and anxious to break the monotony of Seckenheim life, I breezed through all the army official rigamarole required for the trip. Immediately upon arriving there, I headed for a phone to call home but was informed the call would take three days to complete, would cost $15 for three minutes, and would catch up to me wherever I was at the time. Naturally, I had to reverse the charges. If I spent that much my first day, I would have nothing left for the rest of the trip.

When the call finally came through, my mother's excited voice sent a chill through me for a moment. I quickly filled her in on my activities and future. My family had gathered around the phone for they had been alerted in advance that an overseas call was going to be put through in the early afternoon. The three minutes went by as one, but the purpose of the call, to reassure my loved ones that I was alive and well, was achieved.

Switzerland was enchanting and I thoroughly enjoyed a week of mountain-top sleigh rides, gallons of hot chocolate, skating, skiing and sight-seeing in all of Switzerland's major cities.

But, all too soon, it was back to reality.

Rumors were rampant that 45-pointers would ship home soon, but this didn't apply to me since I had signed on for the one-year extension of duty. But I kept my bags packed, just in case. As time went by, the rumors became more prevalent. Each one brought on a euphoria; each delay a depression. Week after week, I looked in vain for my name on the occupation unit transfer rosters.

Then, one day, the wait was over; my orders were posted. I was assigned to an Engineer Forestry Company shipping stateside from Bremerhaven, a seaport on the North Sea. Suddenly, it dawned on me. The Army had screwed up my records again, perhaps by the same clerk named SNAFU who had missed my bandsman classification months earlier, and my extra year's commitment was apparently lost in the shuffle of paperwork. Far be it from me to tell the Army it didn't know how to do its job.

On March 1, the convoy headed north and after two days on the road, we pulled into a bomb-ravaged city where I yelled to the first civilian I saw, "Wohin Sind Wir?" (Where are we?)

"Bremerhaven beim Nord See" (Bremerhaven by the North Sea), a stevedore replied. We could see an entire flotilla of Liberty ships, Victory ships, troop transports and freighters. Somewhere on the waterfront was a ship with my name on it, but which one?

We were instructed to watch the bulletin board daily for our unit name, ship designation and departure date. When our service records finally caught up to us, it touched off a series of baggage and equipment checks, shots, physical exams, "short arm" inspections, VD movies and uniform issuance.

Finally, the notice we had been waiting for was posted on the bulletin board. The 1391st Engineer Forestry Company was slated to ship out on the Frostburg Victory ship March 10 for New York. I ran into the city and sent a cablegram home: "Sailing Sunday 10th Victory Frostburg Bremerhaven Happy Birthday Mom Love." Reluctantly, I accepted the fact I couldn't make it home in time for my mother's birthday, but there still would be the delayed Christmas celebration.

On the assigned departure date, formations of impatient GIs lined up early on the docks and began snaking their way to a gangplank a block away. I looked at the prow of the ship to make sure it said Frostburg. It did. I didn't want to risk winding up in some foreign port.

Even as the Victory ship was tied to the pier, my stomach started reacting to the harbor swells. I was becoming seasick and we hadn't even left the pier yet.

As I settled into a hammock and waited for the ship to get underway, I vowed that if this was another Army foul-up, they would have one helluva battle getting me off that ship again, or even finding me, for that matter.

I attended a church service aboard ship on Easter Sunday, my mother's birthday. Even though still thousands of miles apart, I could at least in spirit celebrate her birthday. I knew she would be thinking of me.

The pitching and rolling of the ship made life below deck abominable. I tried to eat Saltine crackers, or candy bars, or an orange or anything that anyone offered me. But nothing stayed down more than a few seconds.

A week into the voyage, I became aware of a strange shipboard sound, even louder than the pulsing engines. It was the distant roar of men yelling. Shakily, I made my way to the deck and there it was, the distant New York skyline and the Statue of Liberty I had missed on the way overseas. We were finally home and all the horror, the devastation was behind us and gradually becoming only a memory.

On solid ground once again, many men went to their knees to kiss the American soil—or more accurately, the rotted New York harbor pier. I just wanted to get away from the ship, the other men, the docks, the motion of the sea, everything. We were herded onto trains, caring little whether it was the right one, for at least it was in America and any place it transported us would be OK, as long as it was far away from the bilge-smelling rust bucket that had brought us home.

When the train slowed, I saw a sign on a siding: "Camp Kilmer," the same camp from which we had departed 18 month previously. We were assigned to temporary barracks and told our time was free until the next morning. I legged it for the nearest phone. When I dialed 56264, the phone rang only twice before my mother answered. "I'm home," I stated simply. She could not comprehend immediately what I was saying and then, when she did, she couldn't contain the excitement in her voice.

"Where are you? Are you safe? Are you in this country?" The questions tumbled over each other.

"I'm fine and in New Jersey and should be home in a couple of days," I explained quickly, trying to calm her down. Then I heard her crying softly. She put my dad on and he was calmer, at least from the sound of his voice. Before he hung up, he promised, we would resume our meditative man-to-man talks, one of the things that I had missed most while we were apart. There was so much to tell him, but also so much that I couldn't.

Everything moved quickly; as fast as the Army had ensnared me, it was just as eager to get rid of me.

The 12-hour train trip to New England was long and tedious and extended into the night. When I awakened from a series of cap naps, the train was stopped on a siding.

"Where are we?" I asked the conductor.

"Worcester, Massachusetts," he answered, bored. I sat up straight and looked out the window and as my eyes became accustomed to the dark, I recognized the intersection of Southbridge Street and Quinsigamond Avenue. Without thinking, I sprinted out the car door to search for a phone.

"We'll only be here a few minutes," the conductor yelled after me.

I scrambled blindly down a steep embankment and ran across the street to a nearby railroad roundhouse, grabbed a phone and dialed 56264 hurriedly and again my mother answered. "Are you still in New Jersey?" she asked, her voice rising.

"Nope, in Worcester on Southbridge Street," I answered laughing. I told her I was on my way to Fort Devens and would call her from there as soon as I could. I headed back through the darkness to the train and as I approached it, it was pulling away slowly from the siding. My heart pounded as I scrambled back up the embankment and galloped down the tracks after it. I caught the platform door at the rear of the last car just as it reached my top running speed.

Arriving at Devens in the middle of the night, I sat until dawn outside the barracks, just smelling the clean, fresh New England air and looking at the silent array of stars in the sky. I was eager to get my Army career over with and reunite with my family. The discharge processing took almost all day before I was reclassified from 1-A, military fit, to 4-A, no longer militarily desirable, awarded a "ruptured duck" lapel pin and officially designated as a "civilian." With this, I carried and dragged my souvenir-laden dufflebag toward the post main gate.

As I waited for a ride home, I stared at passing officers. The uniform didn't fool them, for I'm sure they knew that despite the beribboned Eisenhower jacket and combat infantry badge, I was a brand-new "civie." I especially enjoyed the freedom of giving officers only a sideways glance instead of a highball.

Soon, my transportation home came wheeling up to the gate. An hour later, I was home, my odyssey finally over, my duty done.

Fifty Years Later

Perhaps the greatest reward and accolade that can be bestowed upon a combat veteran of the Battle of the Bulge is the enduring gratitude and patriotic affection showered upon him by the Belgian people when he revisits the battlefields fifty years later.

None of the Belgian fervor has diminished. If anything, it has intensified with the passing of time. Monuments to American military forces and Belgian resistance freedom fighters dot the Belgian landscape everywhere. Perhaps more remarkably, most are adorned still, yet these 50 years, with fresh flowers of remembrance, maintained daily by the villagers or towns-people. And more such monuments are still being constructed along the roadways—some by individuals working alone who, to their dying days, refuse to forget the sacrifice made by the American forces during the worst recorded winter of the century, 1944–1945.

When the Belgian people recall those dark war years in their national history, their eyes sadden and tears fall at the recollection of the German reign of terror. They speak still of the hunger that blighted their small country when the German juggernaut swept west across their land in 1940 to overrun and occupy France, and of the food offered them by the Americans during the Ardennes Campaign.

The return of an American combat veteran to the battlefields of his youth is a joyous event to the Belgian people, a time of unbounded hospitality with open arms of welcome. But, it is also an occasion for solemn reflection in the many Ardennes woodlands still pockmarked by unfilled foxholes or in the peaceful, immaculate military cemeteries where all-too-familiar unit designations and names are found.

The cities, villages and towns have all been rebuilt and, for the most part, are tranquil and beautiful today. Only occasionally can unrestored barns or farms be found in the villages to replay the stark realities of war. The maddening fog that hampered the Allied force's efforts a half century ago still clings stubbornly to the countryside each morning, especially in winter. Crowns of snow still form white mantles over evergreen forests. The ankle-deep mud of the narrow, winding roads has been replaced by high-speed highways.

Belgian historians diligently continue to dissect every phase of the Battle of the Bulge, much as Americans analyze their own Civil War. Members of the Center for Research and Information on the Battle of the Ardennes (CRIBA) quote chapter and verse what each American military unit did, where it was located, who its officers were, how many field artillery pieces and tanks it had for support, how many German tanks were destroyed, and how many lives were lost. In Belgium, the Battle of the Bulge is a lifelong study. As one member of CRIBA remarked to a revisiting GI, "The more we learn, the more grateful we become to America."

Survivors of the Bulge live with their troubled memories. But seeing carefree Belgian children on their way to school, farmers again plowing their fields, and shattered forests replaced now by new generations of towering pines, pushes these memories into the background of consciousness, where they belong. American military forces wrote a tragic page of history. Now it is time for others to read that page and learn from it.

Index

About the Author

ROSCOE C. BLUNT JR. is a veteran of World War II in the 84th Infantry, serving in Central Europe, the Ardennes and the Rhineland, and earning three battle stars. In 1943, he was the youngest soldier in the country to be awarded the Expert Infantry Badge, presented at Fort McClellan, Alabama. A former private pilot, scuba diver, and underwater cinematographer, Blunt was an award-winning investigative journalist for a metropolitan newspaper and was considered by law enforcement agencies in Massachusetts as the dean of police reporters in New England. He has written two other books.

84th INFANTRY DIVISION
From Activation 15 Oct 42 to V-E Day 9 May 45